MINOLTA

International

DYNAX 5xi

U.S.A.

MAXXUM 5xi

HOVE FOTO BOOKS

Harry Hennings

In U.S.A.

the Minolta Dynax 5xi is known as the

Maxxum 5xi

All text, illustrations and data apply to either camera

First English Edition November 1992
Published by Hove Foto Books Ltd
Hotel de France, St. Saviour's Road, St. Helier, Jersey JE4 8WZ

English Translation: Petra Kopp
Editor: Philip Guyton
Minolta Technical Advice: Bernard Petticrew
Production: Georgina Fuller
Typesetting & Layout: Annida's Written Page, Sussex BN43 5HH
Printed in Guernsey by GP Printers

British Library Cataloguing-in-Publication Data.
A catalogue record for this book is available from the British Library.

ISBN 0-906447-51-8

Worldwide Distribution:
Newpro (UK) Ltd
Old Sawmills Road
Faringdon
Oxon
SN7 7DS
Tel: 0367 242411 Fax: 0367 241124

Contents

Expert knowledge and technical intelligence

The launch of the Minolta 7000 in the mid-80s started a new era in SLR photography. By this point the automation of exposure, film advance, and film speed setting had become a matter of course, but many amateur photographers still had a problem with automatic focusing. The Minolta 7000 was the first camera with a truly effective automatic focusing system. Since then Minolta have improved the autofocus control system of their SLR cameras at ever-decreasing intervals. The system used by Minolta became the model for all subsequent autofocus SLR cameras. But it still had its problems, i.e. focusing speed, and functional reliability in low light. Enormous progress was made with the 7000i, which introduced the predictive autofocus system. With the Minolta 7xi, the first in the third generation of autofocus SLR cameras, Minolta once again shifted the goalposts. Many experts consider the 7xi a high point in modern camera technology, and the 9xi is the professional counterpart of this camera. The Minolta 5xi features all the essential elements of this know-how.

The five most important factors - as identified by market research - an amateur photographer makes of a modern SLR camera are perfectly met by the 5xi. These factors are as follows: automatic focusing and exposure, integral flash, easy handling, and a comprehensive range of system accessories to build up the photographic outfit.

The requirements of amateur photographers and the expert knowledge of professional photography incorporated into computer software are the main inspirations for the 5xi. There are many arguments in favour of the Minolta 5xi as a comfortable and fast SLR camera. It provides an easy entry into one of the most successful SLR systems, but it can also serve as a second camera body to go with its parent, the Maxxum/Dynax 7xi.

Arguments in favour of a Minolta 5xi

- The 5xi utilizes the autofocus system familiar from the other xi-series cameras, which is automatically activated as soon as the eye is on the viewfinder. This eye-start automation system substantially increases the speed with which the first picture can be taken.

- The highly sensitive AF sensors respond even in low light. This means that the automatic focusing system is extremely reliable, even down to LV -1 at ISO 100/21°.
- The AF system also recognizes subject movement. The camera continues to adjust the focus, even while the mirror flips up and up until the iris diaphragm opens, on the basis of the calculated speed of the subject. For still subjects the camera automatically locks the focus.
- As with the first Maxxum/Dynax models, the multi-pattern exposure system of the camera is coupled with the autofocus setting. Like that of its parent camera, the metering area is divided into separate finely subdivided segments, albeit into 'only' eight instead of fourteen honeycomb-pattern metering segments. Based on the AF setting the camera knows where the main subject is located. It compares the brightness of the main subject with that of

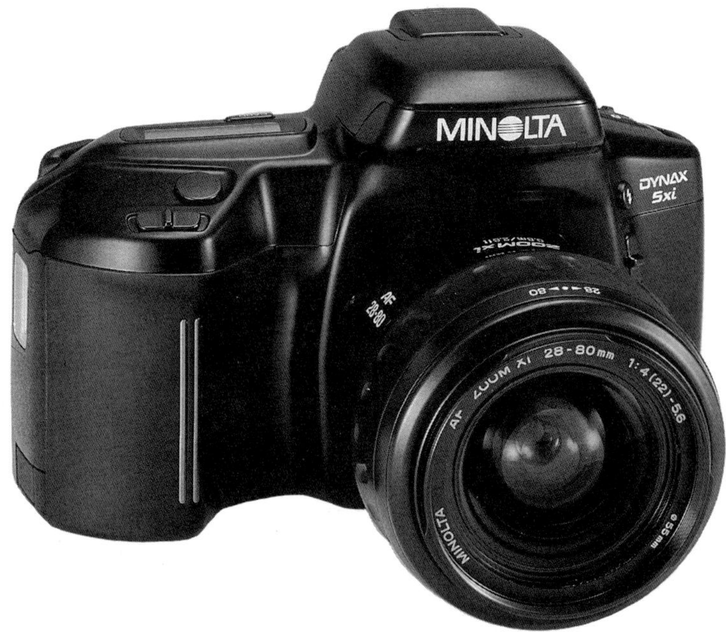

The 5xi meets all the demands an amateur photographer makes of a modern SLR camera.

its surroundings and can consequently determine whether it is evenly lit, whether it is in backlight, or in a cone of light. The camera can adjust the sensitivity of each of the eight honeycomb-pattern segments of the silicon photo cell, which allows a multitude of detailed metering settings. The sensitivity distribution depends on the position of the main subject. Before they are processed further, the measurements are 'evaluated', and with the help of fuzzy logic and the 'expert knowledge' - Minolta's term for the professional photographic experience programmed into the camera - the lighting conditions are then 'interpreted'.

- The 5xi is equipped with a spot metering system for special creative requirements and particularly difficult lighting situations, where photographers want to determine the mood and brightness characteristics of an exposure themselves.
- Minolta's automatic expert program selection is based on, the subject, the subject distance, and the focal length of the lens used: with the special xi zoom lenses the camera automatically suggests

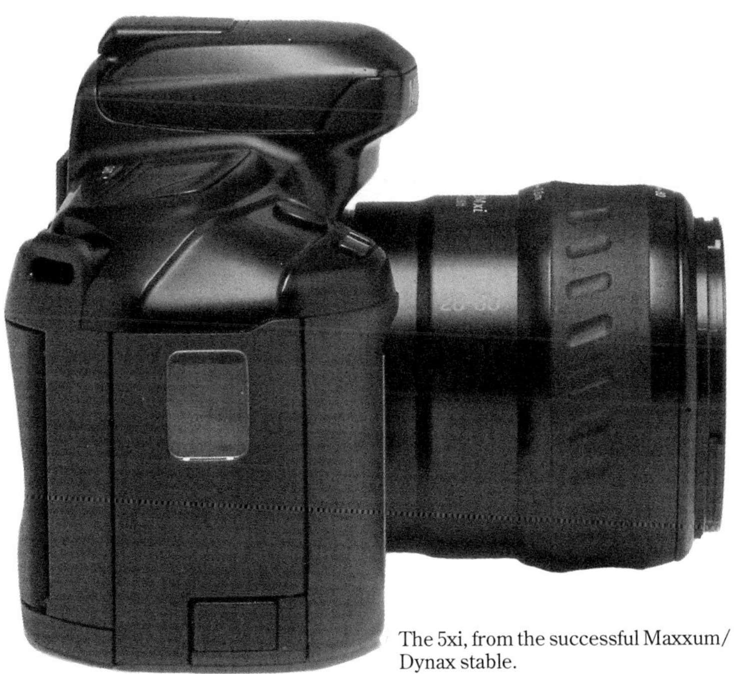

The 5xi, from the successful Maxxum/ Dynax stable.

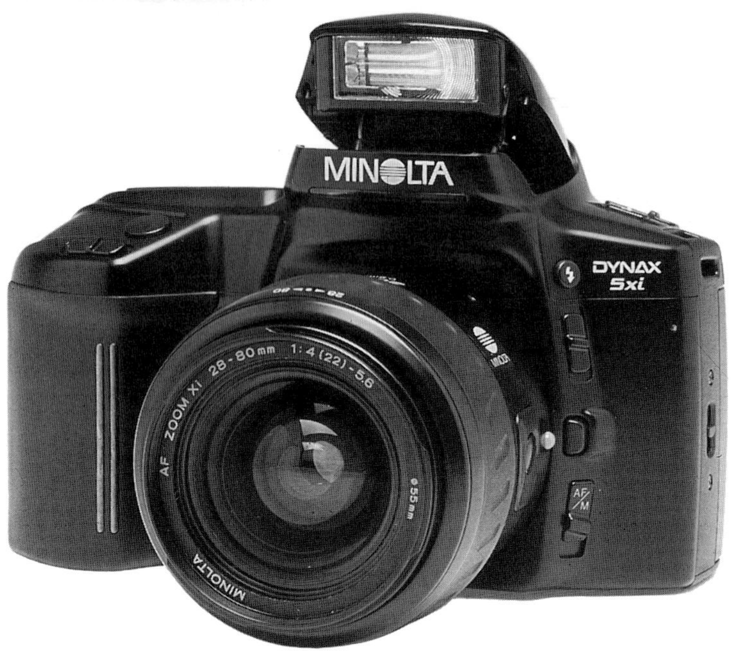

The 5xi, which is equally at home with snapshots and professional photographic techniques, provides easy entry into the Minolta SLR system.

a suitable focal length for the subject. Thanks to their 'expert knowledge' the program selection system and any activated expansion cards have clear ideas about the focal length to be used. The programs are always designed in such a way that the slowest shutter speed is, wherever possible, still fast enough for handheld use. If the shutter speed falls below the handheld limit the photographer is alerted by a camera shake warning and/or the flash is automatically switched on. If the photographer is not happy with the suggestion of the fully automatic program the shutter-setting control can be operated to give preference to a certain shutter speed (PS), or likewise with the aperture-setting control used to select a certain depth of field (PA). And so there is an ability to overriding the 'expert suggestion' made by the camera for the picture about to be taken.

- All flash functions and exposures are also controlled automatically. The integral mini flash unit, although often underrated in its performance, provides guaranteed optimum fill-in. In Program

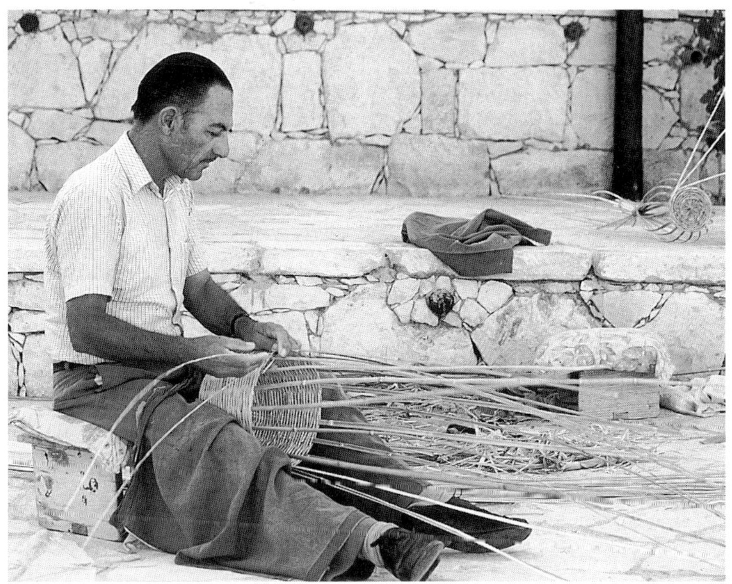

One of the advantages of the autofocus system of the 5xi is its eye-start automation, which substantially reduces the time needed before an exposure can be made.

mode the 5xi also switches on automatically any program flash units - 3200i (now discontinued), 5200i, 3500xi or 5400xi - mounted on the camera. Flash is also used - in the P program - if strong backlighting of the subject requires fill-in flash.

● The unique Minolta expansion card system allows the functions of the camera to be extended step by step, according to photographic requirements. With the help of these cards the camera's computer can be re-programmed for specialist applications, or for certain subject areas, with the required changes regarding depth of field and shutter speeds, or with a different set of priorities regarding these.

● The most up-to-date technology in lens design and manufacture facilitated the development of a range of special zoom lenses for the xi range of cameras, including the 5xi. Whilst providing good reproduction quality, these lenses could be both extremely compact and light and be equipped with special features, such as image size lock. The 35-200mm,f/4.5-5.6 zoom, for example, which measures just 9.3cm and is a lightweight at around 500g, is probably the ideal lens in about 80 per cent of photographic situations. And so this lens is particularly useful if you want to take all your photographs with just one lens.

● Apart from its fully automatic program the 5xi also offers aperture and shutter speed priority modes and a fully manual mode. These modes allow the photographer to stay in complete control of the exposure control parameters. It is also worth noting that the fastest shutter speed of 1/2000 sec will be fast enough for almost all photographic situations.

● In addition to the above features the camera boasts a whole range of characteristics which can make its use an uncompromised pleasure. The near-inexhaustible possibilities of this versatile camera enable it to cope with anything from simple snapshots to creative picture composition with unusual professional photographic techniques. The camera belongs in one of the best AF SLR systems. The 5xi is ideal for people who enjoy photography and want to broaden their knowledge of SLR techniques. With the introduction of this camera Minolta continue on their path towards making sophisticated photography as easy and accessible as possible.

Getting started

The Minolta 5xi is designed so that anybody can easily take photographs with the minimum amount of preparation. However there are still just a few necessary preparations. You need to, ensure a battery is fitted, attach the lens, remove the protective foil from the shutter and, just to be on the safe side, attach a neckstrap. It is also advisable to familiarize yourself with the camera's operating controls with a few practice sessions.

Attaching the neckstrap

One of the first things you should do is attach the neckstrap supplied with the camera - or a quality, comfortable 'Op/Tech' strap. The strap supplied with the camera is attached via two eyelets at the top right and top left of the camera body. The ends of the neckstrap are first pushed through the eyelets and then threaded back through both the rubber clamps and the buckles on the neckstrap. The viewfinder eyepiece cap, which is important for long tripod exposures, or for self-timer shots, is also attached to the neckstrap. This cap blocks off the viewfinder eyepiece to prevent the exposure metering system from being adversely affected by light entering through the viewfinder. The Strap also allows storage for the accessory shoe cap when a flash unit is mounted. When a flash unit is not fitted the accessory shoe cap should always stay on the camera to protect the contacts against dirt and dust. With a quality 'Op/Tech' strap you get extreme comfort, very important if carrying your camera for long periods at a time.

Battery loading

The batteries must be fitted in order for the camera to function at all. Without power nothing will work on almost all of today's modern cameras. The Minolta 5xi uses a 6-volt 2CR5 type lithium battery as its power source. Lithium batteries are now the standard power source for cameras worldwide, and Minolta uses this battery type for all Maxxum/Dynax models. This has the advantage that somebody with two such cameras only needs to keep one battery in reserve should one battery fail. After all, it is unlikely that both batteries will fail at the same time.

The lithium cell is accommodated in the handgrip. When loading the batteries the camera should be switched off, and this is done by pushing the main switch to the **LOCK** position. Then the battery-cover release on the underside of the camera needs to be pushed inwards to open the lid. The lithium cell is shaped to correspond to the shape of the battery chamber, so it's almost impossible to insert it incorrectly. You only have to make sure that the battery poles are pointing towards the top of the camera. This is also indicated inside the battery compartment. If the battery is inserted the wrong way around the body data panel will remain blank and all camera functions are locked. Once the battery has been inserted the lid is simply closed and automatically locked.

Lithium batteries are better suited to cameras than alkaline-manganese types because of their higher resilience, their relatively great tolerance to changes in temperature, and their longer lifespan. Another advantage of the Lithium battery type is its ability to hold a charge during storage for longer periods than alkaline-manganese types. Lithium batteries can retain the power stored in them for up to five years. As they have to be changed less frequently because of their greater capacity, they are also less damaging to the environment. But when changing batteries you should always remember that spent lithium batteries do not belong with household rubbish, they have to be disposed of separately. It's best to give them to your photographic dealer who will ensure that they are disposed of safely.

There is a risk of Lithium batteries exploding if recharging them is attempted, or if they are thrown in a fire or expose to very high temperatures, or if they are short-circuited. They must not be dismantled either, as this would release poisonous chemicals which damage the environment and could cause burns or allergies. Always follow the manufacturers' instructions and remember that batteries do not belong in children's hands.

According to Minolta's data a fresh lithium battery will, under normal temperatures, provide sufficient power to expose approximately 55 rolls of 24-exposure film with the 5xi, provided the integral flash unit isn't used. But depending on how frequently the

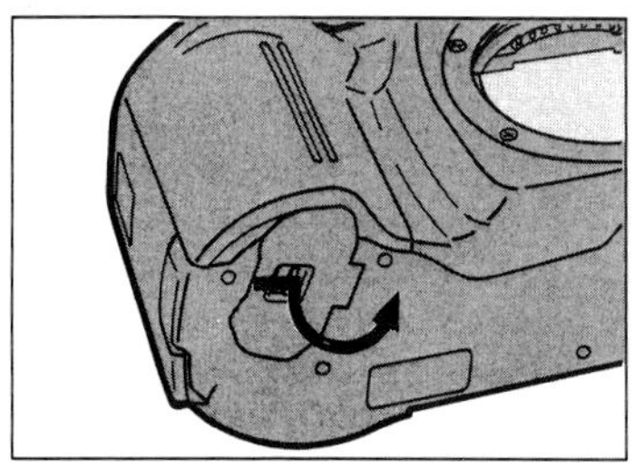

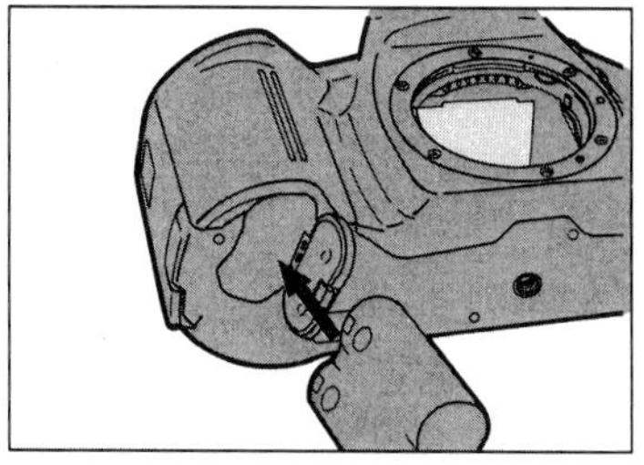

The battery chamber is located in the base of the camera handgrip. The lithium block required to supply the 5xi with power is indented, so that it slots easily into the shaped battery chamber. The battery poles need to point towards the top of the camera.

flash unit is used, the higher amount of power required will reduce this figure. If you use flash for about 50 per cent of your shots the battery's lifespan can be reduced to 20 rolls of 24-exposure film. You should also remember that the first battery may not last even for the minimum figure indicated, as you will use a substantial proportion of power trying out all the different functions.

The state of the batteries charge is indicated by the battery symbol on the body data panel when the camera is switched on.

At full capacity the full battery symbol will light up for four seconds. As the battery charge decreases the low battery symbol indicates that you should have a fresh battery ready. However, the camera will still work and the symbol will still disappear after approximately four seconds. If the battery charge is very weak the symbol will flash continuously and will not disappear during operation. The camera will still function correctly but the battery should be replaced straight away. The remaining charge is no longer sufficient for correct camera functioning if all other indicators disappear and only the battery symbol and the additional **bAtt** indicator flash on the body data panel. This indicator also appears when the camera is switched off and the main switch is set to **LOCK**. Damage may result if the battery is not changed immediately on, or at least very soon after, becoming discharged.

Although lithium batteries perform very well, even in low temperatures, the camera should be kept warm under the coat or jacket in breaks between shots during longer periods of sub-zero use. It is also advisable to keep a fresh replacement battery in a warm interior pocket, in case the power of the camera battery should fail suddenly. Cold batteries can recover once back in normal temperatures, so don't thrown them away.

Attaching the lens

When no lens is attached to the camera the camera bayonet is protected against dirt, dust and mechanical damage by a special cap. This cap can be removed by turning it anti-clockwise, as is the case for the cap on the bayonet of the lens. When attaching the lens to the camera the main switch should be set to **LOCK**. The red index marks on camera and lens bayonet have to be aligned first to enable the lens to be inserted into the camera's lens mount. The lens is locked in the mount by a slight turn clockwise, and a clearly audible click confirms that the lens has engaged and the mechanisms locked. To disengage the lens you need to press the lens release to the right of the camera bayonet, turn the lens anti-clockwise as far as it will go, and then lift it out carefully.

It is important to remember that the lens moves easily in the bayonet. You should never use force as the camera and lens connections could be damaged if the lens is jammed.

If the lens has been attached incorrectly then two small lines appear on the body data panel in place of the aperture display when the camera is switched on. These lines are also visible if there is no lens on the camera, or if the AZ/MZ switch of an xi lens is in the **MZ** position.

When changing lenses be careful not to touch anything inside the camera as the mirror and contacts are particularly delicate.

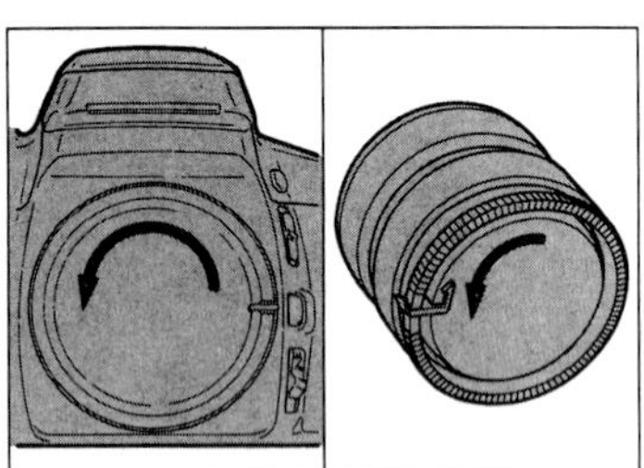

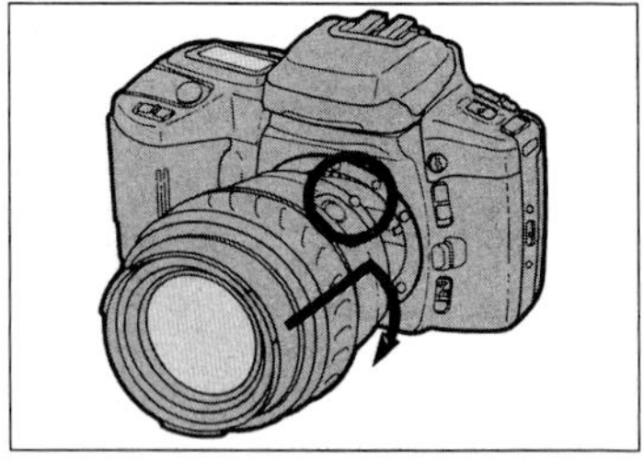

During lens mounting the main switch of the camera always needs to be set to **LOCK**. The lens engages in the mount when it is turned clockwise. The red indices on camera and lens need to be aligned.

You must also never touch any of the glass surfaces with your fingers. Small dust particles can be removed with a bellows brush. And you should only use a clean, dry cotton cloth with a drop of lens cleaner to clean the lens element surfaces or viewfinder eyepiece if this is absolutely necessary. In this case you need to clean the glass surface carefully, wiping in circular movements from the inside to the outside. 'Prophot' is an ideal 'wet' cleaner.

The mirror must never be touched or moved as this could affect its alignment. Small dust particles on the mirror will not affect the functioning of the exposure metering or of the focusing systems. But if the dirt particles do build up, as is inevitable in the course of time, send the camera to a Minolta service centre in order to get the mirror cleaned.

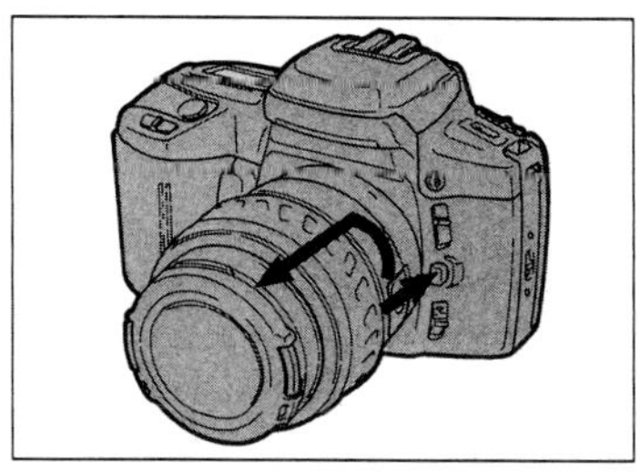

To remove the lens, press the lens release (small arrow on the right), then take out the lens by turning anti-clockwise.

Camera position

The lens is attached, the battery inserted and the neckstrap fastened, so now you can start your first trial runs. One important prerequisite for successful exposures is to hold the camera correctly. None of the automatic programs will help if the photographer's unsteady hand causes camera shake, but fortunately, the 5xi, like all the other Maxxum/Dynax models, is almost built into the photographer's hand. Thanks to its ergonomic shape you will hold it correctly almost automatically. With your right hand you can keep a firm hold on the camera grip, so that your middle finger, ring finger and little finger touch the sensor bar for the automatic

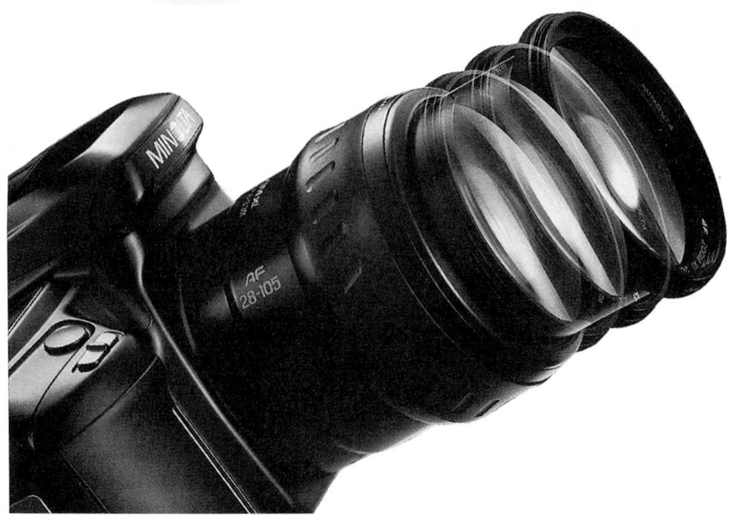

camera activation. The index finger automatically comes to rest in the depression to the side of the shutter release button, and the thumb fits almost perfectly behind the raised form on the back of the camera. This design and the cameras weight means that it can be held comfortably with just one hand. You can then support the base plate of the camera with the palm of your left hand as thumb and index finger grip the zoom ring of the lens. But you musn't touch or hold the focusing ring of AF lenses. The front barrel of the xi series zooms and AF power zoom lenses must not be held either, as this interferes with automatic focusing.

If the main switch is set to **ON** the camera is activated as soon as it is lifted to the eye. It then automatically focuses on the subject area located in the focus frame of the viewfinder, analyses whether it is moving or still, and selects the autozoom setting, AF mode, and exposure program. At first you may find the camera's automatic zooming irritating when you look through the viewfinder. But in practice you will very quickly get used to taking the suggested cropping as a good starting point. In most cases only a minimal amount of adjustment from this point is needed, and often the camera's suggestion coincides with the photographer's preference. Experience has shown that even if the suggested cropping isn't quite what you had in mind, it is still quicker to zoom from this setting to the desired position than from some prior arbitrary setting. However, the auto stand-by zoom function won't work if the sensor bar isn't touched, or if you are wearing gloves. In this case

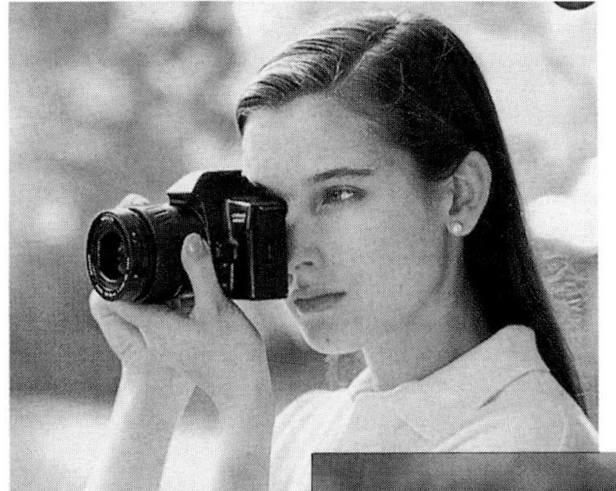

Hold the camera with your right hand; middle, ring and little finger can operate the grip sensor, the index finger the shutter-release button.

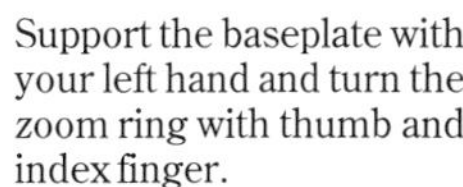

Support the baseplate with your left hand and turn the zoom ring with thumb and index finger.

the framing has to be selected manually. The focusing and exposure control systems, on the other hand, are activated by lightly touching the shutter-release button.

The automatic activation of the camera is achieved with the help of an infrared sensor set next to the viewfinder eyepiece. A transmitter gives out an infrared beam (although it is in fact near

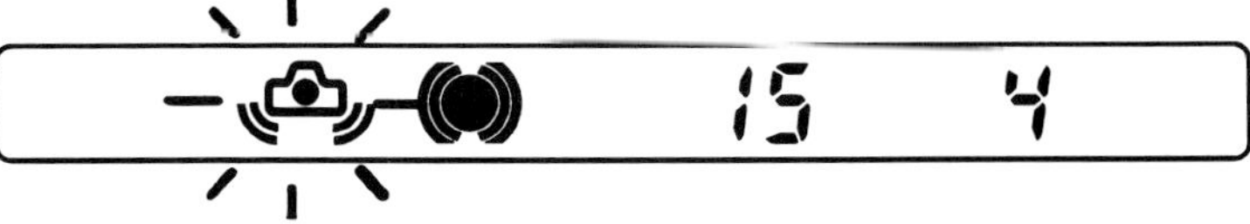

If the flash is de-activated, the camera shake warning will flash below the handheld limit.

infrared and presents no safety hazards) when the sensor bar is touched and as soon as an object approaches the viewfinder eyepiece it reflects this beam back to the second cell, the receiver. This second sensor then activates the automatic system of the camera. However, the eye-start system may not work if you are wearing sunglasses whose lenses absorb infrared light.

The autofocus and automatic exposure system will switch off after about 4 secs if there is no longer an object near the viewfinder.

Nowadays camera shake is one of the most frequent causes of failure. To achieve a steady camera position keep your elbows against your body and, if possible, lean on something. Stand with your legs slightly apart and try to press the shutter-release button as gently as possible, without jerking.

As mentioned earlier, the xi cameras automatically set the focus when you look through the viewfinder; it is not necessary to press the shutter-release button lightly to activate this. But by lightly pressing the shutter-release button the focus can be locked. If, for example, the subject to be focused is not in the centre of the viewfinder, you simply need to aim the camera at it, press and hold the shutter-release button lightly, and re-compose the frame once the focus signal has confirmed the focus. The focus will remain locked for as long as you keep your finger on the shutter release button, or until the shutter is released.

Operating controls

The few buttons and switches for operating the Minolta Dynax 5xi are conveniently placed, and their function can be explained quickly. It doesn't take too much time to familiarize yourself with them but you must do so if you want to make full use of the many possibilities offered.

Main switch

In order to be able to take photographs the main switch must be set to the **ON** position. The power supply is cut off in the **LOCK** position and all camera functions are inactive. If no film is loaded no indicators will be displayed on the body data panel when the camera is switched off, but if film is in the camera the cassette symbol and frame number will appear. If the film is full and rewound the cassette symbol and the number **0** will flash. These two indicators will also flash when the camera is switched on and an exposed and rewound film is in the cassette chamber.

Grip sensor

When in contact with skin the sensor bar on the front of the camera grip activates the infrared sensor on the viewfinder - provided the main switch of the camera is **ON**. However, if you are wearing gloves the sensor on the viewfinder eyepiece will not be activated.

Eyepiece sensor

When the grip sensor is touched the transmitter of the eyepiece sensor emits an infrared beam. As soon as this beam is reflected by an object close to the receiver of the eyepiece sensor, the latter starts the automatic system of the camera. This system includes autofocus, automatic exposure control, and auto stand-by zoom (when an xi zoom lens is used). If the sensor recognizes that there is no longer an object close to the viewfinder eyepiece it will switch off the camera functions after four seconds. It is advisable not to hold the camera by the handgrip or touch the grip sensor if the camera is not in use as this will cause the camera to switch on if it is held close to the body and waste power unnecessarily. Furthermore, many people find it irritating if the autofocus and zoom systems are working noisily when the camera is not in its shooting position at the eye. But the eyepiece sensor is only active when this grip sensor is being touched so the camera will not be switched on when simply hanging from your shoulder.

Shutter-release button

Touching the grip sensor and looking through the eyepiece is sufficient to activate the autofocus, the auto stand-by zoom function and the automatic exposure program. Alternatively, the automatic exposure program and autofocus can be turned on by lightly pressing the shutter-release button. This is necessary, for example, when you have to wear gloves and the grip sensor doesn't activate the eyepiece sensor. Lightly pressing the shutter-release button does not activate the auto stand-by zoom (ASZ) function. If the shutter-release button is held pressed the autofocus setting and exposure are locked for still subjects. The focus lock is indicated in the viewfinder by the focus signal changing from ((o)) to o.

Program-reset button

This button, marked by a bold **P**, is located on the left-hand side of the camera top, in front of the main switch. It is used to cancel most special settings, returning the camera to fully automatic mode with program selection, autofocus and automatic flash. In the P-program the integral flash of the 5xi pops up automatically when necessary. A Minolta program flash unit mounted on the camera is also activated automatically in these situations.

In combination with the shutter-setting control the desired exposure program can be selected while pressing the function button. Apart from programmed autoexposure (P) the 5xi offers aperture priority (A), shutter priority (S), and manual exposure mode (M). By directly adjusting individual settings in programmed autoexposure mode the fully automatic program can be switched to PA (aperture preselection) or PS (shutter speed preselection).

Shutter-setting control

The slide switch in front of the shutter button is used to increase or decrease the shutter speed in PS, S or manual mode. The shutter speed is selected in full steps. The shutter-setting control, when operated in conjunction with the button marked **FUNC** in white on the back of the camera, is also used to select the different exposure functions. Pushing it to the left sets these functions in the following sequence: S (shutter priority), M (manual exposure control), and A (aperture priority). Pushing the switch to the right sets the exposure functions in the opposite sequence.

The operating controls of the 5xi are clearly laid out.

1. Grip sensor
2. Shutter-setting control
3. Shutter-release button
4. Body data panel
5. Flash
6. Self-timer indicator-window
7. Main switch
8. Program-reset button
9. Strap eyelet
10. Flash-control button
11. Aperture-setting control
12. Lens release
13. Focus-mode switch
14. Mirror*
15. Lens contacts
16. Film window
17. Eyepiece sensor*
18. Eyepiece cup
19. Card-on/off button
20. Spot-metering button
21. Function button
22. Card door
23. Card-eject slide
24. Self-timer/drive-mode button
25. Pre-flash button
26. Card-adjust button
27. Remote-control terminal

* Please do not touch

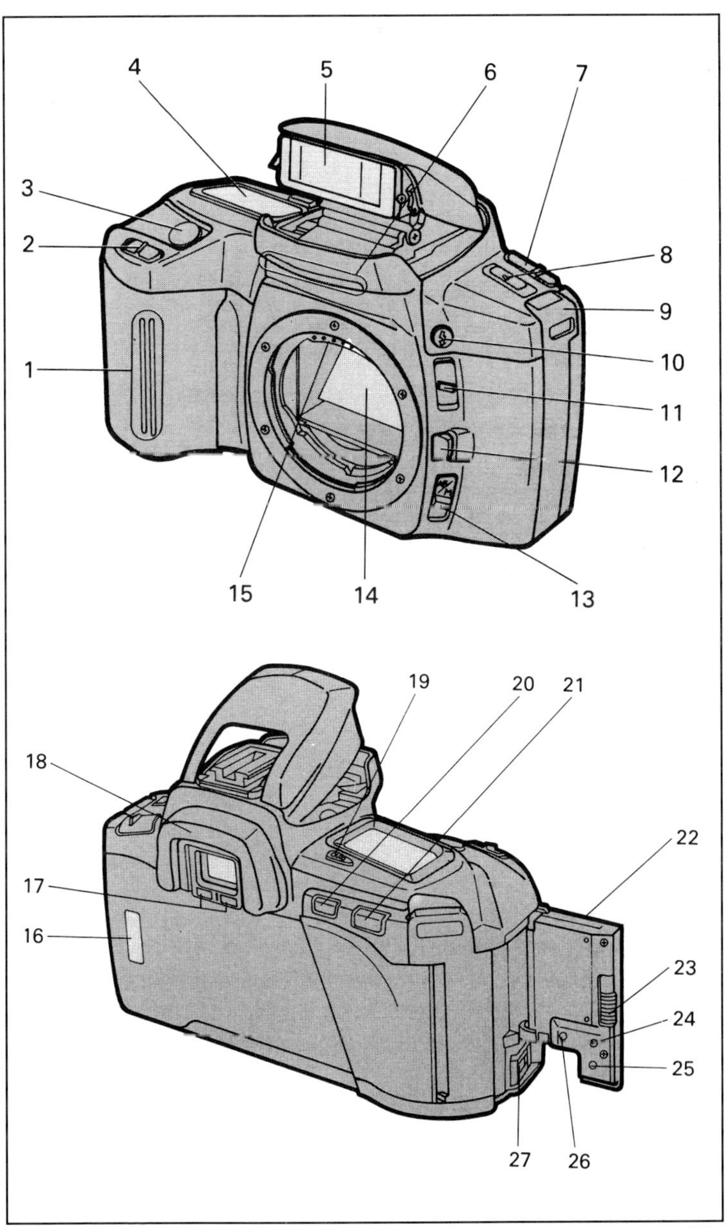
1
2
3
4
5
6
7
8
9
10
11
12
13
14
15
16
17
18
19
20
21
22
23
24
25
26
27

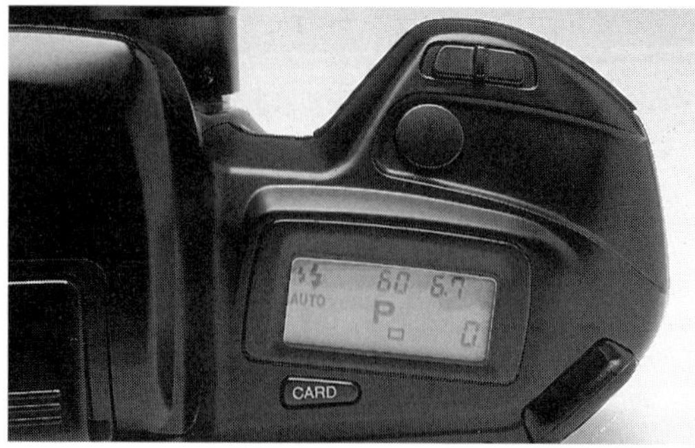

The body data panel displays the different operating modes, e.g. P for programmed autoexposure.

Flash-control button

This button, located above the aperture-setting control and marked with a flash symbol, is used to manually switch on the fill-in flash function, regardless of the lighting conditions. The integral flash unit is popped up by pressing this button; however, in programmed autoexposure mode it will be fired only if the automatic exposure system deems it necessary. It will be fired regardless if the flash-control button is pressed at the same time as the shutter-release button. In aperture priority (A), shutter priority (S), and manual exposure control mode (M) the flash is not activated automatically. In these operating modes it has to be switched on via the flash-

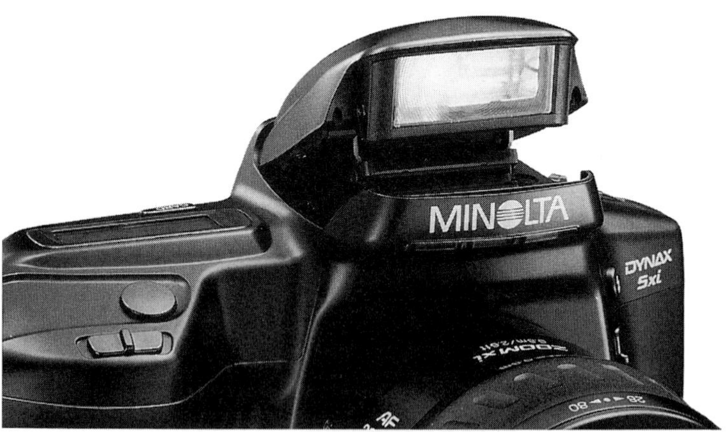

In programmed autoexposure mode the 5xi automatically pops up the integral flash whenever necessary.

control button, but this button does not have to be pressed again for the exposure. In order to switch off the automatic flash function in programmed autoexposure mode hold in the flash control button and slide the shutter setting switch to the right or left. To re-activate the automatic flash function you simply need to press the flash-control button a second time or operate the program-reset button.

Aperture-setting control
To the left of the camera bayonet (when the camera is held normally) you will see a further slide switch at the top. This is used to adjust the aperture setting in manual exposure mode and aperture priority mode. Pushing the switch downwards stops down the aperture (the f/number increases) and pushing it upwards opens up the aperture (reducing the f/number). The aperture is adjusted in half-stop increments.

Lens release
The middle one of the three controls at the side of the bayonet is used to release the lens. This control must first be pushed in before the lens can be turned anti-clockwise and removed from the bayonet. When a lens is mounted this control will lock into position with an audible click.

Focus-mode switch
The bottom control on the side of the lens bayonet is used to switch between automatic and manual focusing. It is needed in situations where low subject contrast or low light make automatic focusing impossible or when the autofocus function fails for any other reason. This will happen only relatively rarely, as the integral flash unit of the 5xi will emit a metering flash to support the focusing system in low light. You can also use a Minolta program flash unit with AF Illuminator for automatic focusing in darkness. To switch the autofocus back on you simply push down the focus-mode button a second time or press the program-reset button.

Spot-metering button
This button, which is located on the back of the camera underneath the card-on/off button, to the left of the function button, is marked **SPOT** and is used to switch from 8-segment honeycomb-pattern metering to spot metering. Pressing and holding the spot-metering

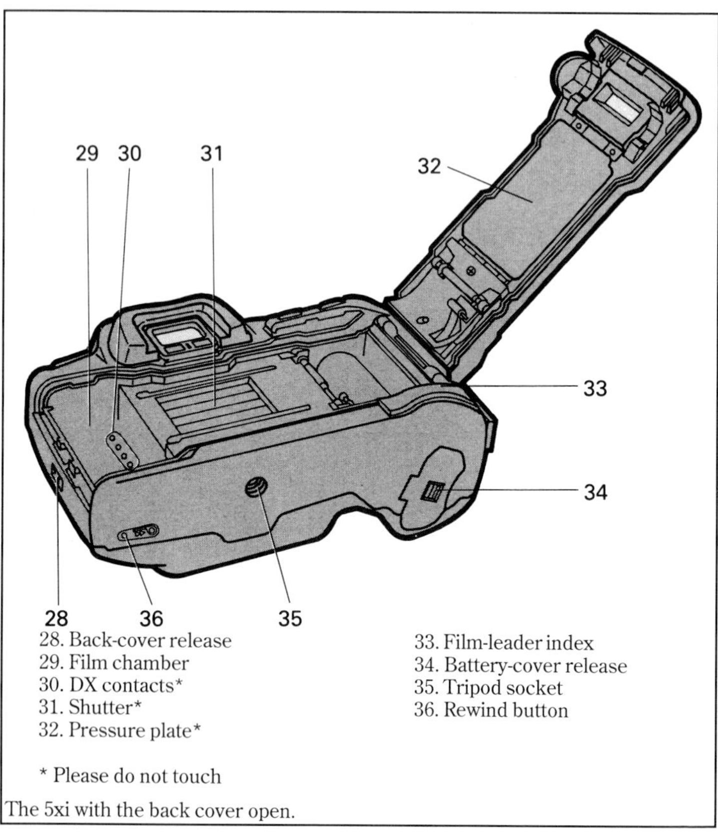

28. Back-cover release
29. Film chamber
30. DX contacts*
31. Shutter*
32. Pressure plate*
33. Film-leader index
34. Battery-cover release
35. Tripod socket
36. Rewind button

* Please do not touch

The 5xi with the back cover open.

button will reduce the exposure metering area to the circle indicated in the viewfinder. If the integral flash unit or a clip-on or remotely controlled system flash unit is used in programmed autoexposure and aperture and shutter priority mode, the spot-metering button is used to activate the slow-shutter sync function. For this function the spot-metering button needs to be pressed and held in during the exposure.

Function button

This button, marked **FUNC**, is located within reach of the thumb towards the outer edge of the camera back and used to select exposure modes and exposure compensation. Pressing the button on its own will allow you to select the different exposure modes - programmed autoexposure (P), aperture priority (A), shutter priority (S) and manual exposure control (M) - via the shutter-setting control. If you operate the aperture-setting control instead of the shutter-setting control you can select manual exposure compensation values between + or - 4 exposure stops. The aperture setting control is pushed up for positive values (i.e. more generous exposure) and down for negative values (less exposure). When compensation is set you will be able to see a plus or minus symbol on the body or viewfinder data panel. The exact value can be displayed on the body data panel and in the viewfinder by pressing the function button. Any exposure compensation selected is cancelled by pressing the program-reset button.

Rewind button
This small button is located on the left of the camera base, slightly recessed to protect it from accidental operation. To rewind a partially exposed film use a pointed object, such as a pencil or ballpoint, to operate the rewind button.

Battery-cover release
The cover on the battery chamber in the base of the camera is secured by a spring clip. To open the chamber simply push the battery-cover release in the direction of the arrow printed on it. The cover locks automatically when it is pushed shut.

Back-cover release
The back cover is opened by pushing down this release, which is on the left-hand side of the camera, and closed by simply pushing it shut. After film loading the camera automatically advances to the first frame after the back cover has been closed.

Viewfinder displays

As the 5xi is intended for easy photography with a high degree of automation, the viewfinder displays were kept to a minimum. When the camera is activated and ready to use you will see, centred below the viewfinder image, a green illuminated LCD panel. These

Viewfinder screen and viewfinder data panel

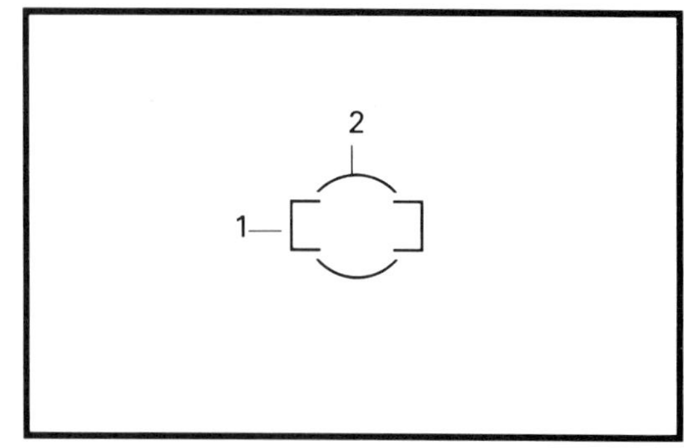

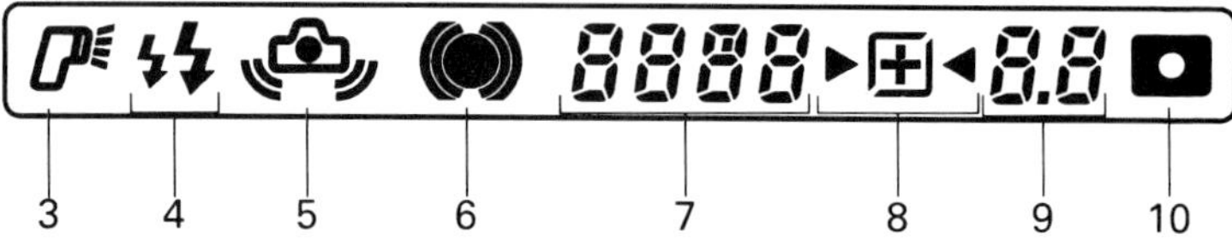

1. Focus frame
2. Spot-metering frame
3. Flash-on indicator
4. Flash-ready indicator
5. Camera-shake warning
6. Focus signal
7. Shutter-speed display
8. Exposure signals/exposure-adjustment indicator
9. Aperture/exposure- adjustment display
10. Spot-metering/slow-shutter-sync indicator

LCDs indicate the autofocus, exposure, and flash functions. The focus and spot-metering frames are shown in the centre of the focusing screen.

Focus signal

A small green dot inside two green brackets indicates that the predictive autofocus function is activated and focusing on the subject inside the focus frame. If only the outer brackets can be seen the system is in the process of focusing. The dot and brackets simultaneously confirm the focus. If the release button is pressed gently, and the subject is static, the green dot will light on its own to indicate that focus is locked and the picture can be re-framed. If the AF system cannot focus the green dot will flash.

Exposure signals
The shutter speed and aperture display, together with the exposure adjustment and spot-metering indicators, enable you to monitor all exposure functions. Shutter speed and aperture are displayed steadily when a correct exposure is to be expected. In programmed autoexposure mode, with expert program selection, all relevant parameters, such as any subject movement as well as the reproduction ratio, are taken into account to determine a suitable aperture/shutter speed combination. If the single green dot is lit, indicating that focus is locked, the shutter speed and aperture are also locked. If two flashing arrow symbols appear between the shutter speed and aperture figures the lighting conditions are outside the camera's range and incorrect exposure may result. Similarly, if you are using Aperture Priority or Shutter Priority mode, or adjusting the Programmed exposure on PA or PS mode, the shutter speed or aperture value will blink if you try to set a value at which correct exposure is not possible. If the automatically determined shutter speed is too slow for shake free handheld use a camera symbol enclosed by two brackets at either side will flash next to the focus signal. In manual mode a square will be indicated between the shutter speed and aperture displays, with a plus or minus symbol lit up in its centre. A small triangular arrow next to the over or underexposure signal will show in which direction the shutter-setting control needs to be pushed to get to the exposure value metered and recommended by the camera. If this value is reached the square will disappear and both arrows will be visible.

Flash symbol
Depending on the flash function different flash symbols, a flash-on indicator and a flash-ready indicator, will be visible in the viewfinder. The latter is shown either as a single or double symbol. These displays indicate a total of five meanings. If only a tiny flash unit is visible the integral unit or a clip-on flash has been activated and the unit is charging. The single or double flash symbol in addition to the flash unit symbol signals that the flash is ready. Flashing after an exposure means that a correct flash shot has been taken.
The double flash symbol indicates that the pre-flash function, for reduction of the 'red-eye' effect, has been activated; if both symbols

are flashing alternately wireless remote flash control is activated. In this case correct flash exposure is indicated by the larger flash symbol flashing after the exposure. When using Remote Cordless TTL flash, the viewfinder indicator only indicates that the built-in flash is ready, not both units.

Focus frame
Two rectangular brackets in the centre of the viewfinder, joined by the two curved brackets of the spot-metering frame, signify the AF metering area. The camera sets the focus on the subject detail located in this square area. In order for the predictive autofocus to be able to follow the subject, all or part of it needs to be located within the focus frame.

Spot-metering frame
The two additional semi-circular brackets in the centre of the viewfinder, above and below the focus frame, enclose the spot metering area of the 5xi. The spot-metering frame is only activated, in P or M mode, if the spot-metering button is pressed. Place the spot-metering frame on the area you wish to meter from, press in and hold the 'SPOT' button, then re-frame the picture if necessary. Spot metering cannot be used when flash is activated. If the spot button is pressed while using flash, 'slow shutter sync' is activated. Two flashing arrows will signal that the metering range is insufficient for spot metering, and that incorrect exposures are to be expected.

Body data panel

The body data panel is the external information centre of the 5xi and indicates all camera, lens, flash, and accessory (such as expansion cards) settings and functions that are relevant for the exposure. Some displays are only visible whilst a function is selected, others only for as long as a certain function is activated or whilst it is running.

Battery-condition indicator
Every time the camera is switched on it automatically checks the charging state of the battery and indicates it via the battery symbol.

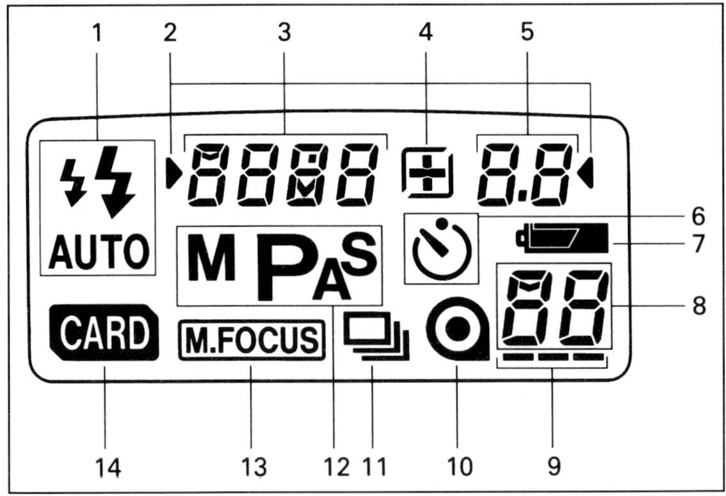

1. Flash-mode indicator
2. Selectable-setting pointers
3. Shutter-speed/card-name display
4. Exposure-adjustment indicator
5. Aperture/exposure-adjustment/card-setting display
6. Self-timer indicator
7. Battery-condition indicator
8. Frame counter/card-setting display
9. Film-transport signals
10. Film-cartridge mark
11. Drive-mode indicator
12. Exposure-mode indicator
13. Manual-focus indicator
14. Card indicator

To change exposure mode:

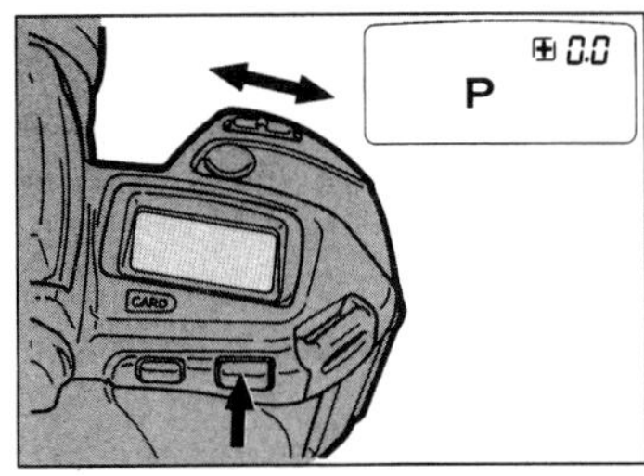

1. Press and hold the function button, then push the shutter-setting control in either direction.

2. The selected exposure mode is automatically entered when you let go of the function button.

Exposure-mode indicator

The display for the currently activated exposure control mode appears almost in the centre of the body data panel:

* P : programmed autoexposure

* PA: creative program control with aperture preselection

* PS: creative program control with shutter speed preselection

Aperture priority (A)

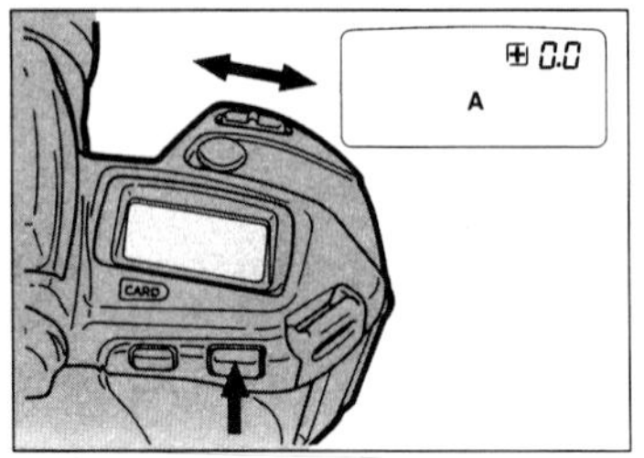

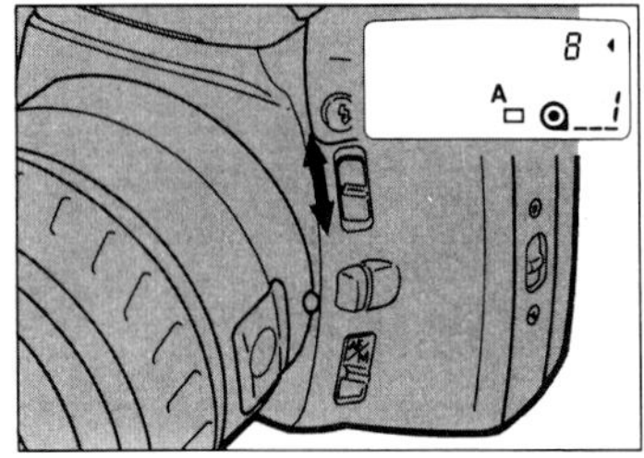

Shutter priority (S)

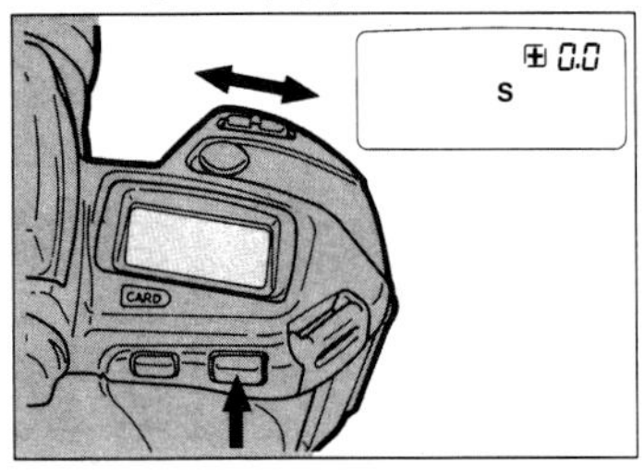

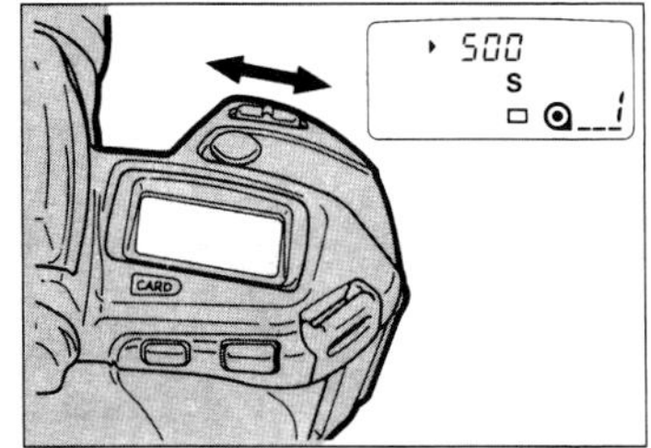

Manual exposure mode (M)

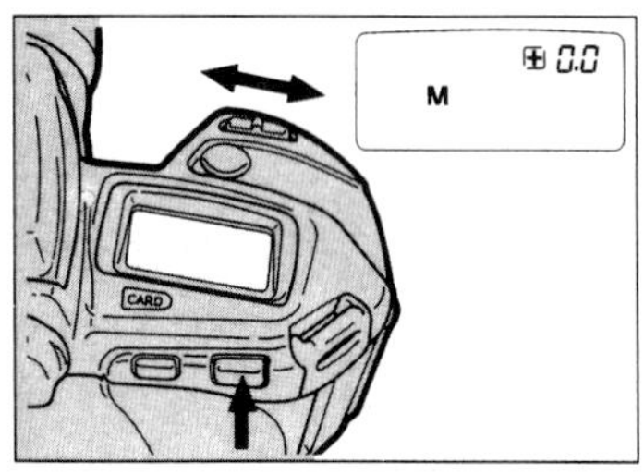

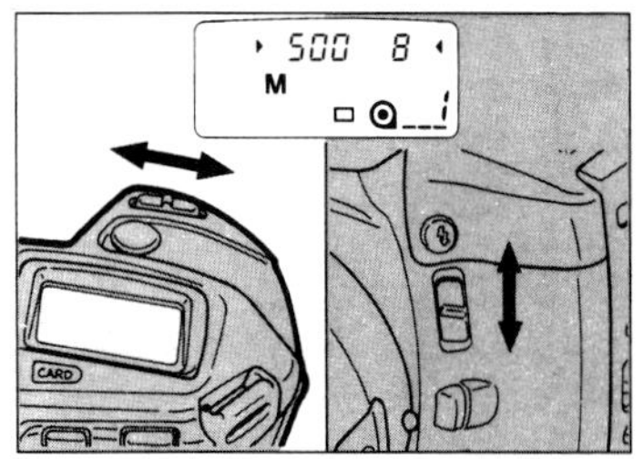

* M : manual exposure control
* A : aperture priority
* S : shutter priority

The **P** for Minolta's expert program selection is unmistakable. The '**P**' symbol appears whenever you press the program-reset button or select this particular mode by means of the function button and the shutter-setting control.

The **P** turns into **PA** for just one shot or a short period of time to signal creative program control with aperture preselection, a mode that works similar to aperture priority. You can switch from

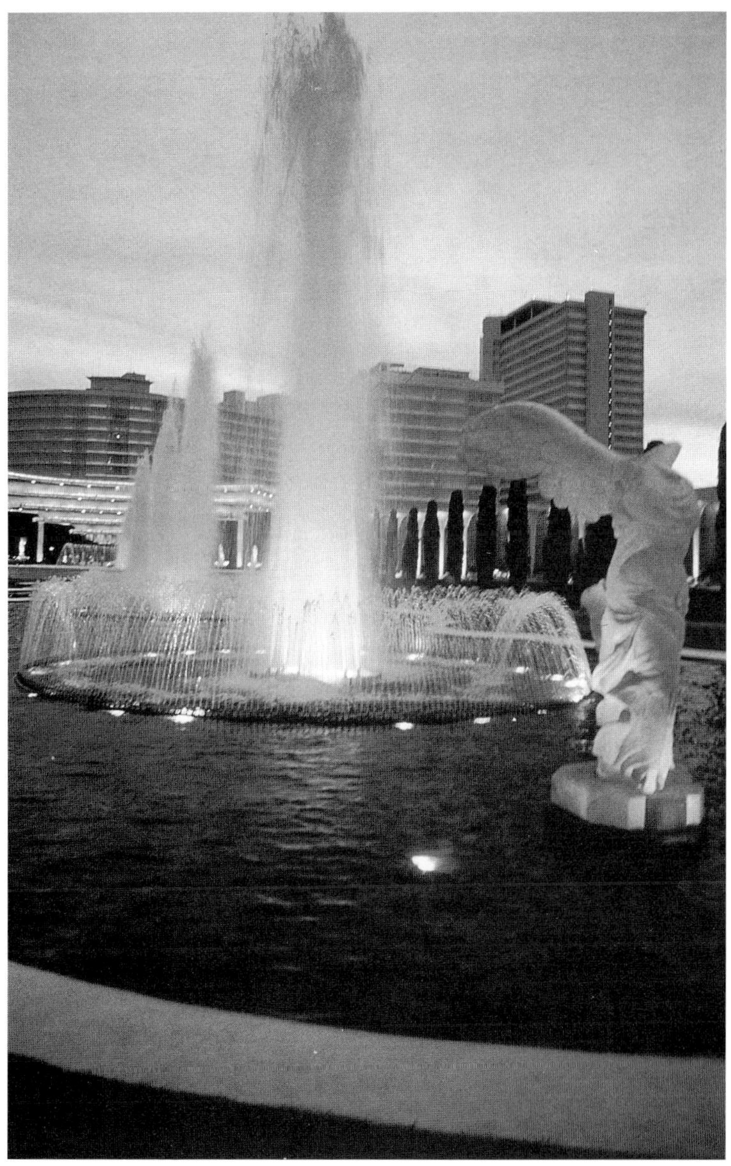

The expert exposure system of the 5xi ensures correctly exposed shots even with strong subject contrast.

Viewfinder exposure signals

Viewfinder signal	Meaning
250 ▸ ◂5.6	Correct exposure set.
60 ▸⊞ 5.6	Overexposure to be expected.
500 ⊟◂5.6	Underexposure to be expected.
2000 ▸ ◂22	Light conditions outside the metering range of the camera.

In manual exposure mode these signals refer to the settings selected by the photographer.

programmed autoexposure mode to PA or PS simply by operating the aperture- or shutter-setting controls respectively. The **P** changing to **PS** signals that creative program selection with shutter speed preselection (shutter priority) has been activated. However, PA or PS mode cannot be selected if flash is required in programmed autoexposure mode. The camera will return to normal Program mode four seconds after you remove your eye from the viewfinder.

Aperture priority is indicated by a large **A**, shutter priority by a large **S**, whereas manual exposure control is signalled by an **M**. The desired exposure mode is selected by pressing the function button on the back of the camera and simultaneously operating the shutter-setting control in front of the shutter-release button.

Manual-focus indicator

The indication **M.FOCUS** appears in a thin frame on the body data panel when the camera is switched from automatic to manual focusing. This is done either by the switch on the camera or by pulling back the zoom ring on one of the new Minolta xi zoom or power zoom lenses.

Flash-mode indicator

A single flash symbol and the letters **AUTO** indicate that the automatic flash function is activated in programmed autoexposure

Page 33
On holiday zoom lenses are particularly useful for continuous framing. A combination of wide-angle and telezoom is ideal.

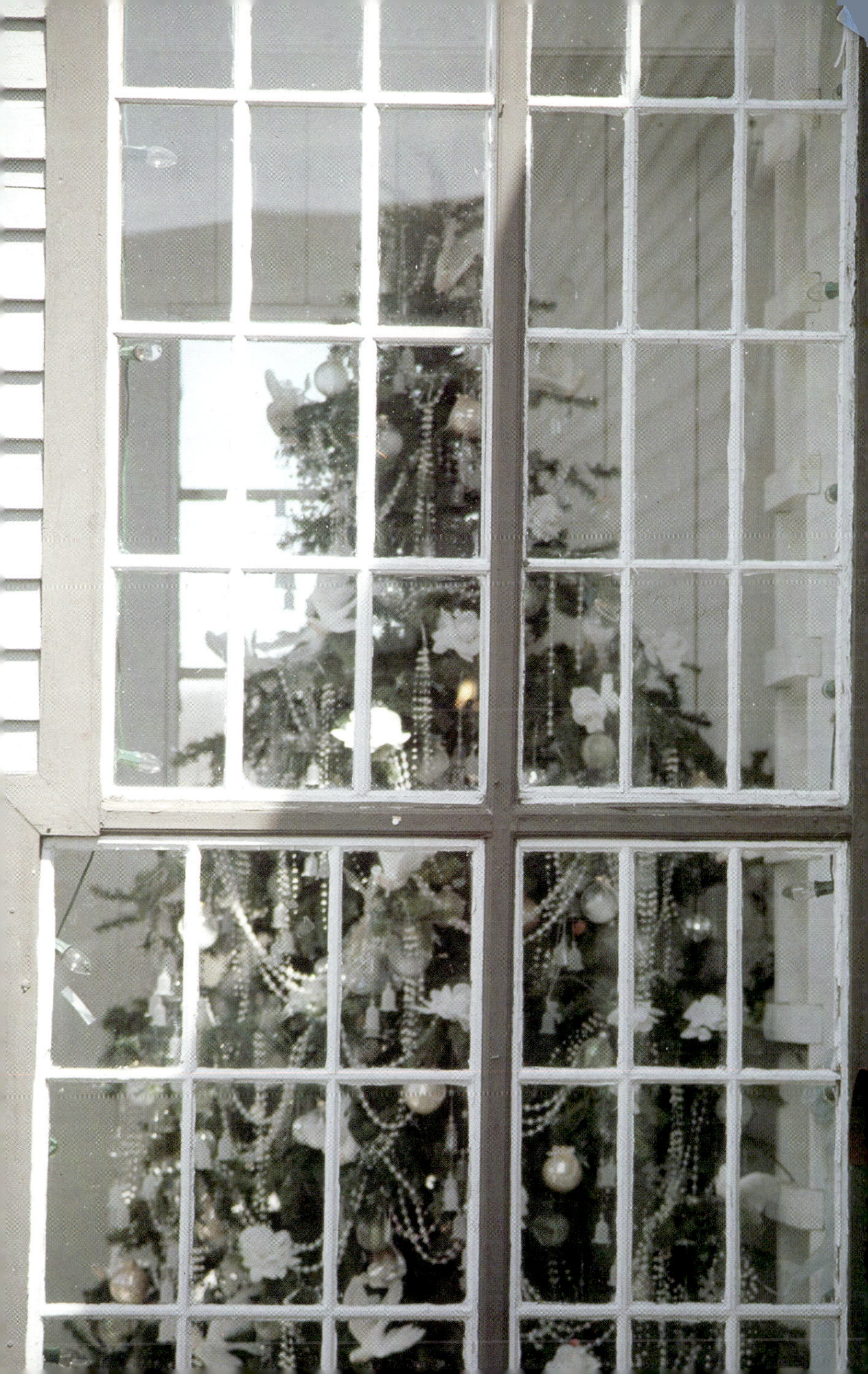

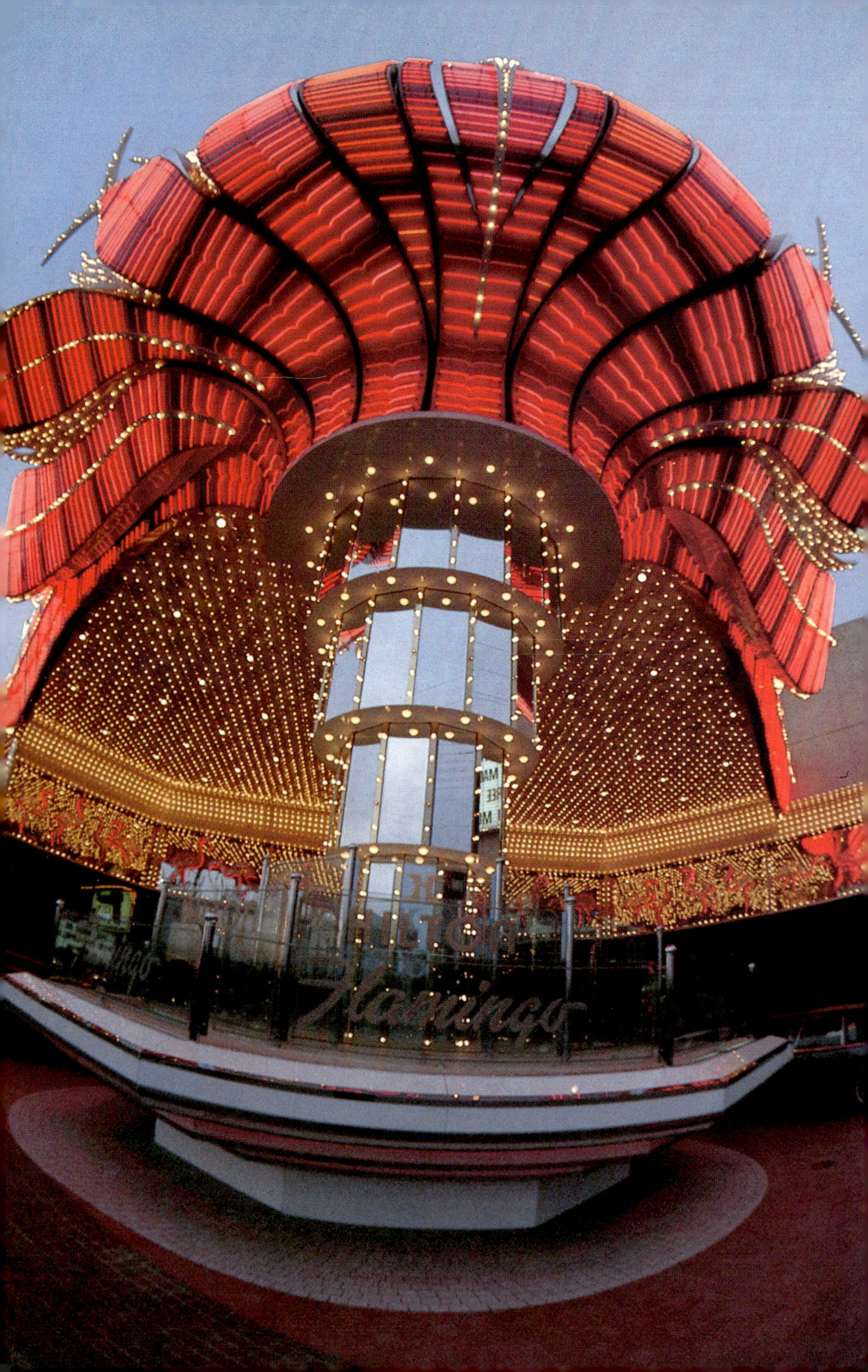
HILTON
Flamingo

mode. If the pre-flash function is also activated the double flash symbol and the letters **AUTO** will appear; alternate flashing of the two flash symbols (without the additional letters) signals that the wireless remote control function is activated. In A, S, and M exposure mode the single or double flash symbol will appear only if both functions have previously been selected by pressing the flash-control button and the pre-flash button inside the card door. The pre-flash function is only carried out with the integral flash unit. The same button that activates pre-flash (when using the built-in flash) will activate Remote Cordless TTL flash if an appropriate xi unit is on the shoe (3500xi or 5400xi).

Aperture and shutter speed displays

Shutter speed and aperture are displayed on the left and right of the top line on the body data panel respectively - provided the shutter-release button is pressed lightly or the camera held in such a way that the viewfinder sensor is activated. If this is not the case the shutter speed/aperture display is switched off quickly to save power. The parameters that can be selected manually in the exposure mode set at any one time are indicated by triangular selectable-setting pointers on the left (shutter speed) or right (aperture) of these displays. The displays of the parameters controlled by the camera will flash if incorrect exposure is likely. Refer to the chapters on the different exposure functions to find out which parameter will flash in which situation. The shutter speed and aperture displays are also used to signal the programming of special functions:

* Lens mounting - two lines (- -) appearing instead of the aperture display means either that no lens is on the camera or that the lens has been attached incorrectly. This indication can also mean that the AZ/MZ switch of an xi lens is set to MZ.

* Image size lock - if the round button (designated function button by Minolta) on the same level as the lens release on the xi lens is pressed, the reproduction ratio of the main subject is locked. At the same time you will see the letters **ISL On** in the viewfinder and on the body data panel. If only two small lines are visible after

---

Page 34
The honeycomb-pattern metering system of the 5xi can master shots at night or in twilight without any problems. Exposure compensation is only necessary in exceptional circumstances.

Switching off the ASZ function

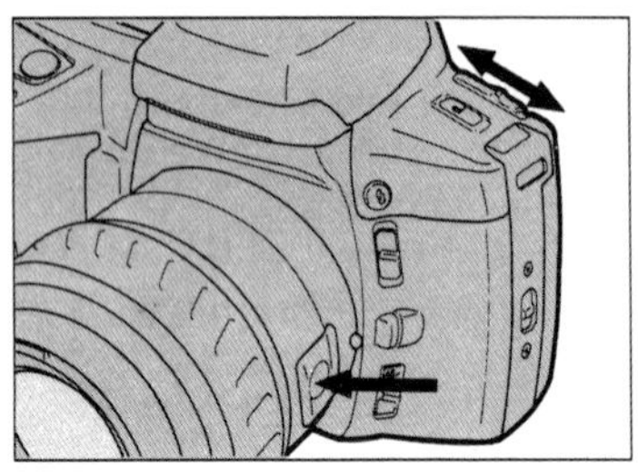

1. Set main switch to **LOCK.**
2. Press and hold the lens-function button on the lens barrel whilst setting the main switch back to **ON.**

* To switch the ASZ function on again, repeat the two steps.

OFF AS

the letters **ISL** (Image Size Lock) the value could not be stored, either because the main subject was too small or because the lens is set to a focal length below 50mm. The image size lock function will only work whilst the button is pressed. The function is interrupted if the subject goes outside the working range of the camera and re-activated if the subject returns into the working range and the button is still held down.

* ASZ function indicator - if the auto stand-by zoom function (ASZ) of Minolta xi auto zoom lenses is switched off, the letters **OFF AS** will appear on the body data panel. To switch this function off press the function button on the lens, also used for the image size lock feature, and push the main switch of the camera from **LOCK** to **ON**. Simply repeat this process to switch ASZ back on - **ON AS** will appear on the body data panel. The display will go out as soon as the function button on the lens is released.

* Remote flash control indicator - to program the 5xi for remote flash control, attach and switch on the 3500xi or 5400xi program flash unit. Pressing the pre-flash button inside the card door will now switch the camera to wireless TTL flash control. At the same time the two flash symbols on the body data panel will flash alternately.

* AF illumination function indicator - on the 5xi the AF illuminator to support the AF system can be switched off. To do this press the pre-flash button inside the card door and push the main switch from **LOCK** to **ON**. The letters **OFF AL** will appear on the body data panel. Switch the function back on by repeating the same

procedure - **ON AL** will appear on the panel. The display goes out as soon as the pre-flash button is released.

The AF illuminator will not work if the flash unit is not required in P mode, or if you have switched it off. It will not work in A, S, or M mode if the flash has not been popped up.

* **bAtt** indicator - if the battery charge is too low and the camera is switched on the flashing **bAtt** indication will appear in place of the shutter speed. Contrary to the instruction manual it will go out as soon as the main switch is set to **LOCK**. The battery symbol will flash even if the camera is switched off.

* **HELP** indication - the film advance function is faulty if the letters **HELP** appear on the body data panel. Usually this can be remedied simply by removing and replacing the battery.

* **CARD** indication - these letters can be seen on a black background at the bottom left of the body data panel if an expansion card is activated. When the card on/off button is pressed to activate the card function, the short name of the card will appear briefly on the display panel. The indication on the panel is cancelled by pressing the card-on/off button for a second time; this will also de-activate the card function, even if it is left in the card door. Resetting by means of the program-reset button or switching the **LOCK** button on and off will not work.

Frame counter

If no film is loaded the figure **0** appears on the frame counter in the bottom right-hand corner of the body data panel. If the figure **0** flashes together with the cassette symbol and the film-transport signals then the film was loaded incorrectly. If only the **0** and the cassette symbol flash, the film was either rewound automatically after the last frame or rewound manually and only partially exposed. The cassette symbol, film-transport signals, and frame number are permanently visible if the camera is switched on and the film is winding on correctly.

Self-timer

The self-timer symbol appears if you press the self-timer/drive-mode button inside the card door. In single-frame

The Minolta 5xi automatically reads off the film speed of DX-coded films in a range between ISO 25/15° and 5000/38°.

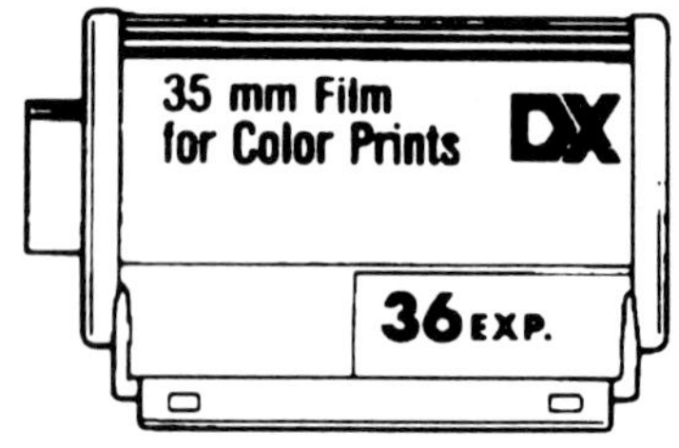

advance mode the self-timer symbol appears after one press of the button. If continuous mode has been selected pressing the button will first reset the camera to single-frame advance and pressing it for a second time will activate the self-timer. The function is once again cancelled by repeating the same procedure, or by switching off the camera or operating the program-reset button. The self-timer symbol on the body data panel will flash during the count-down, and immediately prior to the exposure three red flashes will be fired. The self-timer has to be re-activated after each shot.

Film loading

Film loading is a sheer pleasure with today's motorized cameras sporting automatic threading and advance. It's easy to forget the 'good old days' when fiddling around trying to stick the film leader into take-up spool slots was normal. With Minolta's Maxxum/ Dynax cameras all you need do is open the back cover, place the film cassette in the film chamber and pull the film leader to the right until it reaches the red film leader index. Then simply close and press down the back cover and, the film will be advanced to the first frame. You are ready to 'go'!

If you accidentally pull the film leader too far out so that it extends beyond the red film leader index, take the film cassette back out of the camera and carefully rewind it a little. Films with torn or creased film leaders can also cause problems for the threading mechanism because the sprockets of the transport spool in front of the index mark must engage with the lower perforations of the film.

The film speed is automatically read off the film cassette and transmitted to the computer for exposure control purposes. Because of automatic film speed registration only DX-coded films can be used in the 5xi, although with un-coded films the camera automatically sets ISO 100/21°. The automatic film speed registration works in one-third increments on films between ISO 25/15° and 5000/38°, but the automatic flash control system is only designed to work up to ISO 1000/31°.

Before loading a film, or rather before opening the camera back, it's a good idea to look at the body data panel and through the film window. If there is still film in the camera opening the back cover can spoil the pictures you've already taken. The light entering during accidental opening becomes visible as a wide bright stripe on the affected frames. The frame counter also returns to **1** when the back cover is closed.

Partially exposed films have to be rewound before they can be taken out. Film rewind is activated by pressing the rewind button on the underside of the camera. Once rewinding has been completed the figure **0** and the cassette symbol flash on the body data panel. Films are automatically rewound after the last exposure. With a 36-exposure film this takes around 18 seconds while a 24-exposure film will be rewound in 12 seconds. If the battery is too flat to complete rewinding the process will continue as soon as a fresh battery is inserted; there is no need to press the rewind button again.

To prevent light from entering through the opening in the film cassette, don't change films in bright sunlight. If this can't be avoided then at least do it in your own shadow.

Whatever you do, don't forget to remove the protective foil from the film channel of new cameras.

If the film has been loaded correctly the figure **1** will appear on the body data panel once the back cover has been closed, indicating that the first shot can be taken. When loaded incorrectly the frame counter stays on **0** and this and the cassette symbol on the body data panel flash. Just open the back cover and re-load the film. The camera has to be set to **ON** for film loading.

Expert autofocus

If you've never worked with predictive autofocus you can't even begin to imagine how comfortable and easy focusing can be with a modern Maxxum/Dynax camera like the 5xi. And it's not just that you gain time for frame composition; for many photographs automatic focusing is a guarantee for improved technical quality. Autofocus reduces the technical error rate to a hardly imaginable minimum. And if you take the camera shake warning indicator seriously, you'll rarely get any technically deficient exposures.

Minolta offer two types of focusing, one for still subjects and the other for moving subjects. Unlike many other AF cameras the Minolta 5xi switches between exposure lock and predictive autofocus automatically: it is not necessary to select the suitable operating mode manually. The camera recognizes whether a subject is moving or still and selects the appropriate operating

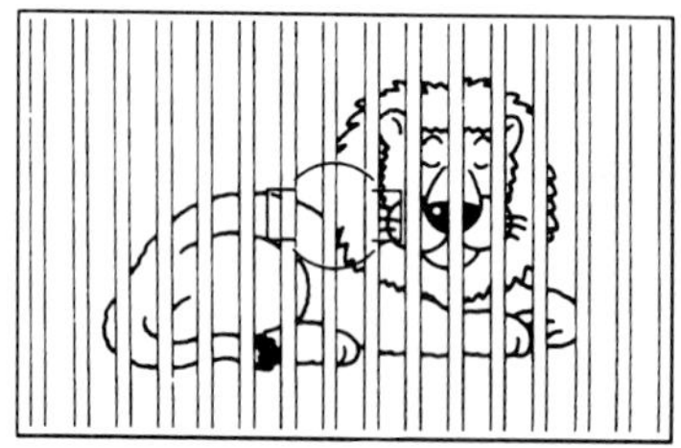

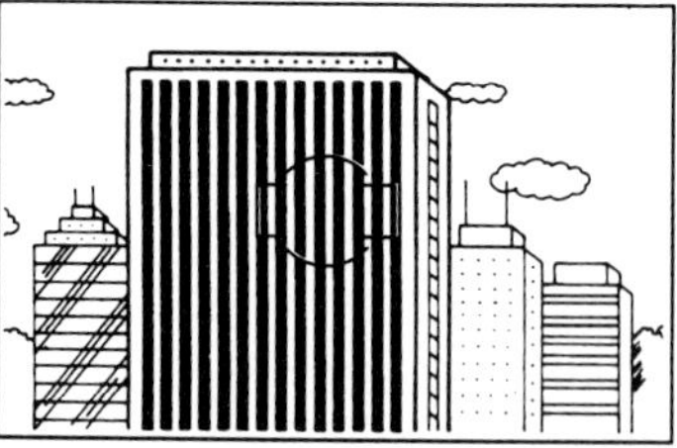

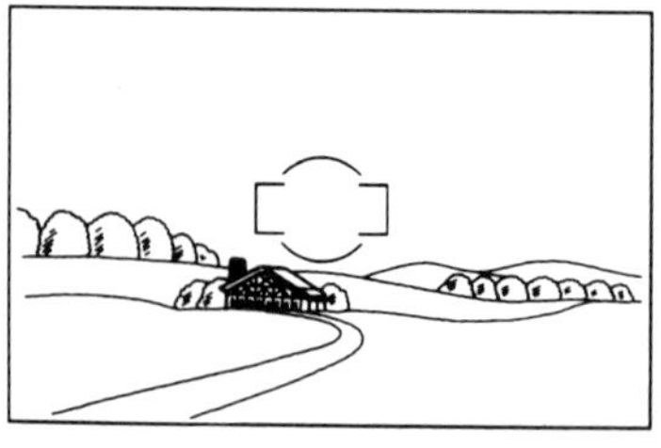

Subjects with regular patterns, objects at different distances in the metering area and with portions lacking in contrast can interfere with the functioning of the 5xi's AF system.

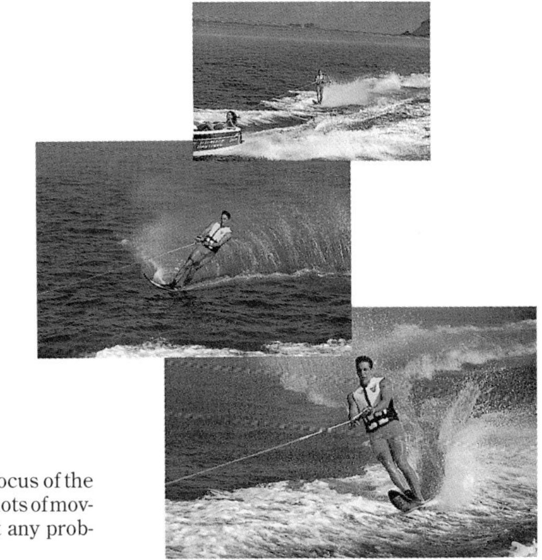

The predictive autofocus of the 5xi achieves sharp shots of moving subjects without any problems.

mode itself. The expert predictive autofocus is activated as soon as you look through the viewfinder. If the cameras computer recognizes that the subject is moving it will also calculate the speed at which it is moving. When you press the shutter-release button the camera will use its calculation to focus on the position the subject will be in at the point of shutter release. This means that the autofocus system of the 5xi calculates the distance a subject will cover in the period between the pressing of the shutter-release button and the mirror swinging up and the iris diaphragm operating, anticipating the position of the subject at the actual time of exposure. This automatic focusing system, marketed by Minolta under the name predictive autofocus, delivers excellent results even with fast subject movement.

The autofocus area is fairly large compared to those of other manufacturers' camera, which makes it easy to aim at a moving subject and keep it within the focus frame. Like those of almost all other AF SLR cameras, the AF system works with CCD sensors

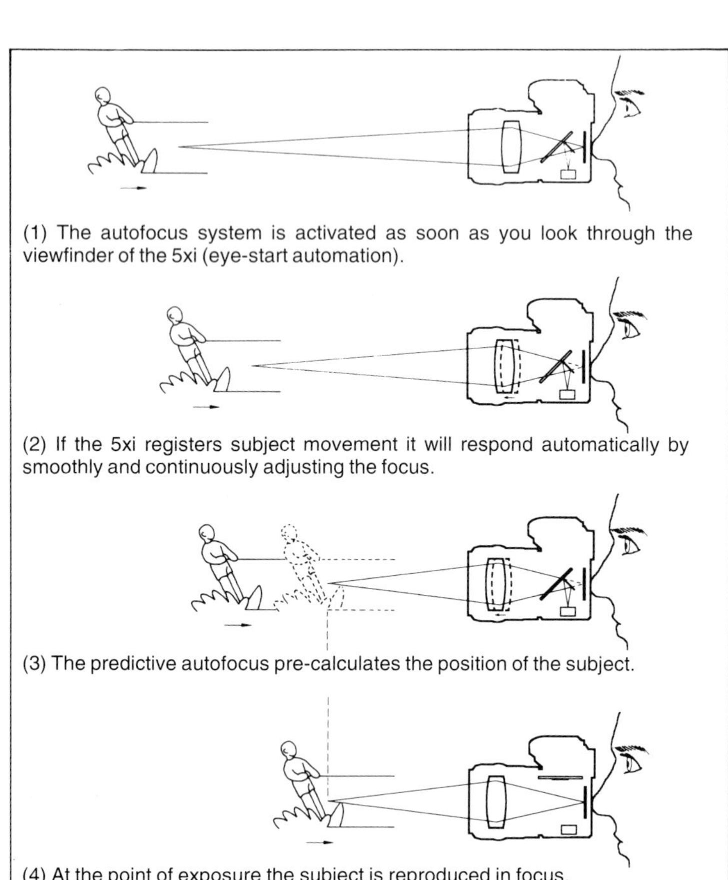

Calculations of the predictive autofocus.

using the phase-detection principle. Here part of the light entering through the lens is not directed to the viewfinder but falls through the mirror onto an infrared block filter instead. It is then concentrated by a collecting lens and re-directed onto two rows of sensors through a separating mask and a divider element via a secondary mirror. If the subject is in focus the divided light-rays hit the same sensors on each of the two CCD rows. Accurate and fast focusing, even in low light, is guaranteed by the high sensitivity of the sensors and the high calculating capacity of the integral computer control system. The system is also aided by advanced fuzzy logic software and the fast response of the AF motor. Although Minolta state that extremely fast subjects and abrupt changes in speed and direction can prove too much for the predictive autofocus system, such situations are extremely rare in practice. The working range of the AF system lies between -1 and 18EV at ISO 100.

To indicate that the subject in the large focusing area is in focus the green LCD symbol **((o))** will appear at the bottom of the viewfinder.

The distance setting is locked when the shutter-release button is pressed lightly, provided the subject is still, and the green LCD symbol **o** will appear in the viewfinder. If the subject in the focus frame is moving the camera will stay in continuous focus mode. If you are using an xi zoom lens or an AF power zoom you can lock the distance setting by pulling the zoom ring towards the camera - in this case it must not subsequently be turned.

AF illuminator

The 5xi can focus automatically not only in low light but also in complete darkness. If the camera registers insufficient subject contrast because the light level is too low for correct automatic focusing, the integral flash unit will emit several visible auxiliary flashes when the shutter-release button is pressed lightly. The light from these pre-flashes enables the AF system to focus even in complete darkness. The range for automatic focusing with the AF illuminator is usually between one and five metres, although there are exceptional situations where you have to do without the AF illuminator. This could be the case, for example, if the pre-flash would intrude on the mood of the scene, or if the subject is outside its range and you have to do without flash and the AF illuminator altogether. In such cases the AF illuminator can be switched off by pressing the pre-flash button inside the card door whilst pushing the main switch from **LOCK** to **ON**. Instead of the two flash symbols in the top line of the body data panel there will now be the letters **OFF AL**. Simply repeat the same procedure to switch the AF illuminator back on - the body data panel will signal **ON AL** until the pre-flash button is released. This setting of the AF illumination

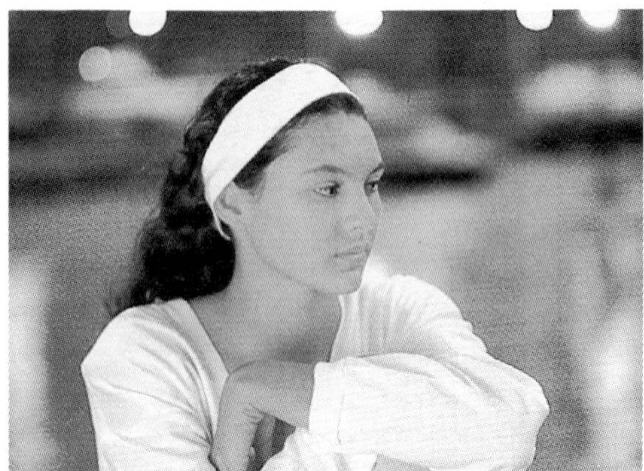

The highly sensitive CCD sensor guarantees perfect shots even in low light.

applies only to the integral flash. The AF Illuminator of an attached program flash will operate regardless of whether the camera's own AF Illuminator has been switched on or off.

In programmed autoexposure mode the AF illuminator is switched on automatically whenever necessary, but it will only work if the exposure also requires flash light for a correct exposure. If the flash function has been switched off, for example to take a slow exposure, the AF illuminator is also switched off. Switching off the red-eye reduction pre-flash function has no effect on the AF illuminator. In manual, shutter, and aperture priority mode the integral flash has to be popped up by pressing the flash-control button, which also activates the AF illuminator.

Manual focusing

There are some situations where even the best autofocus system fails. In this case you need to switch to manual focusing: with Minolta AF lenses this is easiest via the focus-mode switch on the camera body. With Minolta xi auto zoom or power zoom lenses you can simply pull the zoom ring slightly towards the camera. Focusing is then done via the lens motor, similar to the focal length setting, by turning the focusing ring. AF lenses are focused manually by turning the focusing ring. The focus is confirmed by the electronic focus signal in the viewfinder: the round green LED lights up as soon as the subject in the focus frame is in sharp focus.

Manual focusing

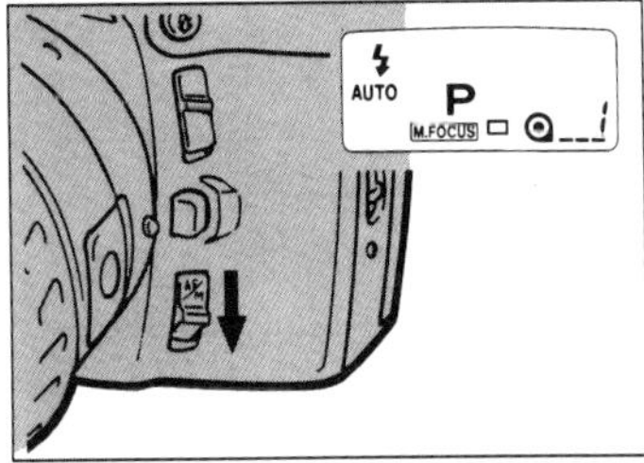

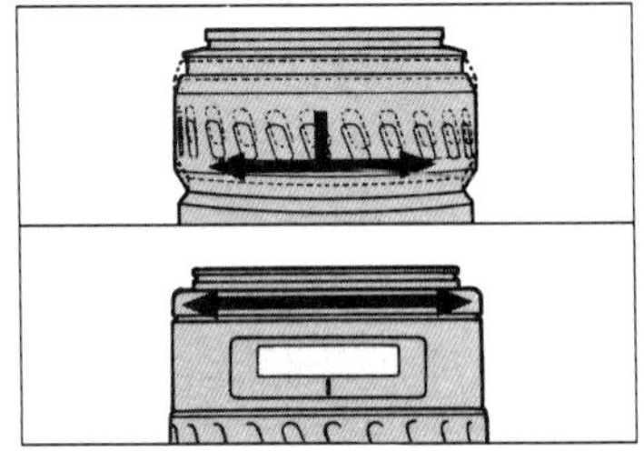

The characters **M.FOCUS** on the body data panel indicate manual focusing mode; you can focus by turning the zoom ring on the lens.

In critical situations the electronic focus signal may not work, in which case you need to determine the focus visually on the viewfinder matte screen.

Situations where you need to switch to manual focusing are when taking pictures of, monochrome areas with little contrast, subjects with alternating dark and light lines filling the focus frame, and when there are objects at different distances in the focus frame. The letters **M.FOCUS** will appear on the body data panel whenever you switch to manual focusing, whether you do so via the focus-mode switch on the camera or by pulling the zoom ring. To switch back to autofocus simply press the switch once more or operate the program-reset button. With manual focusing the shutter can be released at any time, whether the subject is in focus or not.

Exposure metering

The Minolta 5xi has a honeycomb-pattern metering system to determine the correct exposure. A highly sensitive silicon photo cell consisting of eight segments carries out the measurement. The sensitivity of each of the segments is adjusted automatically in order to adapt the metering characteristics to the subject in terms of reproduction ratio and autofocus. When spot metering is activated only the centre honeycomb segment is used, which is why spot metering fails more quickly in low light than honeycomb-pattern metering. The 5xi has a further silicon photo cell for TTL flash control.

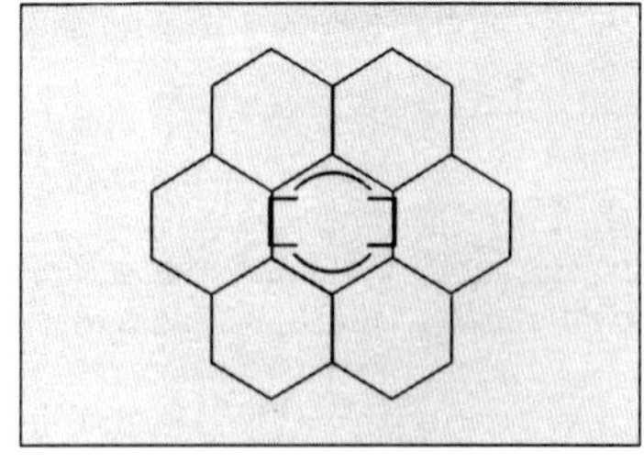

The 8-segment honeycomb-pattern metering system precisely determines the exposure values.

Honeycomb-pattern metering

The silicon photo cell of the 5xi divides the image into seven hexagonal areas arranged in a honeycomb pattern, plus a further segment to evaluate the background brightness. The brightness in each segment is then measured separately. The data from the AF sensors helps the automatic exposure system to determine the position of the main subject and to adjust the sensitivity of the metering segments in relation to this. The honeycomb-pattern system determines not only how much light is available for the exposure in order to adjust aperture and shutter speed accordingly, but also recognizes the differences in subject brightness and uses these to try and ensure that both the bright and dark portions will still have contrast. The working range of the honeycomb-pattern metering system of the 5xi lies between 0 and 20EV with ISO 100/21° films and a 50mm,f/1.4 standard lens.

In programmed autoexposure mode the 5xi automatically uses its integral flash to fill in overly dark subject portions in order to reduce excessive contrast. When a program flash unit is attached

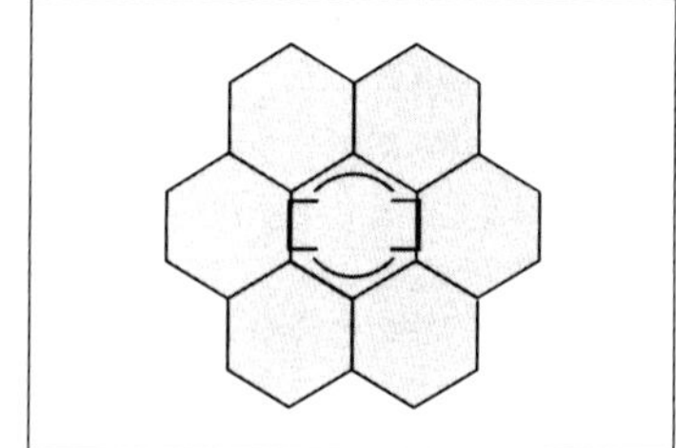

The image area of the camera is divided into seven honeycomb segments and one background segment.

in programmed autoexposure mode, it takes on the job of automatic fill-in. The operation of fill-in flash is covered in the chapter on flash photography.

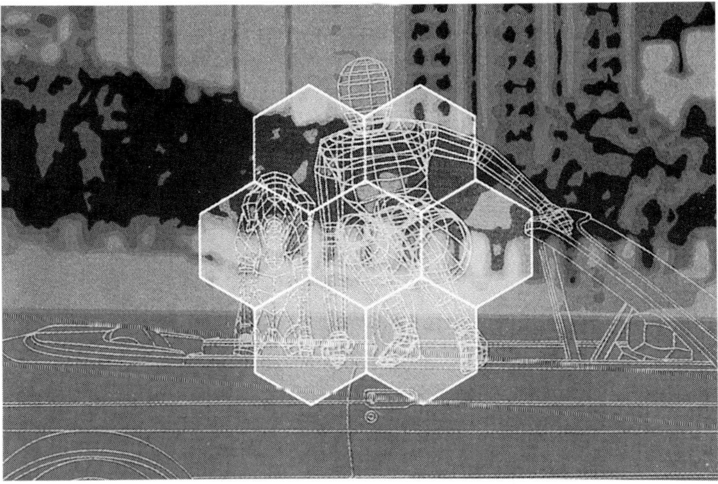

The Maxxum/Dynax expert exposure system masters a wide variety of shooting situations.

Spot metering with the 5xi

In addition to the honeycomb-pattern metering system the 5xi offers spot metering for precise exposure control. This metering mode makes sense whenever certain parts of the subject are to be emphasized and must receive optimum exposure. In the spot metering system of the 5xi the metering area is reduced to the centre segment of the honeycomb pattern, where it takes up approximately 2.7 per cent of the entire image area. The metering area is indicated by the two semi-circles engraved on the viewfinder screen.

Spot metering requires some experience in exposure metering and only really makes sense when slide film is used and you want to make creative use of certain lighting situations. In other situations the honeycomb-pattern system is unsurpassed and delivers a technically correct metering result in virtually every case. On a backlit portrait photograph, for example, the honeycomb system produces good detail in the shadow portions by reducing any excessive contrast with fill-in flash. The person will always be rendered in good contrast and the mood of the picture maintained. Spot metering, on the other hand, can produce at least five different exposures in the same situation, from a 'high key' mood to a dramatic silhouette. But as has already been stated, these subtle differences will only be noticeable on slide photographs, unless the picture is enlarged, and so a high contrast negative exposed in the honeycomb-pattern mode will often be sufficient. To know when to use the spot-metering button to maximum effect you need to know the basics of exposure.

Every exposure measurement is adjusted to the reflectance of medium grey subjects, more precisely a reflectance of 18 per cent. But our world isn't grey, it's full of colours and different colours reflect light to different degrees. So if spot metering is used you have to meter a colour with roughly the same reflectance as a medium grey in order to prevent incorrect exposure. Dark colours reflect less light, so the camera will think the scene is darker than it really is and will expose more generously. The consequence is a more or less pronounced tendency towards overexposure. Conversely, metering strongly reflecting bright colours will lead to underexposure, as the camera will think the scene is more brightly lit than it actually is. So when using spot metering you should be careful which subject detail you measure. Colours whose reflectance roughly corresponds to a medium grey are green fields (not too dark) and the asphalt or pavements of streets. Skin tones are not 18% grey. Average white skin is about half to one stop lighter, whereas average black skin is about three quarters of a stop

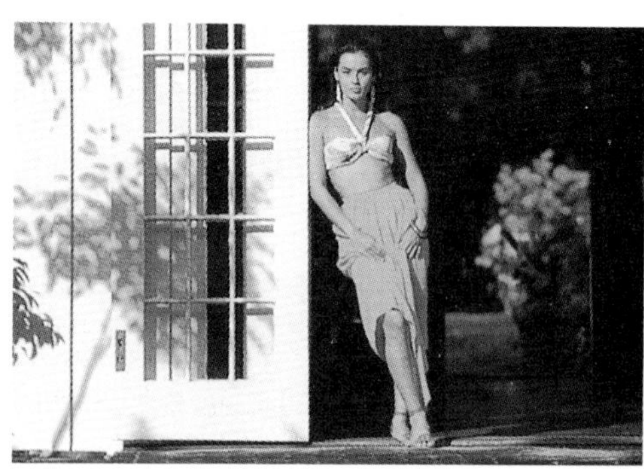

Half-stop exposure adjustments are also possible with the 5xi exposure system.

darker. Taking this into account it is possible to meter from your palm held in front of the camera or from the face of a subject, but only if you make the necessary correction thereafter.

For an accurate measurement the metered detail should fill the entire spot-metering frame in the viewfinder. You may need to go closer to the subject and then recompose after metering. The measurement remains locked for as long as the spot-metering button remains pressed. This button also has to remain pressed when the shutter is released.

Spot metering is done as follows: first aim at the subject and place the relevant detail in the viewfinder so that it fills the entire metering area. Go closer to the subject if necessary. And then, while holding in the spot-metering button, compose the image and releasing the shutter.

The working range of the spot metering system lies between 3 and 20EV with an ISO 100/21° film and a 50mm,f/1.4 standard lens. Spot metering sensitivity is slightly less than that of the honeycomb pattern metering. Spot metering activation is indicated on the lower right-hand side of the viewfinder. In TTL flash control mode spot metering cannot be used for flash exposure metering. When flashing in aperture or shutter priority mode, as well as in program mode, the spot-metering button is used for slow shutter sync.

Exposure control

The 5xi has five (including flash) different exposure control modes. Depending on the photographic situation you can choose between

Autoflash function (P)

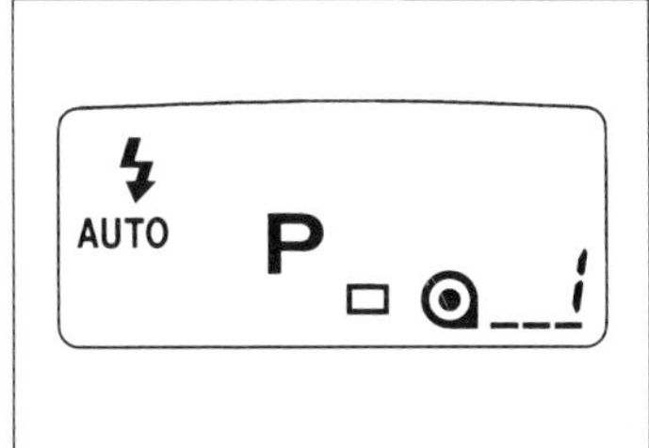

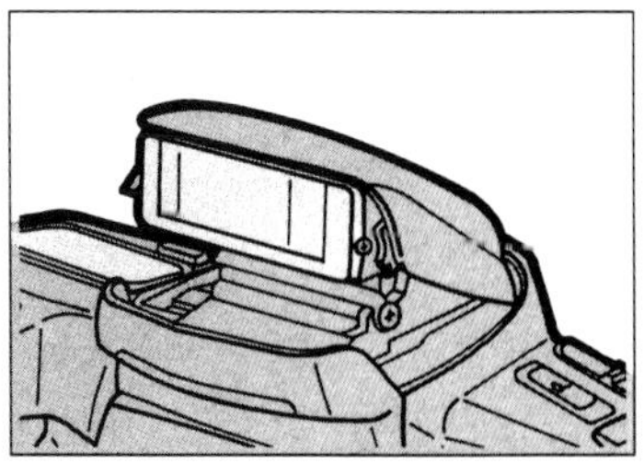

If it's too dark, the integral flash will fire automatically to achieve better illumination.

programmed autoexposure (P), aperture priority (A), shutter priority (S), and manual control of shutter speed and aperture (M). TTL automatic flash can be used in all these modes, either with the integral flash or with an external program flash unit. The integral flash can also be used for wireless remote control of a second external flash unit.

To set the standard exposure metering mode - Minolta's Maxxum/Dynax expert program selection - simply press the program-reset button in front of the main switch.

If you want to select one of the five modes, press and hold the function button and set the desired mode with the shutter-setting control. The selected mode is maintained when the function button is released, and will be displayed on the body data panel.

Programmed autoexposure

To set a Maxxum/Dynax camera, including the 5xi, to programmed autoexposure mode, simply press the program-reset button. The large **P** in the viewfinder indicates that the camera will now control all functions automatically. Programmed autoexposure is probably the standard setting for most work with the 5xi.

The camera will select the focus mode and control the shutter speed and aperture necessary for a correct exposure. But whilst most SLR cameras will base the aperture/shutter speed combination in the automatic program on the focal length of the lens used, the Maxxum/Dynax xi models - including the 5xi - are not limited to a single program characteristic but select shutter speed and aperture from a whole range of possible exposure setting. With the help of its software, based on the principles of fuzzy logic, the expert exposure program adjusts its settings to the entire photographic situation. To optimize the setting of aperture and shutter speed the Maxxum/Dynax cameras take into account the shooting distance, reproduction ratio, lens focal length, and camera movement, as well as the subject brightness. The camera recognizes, for

---

Page 51
The AF 20mm, f/2.8 super wide-angle was used for the shot top right, the photograph bottom right was created with a 35-105mm wide-angle.

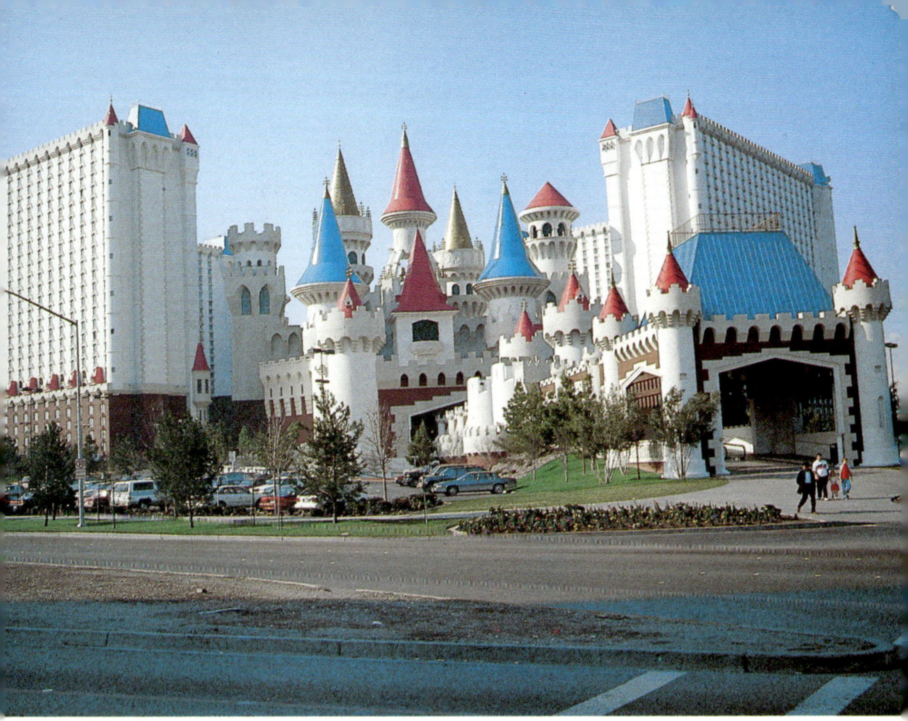

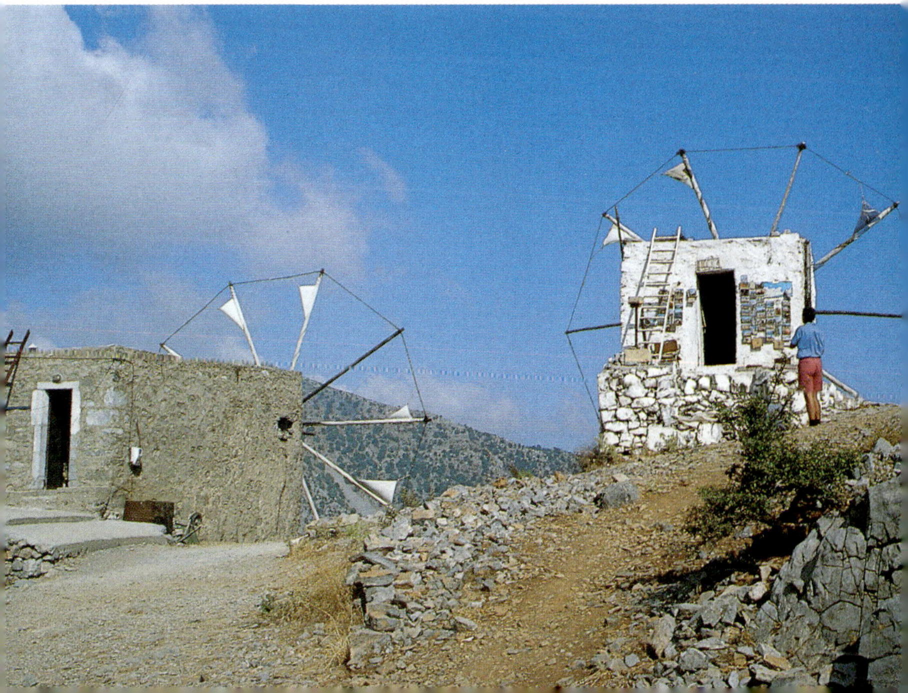

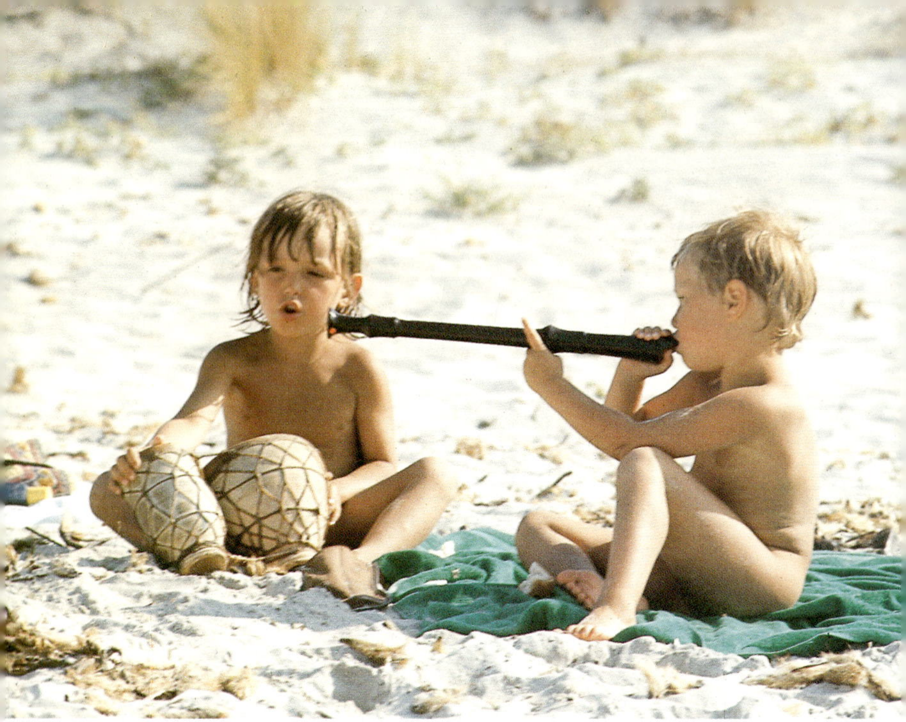

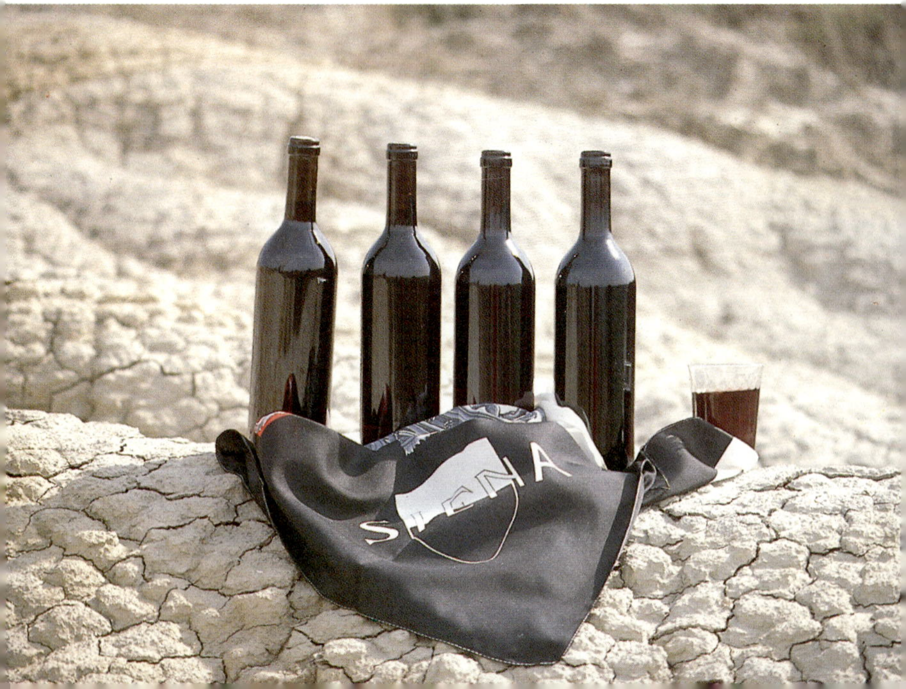

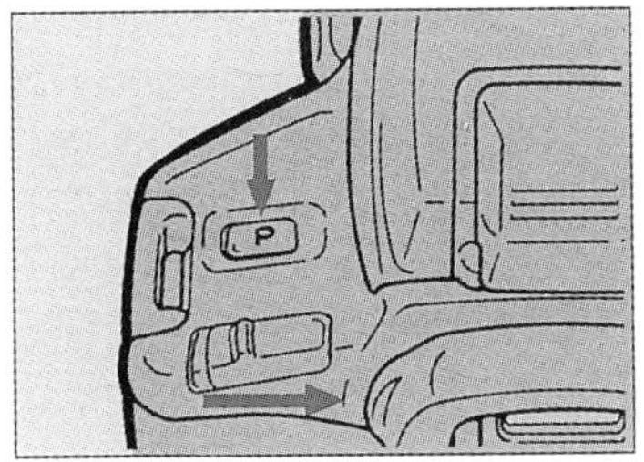

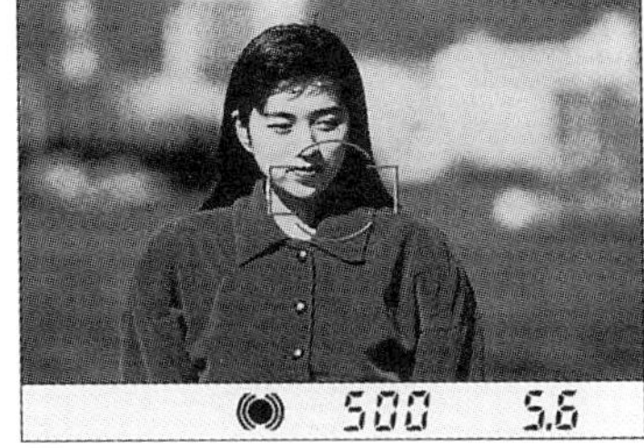

In P mode all camera functions are controlled automatically. The photographer can concentrate fully on the subject.

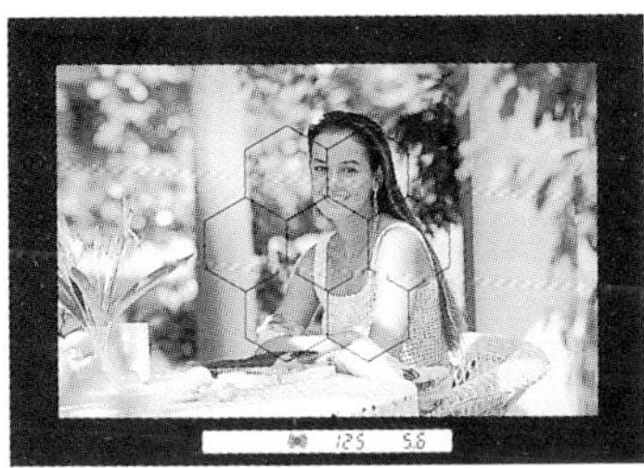

Honeycomb-exposure metering. The advanced exposure metering system determines the optimum exposure value for your subject by means of the honeycomb-pattern system. This value is based on the assessment of the seven individual segments and the background brightness.

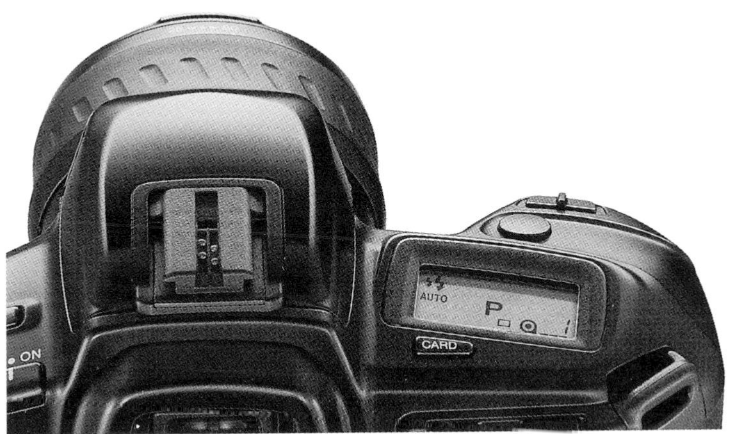

Page 52
With telelphoto lenses you can watch children from a distance without being noticed (top left). The macro function available on most telephotos enables you to take detail shots such as the one bottom left.

example, whether it is dealing with an action, landscape, or close-up photograph.

It even recognizes whether or not excessive differences in subject brightness necessitate fill-in flash, and if necessary automatically switches on the integral flash. The flash is also activated in low light situations. In this mode a program flash unit attached and switched on will also be fired automatically as necessary.

The viewfinder displays indicate the current state of the flash unit. The flash unit 'pictogram' will be lit on its own whilst the flash is charging. The flash symbol will light up when the flash reaches full charge, and it will flash after the exposure to indicate a correct flash exposure. If the pre-flash function is activated the viewfinder data panel will display the double flash symbol. And with wireless TTL flash control the two flash symbols will flash alternately; a correct flash exposure is then signalled with the larger flash symbol, up until both symbols once again flash alternately to indicate that full flash charge has been reached.

You can also suppress the automatic fill-in flash and autoflash in low light, but because the camera may well have employed the flash to avoid the risk of camera shake it is advisable, in these instances, to support the camera. Simply press the flash-control button on the front of the camera whilst operating the shutter-setting control in front of the shutter-release button. Autoflash is reactivated by operating the two buttons once more, or by pressing the program-reset button. In autoflash mode the letters **AUTO** will appear underneath the flash symbol on the body data panel. If you activate the flash manually only the flash symbol will appear (the double flash symbol if the pre-flash function is activated). No indication is given if the autoflash function is switched off.

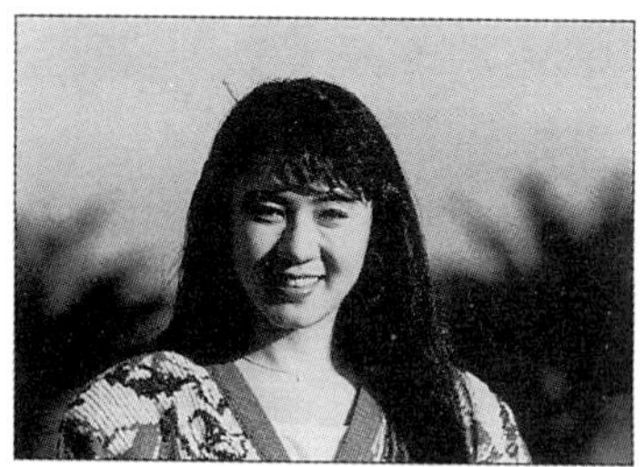

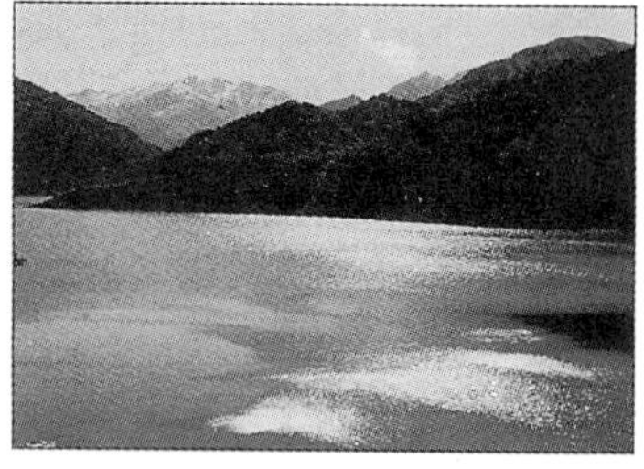

In aperture priority you can choose between great (right) and shallow (left) depth of field by preselecting the aperture.

If the 5xi recognizes a situation where fill-in flash is required it will switch it on automatically, as mentioned earlier. But you have the option of activating this function manually if the camera itself does not deem it necessary. Simply pop up the flash unit by pressing the flash-control button and to ensure the flash is fired hold the button during the exposure.

In programmed autoexposure mode the 5xi works with shutter speeds between 1/2000 sec and 30 seconds continuously, utilizing all available lens apertures in half-stop increments. When flashing the fastest flash sync speed is 1/90 sec, although in the P mode the camera can set anything up to this speed and with shorter focal lengths slower speeds will often be set. Shutter speed and aperture are indicated in the top line of the body data panel when the two-step shutter-release button is pressed lightly.

Aperture priority

In this mode you can preselect the aperture - hence the term 'aperture priority' - and the camera will automatically select a suitable shutter speed. To switch to aperture priority press and hold the function button and push the shutter-setting control to the right - **A** will be displayed on the body data panel. If you forget which way you need to push the shutter-setting control just push it in either direction until the **A** appears. Aperture priority is then activated as soon as you release the function button. The aperture display appears next to an arrow in the top right-hand corner of the body data panel. You can now preselect the aperture in half-stop increments with the aperture-setting control, located on the top left of the camera body (held normally) next to the camera bayonet. As you push the aperture-setting control up, the aperture becomes wider, pushing it down reduces the aperture. Lightly press the shutter-release button and the shutter speed automatically selected by the camera to suit the aperture will be displayed to the left of the aperture on the body data panel. The available aperture range is determined by the lens used, whereas the shutter speed range lies between 1/2000 sec and 30 seconds; the latter is controlled steplessly and displayed to the nearest half-stop increment. Depending on the lighting conditions the display for the slowest or fastest shutter speed will flash on the body data panel if there is a danger of incorrect exposure because a sufficiently slow or fast shutter speed is not available to match the preselected aperture. If the fastest shutter speed is flashing, stop down the aperture to achieve a correct exposure. If this is impossible you can solve the problem by using a slower film. Another possibility might be to reduce the light intensity, although this cannot always be done. If the display for the slowest shutter speed is flashing you either need to open up the aperture further, use a faster film, increase the light intensity, or use flash.

In parallel with the displays on the body data panel the relevant exposure signals in the viewfinder will also flash - either to warn of over or underexposure, or to indicate that the light is too dim or too bright for the working range of the exposure metering system.

If the flash unit is switched off the camera symbol, bottom and left of centre in the viewfinder, will flash to warn that the shutter speed is too slow for shake-free handheld use. In such cases you need to either use a tripod or select a wider aperture to achieve a faster shutter speed.

Shutter priority

To switch to shutter priority press and hold the function button and push the shutter-setting control to the left. Shutter priority is then activated when you release the function button - **S** for shutter priority will appear on the body data panel and, directly above it, next to a triangle pointing to the right is the preselected shutter speed. Pressing the shutter-release button lightly will now cause the camera-controlled aperture to be displayed next to the shutter speed. Underexposure is likely if the maximum aperture (smallest figure) of the current lens is flashing - you need to either select a slower shutter speed, increase the light intensity, or use a faster film. To avoid the danger of overexposure, signalled by the narrowest aperture (largest figure) of the lens flashing, select a faster shutter speed or slower film, or reduce the light intensity (although usually you will have no influence over this parameter). In both cases, over and underexposure, and when the metering range of the camera is exceeded, the relevant parameters will also flash in the viewfinder. As the shutter speed is preselected the camera will not give a camera shake warning. The reciprocal of the focal

Manual exposure mode (M)

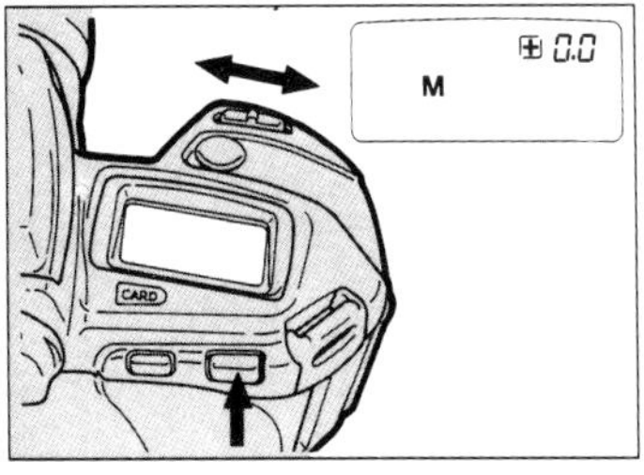

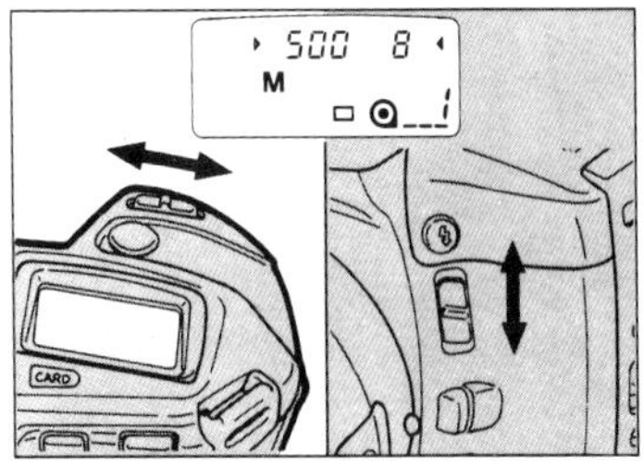

Viewfinder exposure signals

Viewfinder signal	Meaning
250 ▸ ◂5.6	Correct exposure set.
60 ▸⊞ 5.6	Overexposure to be expected.
500 ⊟◂5.6	Underexposure to be expected.
2000 ▸ ◂22	Light conditions outside the metering range of the camera.

To create certain effects you can set your 5xi to **M** for manual mode and determine shutter speed and aperture yourself.

length is taken as the slowest speed for handheld use, for example 1/500 sec for a 500mm lens.

The long exposure setting **bulb** can be selected in shutter priority mode, but will not produce a correct exposure. As soon as **bulb** appears on the body data panel the narrowest aperture will flash in the viewfinder and on the body data panel. Correct exposure can't be guaranteed.

Manual exposure control

If you want to select shutter speed and aperture freely to achieve certain effects, select the manual exposure control mode. This is done by pressing and holding the function button and pushing the shutter-setting control to the left until **M** and the shutter speed and aperture displays, enclosed by two triangles, appear on the body data panel. You can now select the shutter speed, using the shutter-setting control, in whole steps between 1/2000 sec and 30 seconds, as well as **bulb** for long exposures. (If the integral flash or an

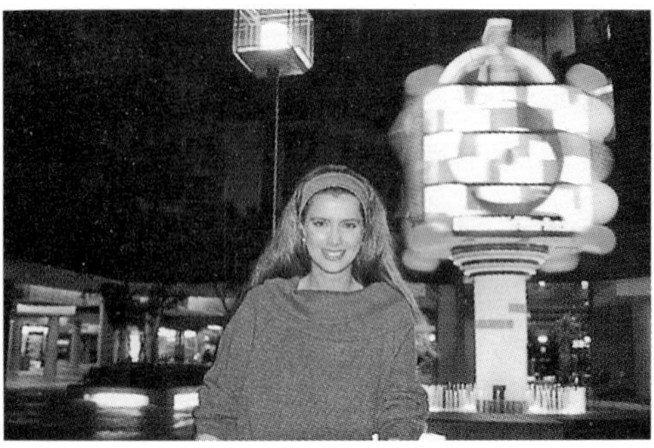

Slow- shutter sync
Holding the spot-metering button increases the background exposure.

attached system flash unit is switched on, the fastest shutter speed you can select is 1/90 sec; the camera will also default to this speed if the flash is switched on whilst a faster speed is selected.)

The aperture can be controlled, within the limits of the current lens, in half-stop increments using the aperture-setting control next to the camera bayonet. The aperture/shutter speed combination can be freely selected and the viewfinder of the camera will indicate whether the selected exposure is correct according to its own measurements, or whether it would lead to over or underexposure. If the selected setting is correct both triangular LCDs in the viewfinder will be lit; if overexposure threatens the left-hand triangle will point to a plus symbol in a small square. With impending underexposure the right-hand LCD will be lit and a minus symbol will be visible inside the square. The tip of the arrow LCD will also indicate in which direction the shutter-setting control needs to be pushed in order to achieve the exposure parameters determined by the camera. If both LCDs flash then the lighting conditions are outside the metering range of the camera.

In the **bulb** setting the shutter of the camera remains open for as long as the shutter-release button remains pressed. For photographs of this kind you need to mount the camera on a tripod and set the camera to **bulb** with the shutter-setting control. As long exposure photographs are generally taken in very low light, the autofocus may not work, so you may need to switch to manual focusing and check the focus on the viewfinder screen. Once focused, it is advisable to cover the viewfinder eyepiece with the eyepiece cap to prevent stray light entering during the exposure.

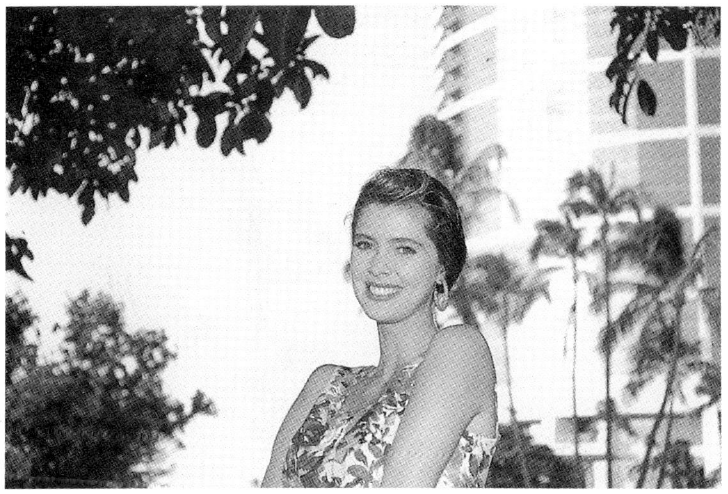

The integral flash automatically fires fill-in light in critical shooting situations.

Which exposure function is best?

The 5xi will master most photographic situations with its expert program selection in programmed autoexposure mode. Unlike most other cameras its fuzzy logic control software, programmed with expert knowledge, will not only take into account subject brightness and lens focal length, but also subject-specific parameters such as reproduction ratio, subject movement and position - just like an experienced photographer. This type of exposure control will certainly produce the highest success rate; as long as the camera is held fairly steady it will deliver correctly exposed shake-free photographs with no speed blur. Programmed autoexposure is excellent for 'snapshots', photojournalism, group photography, and photographs of family events. But whether the correct exposure is always the right choice for the intended effect is a different matter altogether. Sharpness and unsharpness can be used as important creative tools: unsharpness caused by fast movement of a subject can evoke an impression of speed. On the other hand you might want to precisely influence the depth of sharpness, to limit it or extend it as you choose. Shutter priority gives you the opportunity to render subjects sharp or blurred by allowing you to select a shutter speed that is either fast enough to freeze the movement or slow enough to show a moving subject as a mere blur. How slow or fast a shutter speed you need to select to achieve this depends on both the speed and the direction of the subject movement. If the subject is moving towards the camera the shutter speed can be a little slower than for a movement at right angles to the lens axis. Freezing the explosive start of a 100m sprinter, for example, is often the only way to make certain phases of a movement visible.

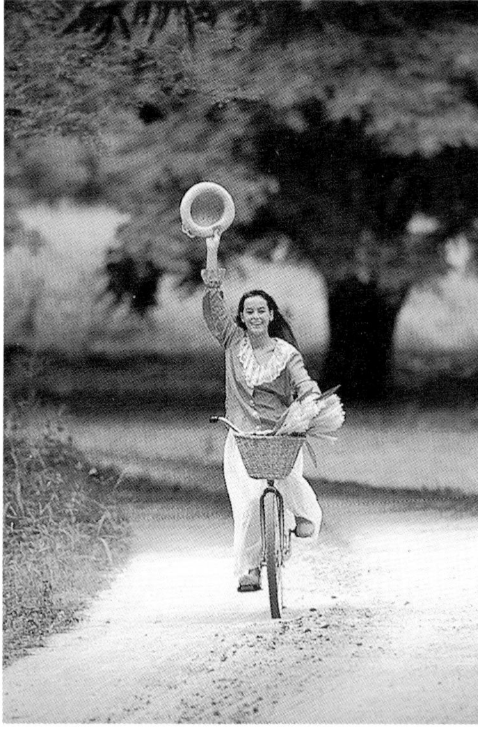

In P mode you will master most shots of moving subjects.

For such action pictures its best to load an ISO 400/27° colour negative film, set shutter priority and preselect a shutter speed between 1/500 and 1/2000 sec, depending on the speed of your subject. In critical light situations you can also work with aperture priority, preselecting the maximum aperture (smallest f/number) and leaving the camera to automatically set the fastest possible shutter speed.

But if you want to give a subject the impression of speed through unsharp streaking effects, stop down the aperture in aperture priority until you reach a shutter speed of 1/30 sec or slower. However, photographs where the subject itself is sharp and the background blurred are usually more effective. You can achieve this with the same exposure setting by tracking the subject with the camera during the exposure. This technique is known as panning and to get even movement of the camera, following the speed of the movement, you can use a tripod with a panning arm. So to freeze movement select shutter priority and preselect a sufficiently fast shutter speed. In critical light conditions set aperture priority, preselect the maximum aperture and leave the camera to automatically set the fastest possible shutter speed. For streaking effects, on the other hand, use shutter priority.

Aperture priority is best for controlling the depth of field, the zone in front of and behind the point of focus that will be rendered sharp on the final picture. The more you open the aperture, the narrower this zone is and vice versa. Good photographers use this technique for creative picture composition, selecting a sufficiently wide or narrow aperture whilst the camera takes care of the shutter speed automatically. Applications for this technique are landscape photography with wide-angle lenses, where there is no danger of camera shake or speed blur, or situations where you want the background of a photograph to disappear in unsharpness.

Using PA or PS mode:

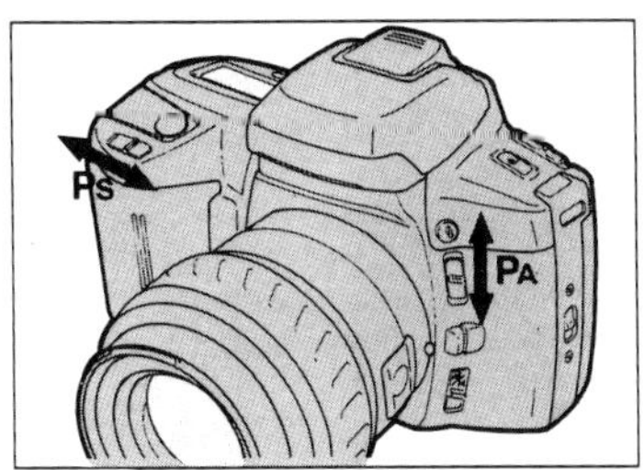

In programmed autoexposure mode you can select a different aperture or shutter speed by simply operating the aperture-setting control (PA) or shutter-setting control (PS). PA or PS will appear on the body data panel.

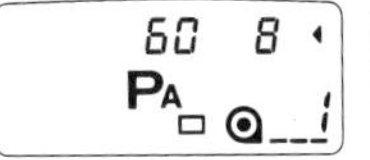

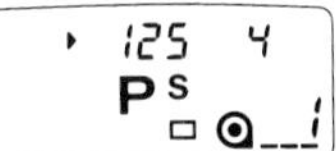

So controlling the depth of field zone is the domain of aperture priority, allowing you to create deliberately slow shutter speeds with the camera on a tripod or if a wide-angle lens is used. The technique can also help to eliminate unwanted details in the foreground or background. Landscape or architectural photography require great depth of field, whereas shallow depth of field can be used to great effect in portrait photography. The ability to separate a subject from its surrounding is also a great bonus in action photography or photojournalism where you can't freely choose or create you setting.

If you're wondering which of the two priority programs is better or more meaningful, remember that you are more likely to come up against the limits of correct exposure with shutter speed preselection. This is because in this mode the camera will automatically select a suitable aperture, but will only have a maximum choice of seven stops between the narrowest and the widest setting (although this number may vary depending on the lens). But with aperture preselection where the camera selects the shutter speed, it has more than twice as many settings - namely sixteen - at its disposal.

Under or overexposure will result if the limits of the lens aperture are reached. This is rarely the case in aperture priority mode, although you are more likely to get camera shake in this mode. But you will get a visible camera shake warning in the viewfinder if the shutter speed is too slow and you will usually be able to take a second exposure, after having made the necessary adjustments such as switching on the flash. As you will see when we get to the relevant expansion card, even sports photographs are nowadays often taken with aperture priority rather than the traditionally preferred shutter priority mode.

You can, of course, achieve all the above effects by selecting both shutter speed and aperture manually, although this demands a great deal more attention from the photographer who would have to be alert to very change in lighting. But manual mode has additional advantages. Many photographers expose certain films at speeds that differ from their manufacturers' ratings. With the 5xi you can't see the amount of the deviation, but you can still determine it precisely, although it is a little complicated. First meter the light conditions in programmed autoexposure mode, read the settings off the body data panel and finally select the values

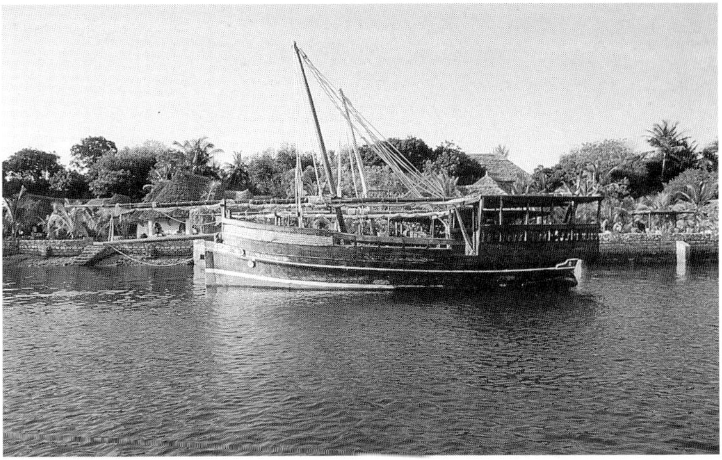

With automatic exposure metering you don't need to watch out for changes in the light, such as clouds passing by overhead.

corresponding to the desired deviation manually. Alternatively work with a manual exposure meter.

If you want to expose a slide film by a half-stop less, or a colour negative film more generously, this is easily achieved. Once the two triangular LEDs in the viewfinder light up to confirm the correct exposure, simply stop down the aperture by half a stop, or use the shutter-setting control for adjustments in full-stop increments. Although to over or underexpose a film more easily you can use exposure compensation.

Manual exposure mode will probably only be used in exceptional circumstances. After all, the 5xi is primarily designed for easy photography without technical constraint. But if you want to explore the boundaries you still have a great deal of scope for experimentation.

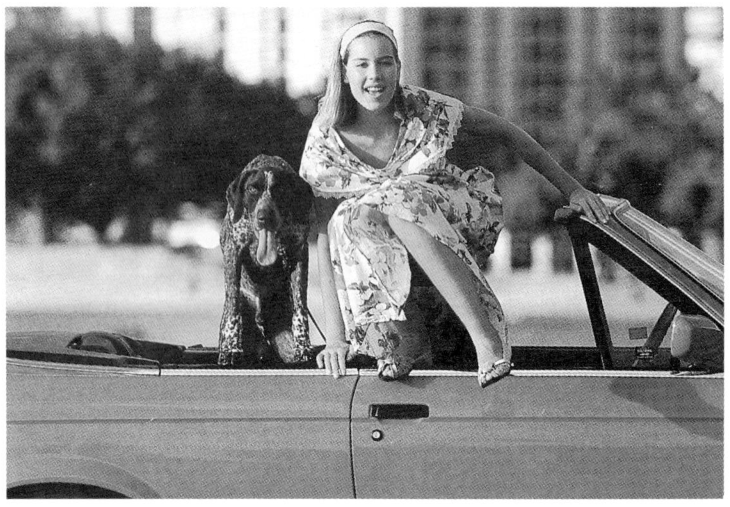

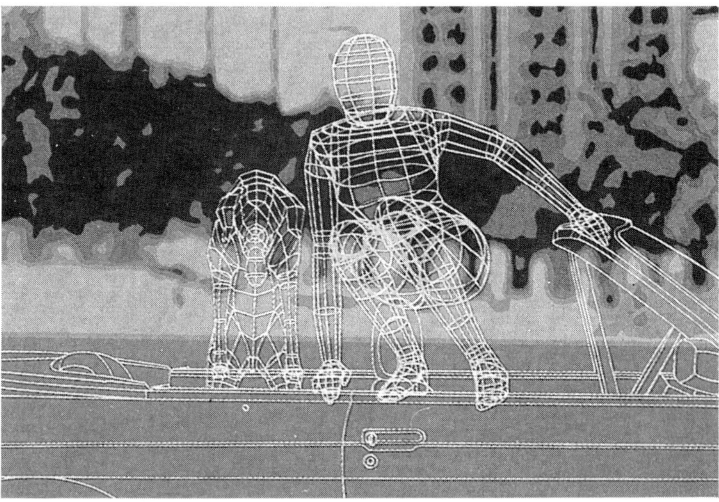

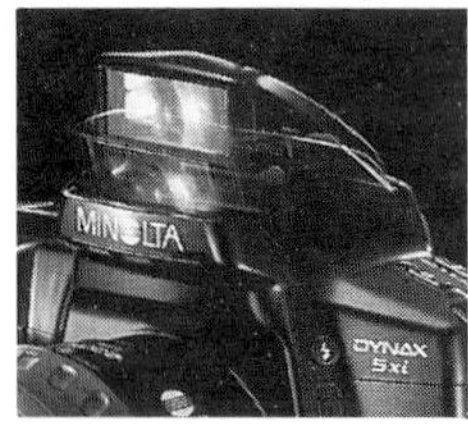

To ensure better illumination the powerful integral zoom flash will fire automatically if it is too dark.

Expert flash system

The integral flash of the 5xi in conjunction with expert flash control makes flash photography in critical light situations and for creative effects a sheer pleasure. It can help you achieve perfect flash exposures automatically in most light conditions, offering flash functions such as automatic and manual fill-in flash, pre-flash for suppressing the notorious 'red-eye' effect, and slow shutter sync, as well as, in conjunction with a Minolta Program Flash xi unit, wireless TTL flash control for flash illumination. The small integral flash does allow exposures at night or in very low light (although its power is limited), but even just used for filling in backlight it produces technically and, thanks to its professional illumination, creatively improved photographs in a variety of situations. You can use the small integral flash for remote control of the 3500xi and 5400xi Minolta program flash units without giving up the benefits of TTL flash control.

In programmed autoexposure mode the 5xi automatically activates the integral flash, or a unit mounted on the camera, whenever the light conditions make this necessary. If necessary, just press the program reset button to re-program the unit(s) for fill-in and autoflash. As soon as the camera registers that additional flash illumination could improve the final result and compensate for differences in subject brightness, the small integral flash is popped up, charged, and fired on release of the shutter. The same goes for a program flash unit that is mounted and switched on. The flash of the 5xi is so cleverly integrated into the camera that it isn't even noticeable at a first glance. For its size it is surprisingly powerful, managing a guide numbers of as much as 14 at ISO 100/21° and 28mm focal length and 17 at 80mm focal length. This means that it can achieve a guide number of as much as 28 and 44 in the wide-angle setting when used with high-speed films such as ISO 400/27° or ISO 1000/31° respectively, and can therefore provide fill-in light even in larger rooms. Its angle of coverage is sufficient for a 28mm lens, and thanks to its surprisingly fast recycling time of only 2.5 seconds you are ready to shoot again extremely quickly when using fill-in flash.

The power zoom reflector of the 5xi adjusts the coverage angle to the focal length.

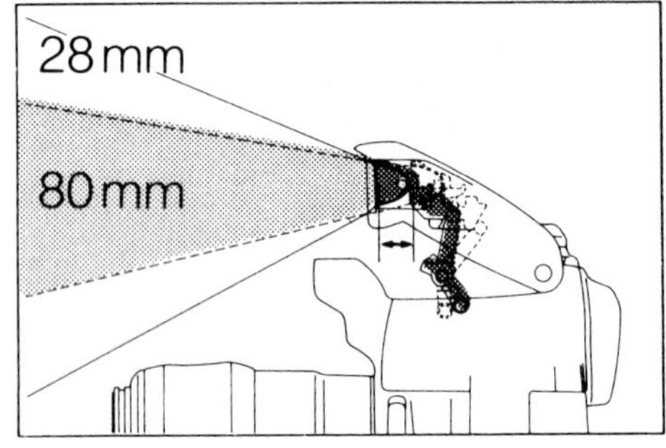

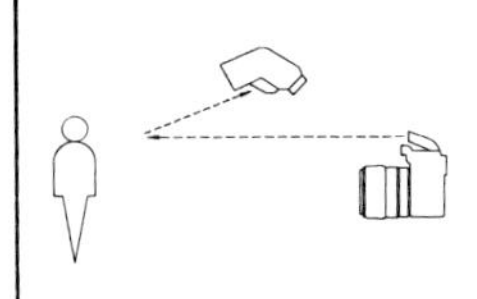

Start signal from the 5xi.

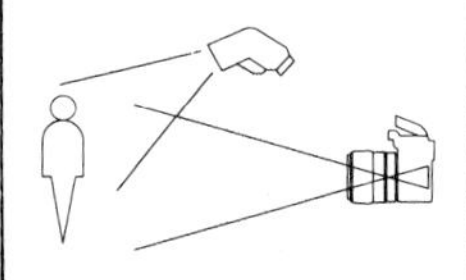

3500xi starts firing.

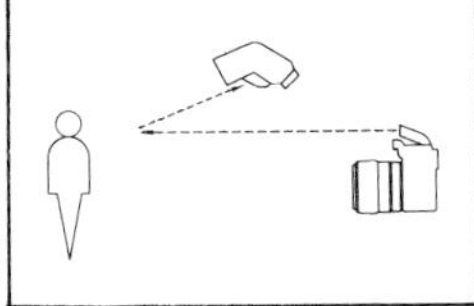

Stop signal sent when TTL metering detects sufficient exposure at the film plane.

But you don't have to wait until the automatic system of the camera registers a backlight situation or excessive subject contrast to use the flash, you can switch on the fill-in flash function manually at any time by pressing the flash-control button on the front of the 5xi. Although you need to hold the button pressed during the exposure, otherwise programmed autoexposure mode will fire the popped-up flash only if the expert exposure system of the camera deems this necessary. In aperture and shutter priority the integral flash is fired only if it has been activated manually by pressing the flash-control button. Once it is popped up it will fire every time and will not allow the camera to select an incorrect sync speed. As long as you don't activate a different exposure function by pressing the spot-metering button, the camera will always default to 1/60 or 1/90 sec.

Regardless of the exposure function selected, the Minolta 5xi can only be released once the flash unit is fully charged. A correct flash exposure is indicated to the photographer by rapid flashing of the flash symbol in the viewfinder.

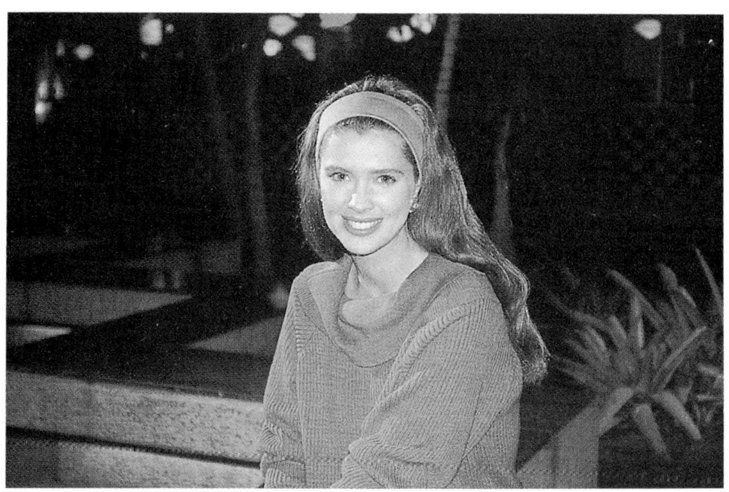

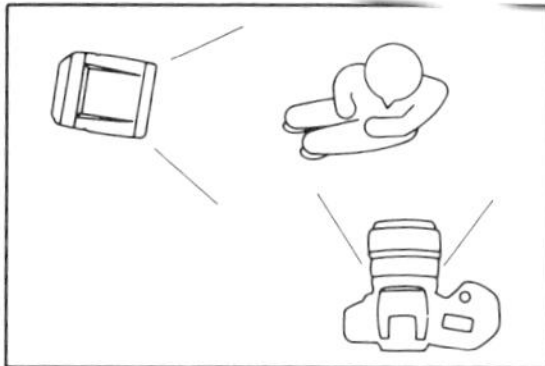

You can take a variety of different flash shots with wireless remote TTL flash control.

You can suppress the autoflash function of programmed exposure mode at any time by operating the flash-control button and shutter-setting control simultaneously to retract the popped-up flash. Re-activate autoflash by pressing the program-reset button or switching off and on again at the main switch.

Remarks on the integral flash

Because of their constructions a few lenses may cast a shadow on the lower portion of the flash emission of the 5xi integral flash. This applies to the AF 28-85mm,f/3.5-4.5 and the AF 28-135mm,f/4-4.5, as well as the 300 and 600mm APO lenses. If in doubt, remove the lens hood from other lenses and make sure the main subject is at least one metre away from the camera.

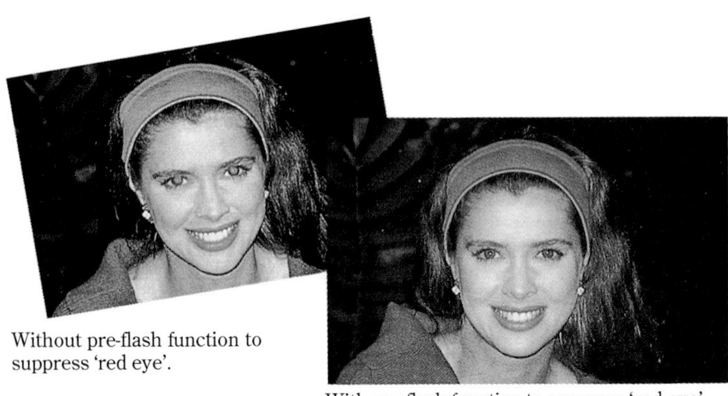

Without pre-flash function to suppress 'red eye'.

With pre-flash function to suppress 'red-eye'.

Pre-flash function to suppress red-eye

Flash portraits often suffer from so-called 'red-eye'. This effect is caused by a reflection of the flash light from the back of the eye. It is particularly pronounced when the flash unit is positioned close to the optical axis of the lens. If ambient light levels are very low the pupils of the eyes dilate and the flash light hits the retina at the back of the eye. With the 5xi you can trick the eye about the actual brightness by using a series of pre-flashes which cause the iris to contract so that the flash is less likely to reach the retina. Use the pre-flash function of the 5xi especially for portraits in badly lit rooms, although it's not needed for fill-in flash, where red-eye is rare.

The pre-flash facility is activated by pressing the recessed pre-flash button inside the card door. A second, smaller flash symbol will appear next to the standard symbol on the body data panel. Cancel the function by pressing the button a second time. The 5xi can flash with or without pre-flash in all exposure modes.

Manual flash Photography

For maximum creative freedom all shutter speeds of 1/90 sec and slower - including **bulb** - can be used for flashing in manual exposure mode, and the automatic flash control system of the 5xi

Flashing in A, S and M mode

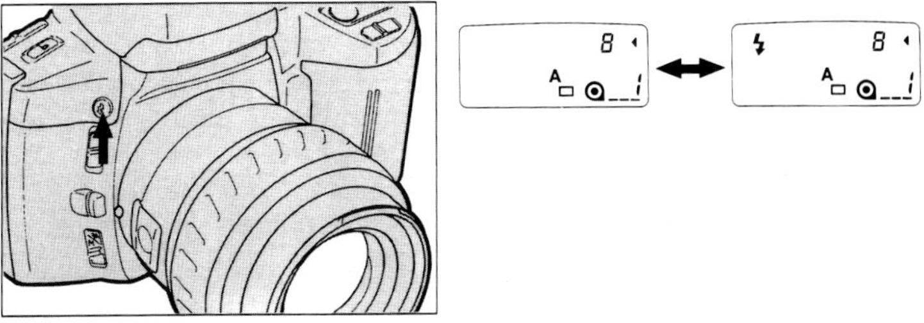

Flash ranges (at ISO 100/21°)

Focal length / Aperture	28-50mm	50-80mm	above 80mm
f/2.8	1.0 5m	1.0-5.4m	1.0-6.1m
f/4	1.0-3.5m	1.0-3.75m	1.0-4.25m
f/5.6	1.0-2.5m	1.0-2.6m	1.0-3.0m

The maximum flash ranges are doubled if an ISO 400/27° film is used.
The 5xi offers three different flash functions.

will work without any problems. If you have accidentally selected too fast a shutter speed in this mode the camera will automatically default to the correct sync speed of 1/90 sec, whereas slower speeds right down to 30 seconds are maintained.

On focal plane shutter cameras - which includes almost all 35mm SLR cameras nowadays - correct flash exposure is only possible with a limited shutter speed range, because they control their shutter speed by means of two curtains which expose the image area for the duration of the exposure. Shutter speed faster than 1/90 sec are achieved on the 5xi by no longer opening the shutter completely, but by means of a small slit between the first and second curtains scanning the film surface and exposing it to light for a short period of time. This means that for fast shutter speeds the first curtain starts to move, opening a proportion of the film surface, and the second curtain starts to run before its counterpart has reached the other end of the frame and uncovered the entire image area. The time required by the slit to travel across the whole image area is longer than the flash emission, which means that the light will only reach that part of the image which is uncovered

Slow shutter sync

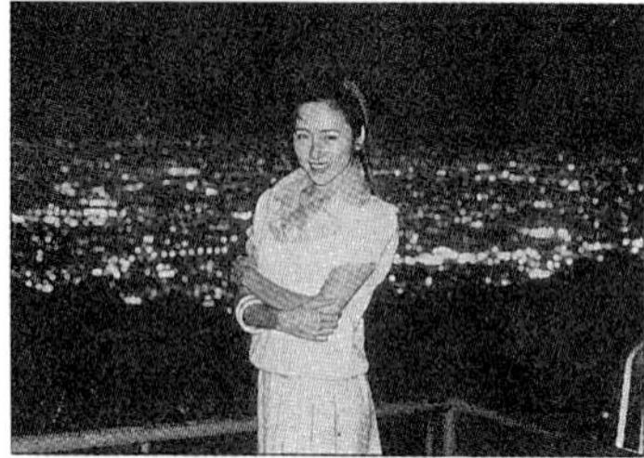

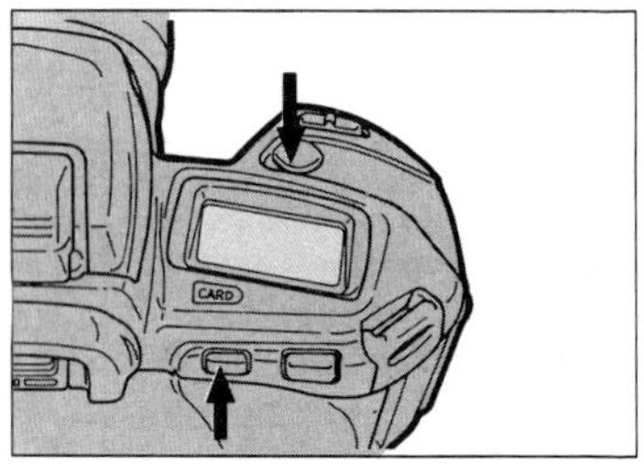

The spot-metering button has to be held down during the exposure.

during the actual flash emission and only part of the frame is correctly exposed. With slower shutter speeds, on the other hand, the first curtain completely clears the image, which is only covered by the second curtain after the exposure. So the flash emission, usually fired as soon as the shutter is opened, can illuminate the entire image area, resulting in a combination of ambient and flash illumination.

Slow shutter sync with the 5xi

Slower flash sync speeds can be achieved by metering the subject background. Take this approach whenever the atmosphere of a room or nocturnal surroundings provide the mood of a scene and the flash is only to illuminate a detail in the foreground. To do this first focus and frame your subject, then press in and hold the spot-metering button. The long exposure obtained in this way is maintained even during flashing, provided you hold the spot-metering button when the shutter is released. The camera then correctly exposes the surroundings using a relatively slow shutter speed, reducing the flash exposure so that the main subject in the foreground is correctly exposed without destroying the mood of the scene. The camera is programmed to take account of the need for the background of such a photograph to be slightly underexposed, so no corrections are necessary. Slow shutter sync prevents the subject background from merging into blackness as it does with fast shutter speeds. You don't need to worry about camera shake too much as the short burst of flash gives a sharp main subject - but use a tripod if the background needs to be sharp too.

In such situations a very bright background or wide aperture may mean that the sync speed is limited to 1/90 sec as the background might otherwise be overexposed. With slow shutter

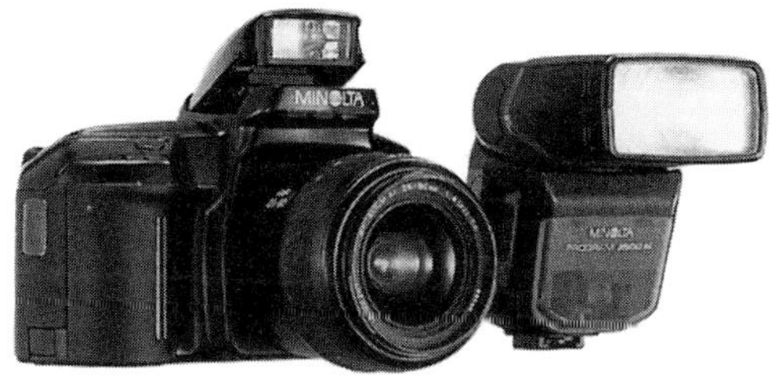

3500xi program flash

sync the correct flash exposure is again indicated by rapid flashing of the flash symbols in the viewfinder.

Wireless remote flash control with the 5xi and Minolta program flash units 3500xi and 5400xi

Apart from the pre-flash facility, all flash techniques described so far can be carried out either with the integral flash of the 5xi or with one of the i or xi series Minolta program flash units. Used with the Minolta program flash unit 3500xi or the new 5400xi, the 5xi offers the additional option of wireless remote TTL flash control which produces precisely lit flash photographs every time, no matter which exposure function you use or whether it is used on- or off-camera. To set the 5xi to wireless remote control attach a program flash 3500xi or 5400xi to the camera and switch on or press the program-reset button. All you need to do now is press the pre-flash button inside the card door and **Wireless** (on the 3500xi) , or **W.L.** and **F1**, **F2**, **F3**, or **F4** (on the 5400xi), will be indicated on the flash. You can now take the flash off the camera and attach the 'feet' it is supplied with for easier positioning. The off-camera flash is now fired from the integral flash of the 5xi. To ensure the external unit can recognize the control signals, it mustn't be obscured by the subject.

Full charge of the off-camera unit is indicated by the flashing of its AF illuminator, and the single and double flash symbol in the

Wireless remote flash control

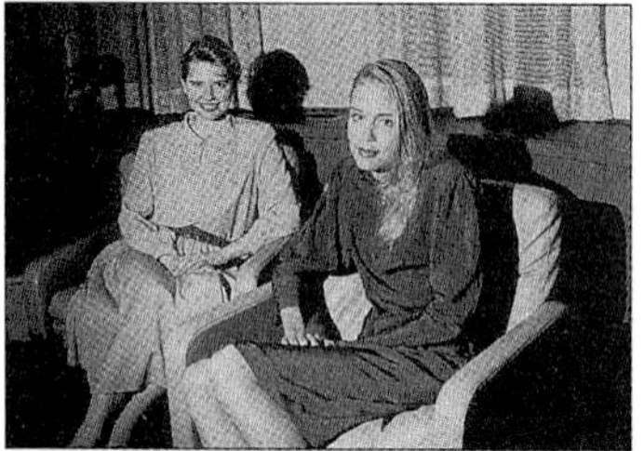

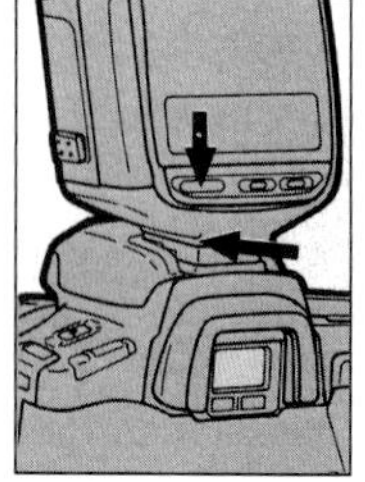

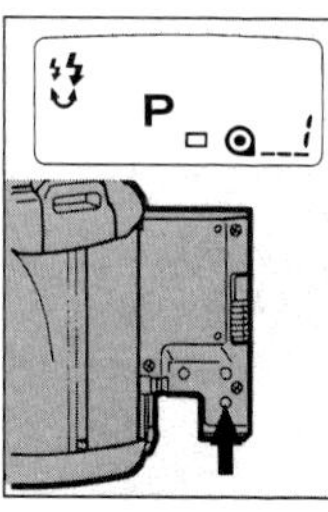

Wireless remote flash control provides three-dimensional lighting by allowing the flash to be taken off the camera and giving the option of controlling several flash units. To program wireless remote flash control you have to set the flash to **CH1** and press the pre-flash button inside the card door. Then detach the program flash from the camera and position it for optimum flash illumination.

viewfinder will flash alternately if the integral flash is fully charged. You can now fire a test flash from the external unit, to check that it is in range of the control signal from the camera, by pressing the spot-metering button, provided the viewfinder is not activated. Once both units are again fully charged you can release the shutter. The integral flash again sends the firing signal and, having successfully received its signal, the 3500xi or 5400xi will start to illuminate the subject with a series of light impulses. As soon as the TTL metering system of the camera has registered sufficient light on the film surface, the integral unit of the 5xi will emit a second signal to stop the 3500xi or 5400xi.

In this operating mode the off-camera unit will fire every time in programmed autoexposure mode, regardless of whether or not the ambient light would be sufficient for an exposure without flash. The fastest flash sync speed in this situation is 1/45 sec, reduced in comparison to the other flash setups. Unless set to a different value manually, the zoom reflector will always be at the maximum wide-angle setting in situations such as this.

For a more three-dimensional effect the external and integral units can also illuminate the subject at different light intensities, at a ratio of 2:1, simply by pressing the flash-control button on the front of the camera during the exposure. Roughly one-third of the light reaching the subject comes from the integral flash, and the remaining two-thirds from the more powerful off-camera unit.

Notably, the slow shutter sync facility is also available with wireless remote flash control. This is activated in the same way as with the integral or pushed-on system flash units, that is by pressing the spot-metering button in P, A and S mode and hold it in during the exposure. But make sure the eyepiece sensor is activated, otherwise the off-camera unit will first show that it is functioning by firing a test flash.

To suspend wireless remote TTL flash control momentarily, press and hold the flash-control button on the camera front whilst operating the shutter-setting control. The flash symbols will disappear from the body data panel, even if the external unit is still flashing. To resume remote control mode press the flash-control button once.

Pressing the program-reset button is the easiest way to switch off remote control mode completely. Alternatively you can re-mount the unit on the camera and press the pre-flash button inside the card door. The 3500xi, 5400xi, and 5200i program flash units can, of course, also be used as clip-on units for the 5xi; these units have guide numbers of 35, 54 and 52 respectively. In this case the flash reflector is automatically adjusted to the selected focal length on the lens, in the range between 28mm to 105mm (3500xi), or 24mm to 105mm (5400xi), or 24mm to 85mm (5200i).

Off-camera flashing allows effective lighting techniques familiar from professional photographs. It can produce good flash effects and better lighting, particularly in the close-up range, still lifes, portraits, and interiors.

The instruction manual states slight restrictions in terms of distance and functioning - for reasons of product liability. It says, for example, that in such instances the ambient light should be kept as low as possible. But the integral flash unit has a substantially greater range than Minolta indicate: in normal light conditions it can fire the 3500xi program flash unit across a distance of up to five metres without any problems, and the 5400xi at a distance of up to seven metres. But the further away it is from the subject the more important it is for the additional flash unit to receive the firing impulse directly. So make sure the units AF Illuminator is pointing towards the camera.

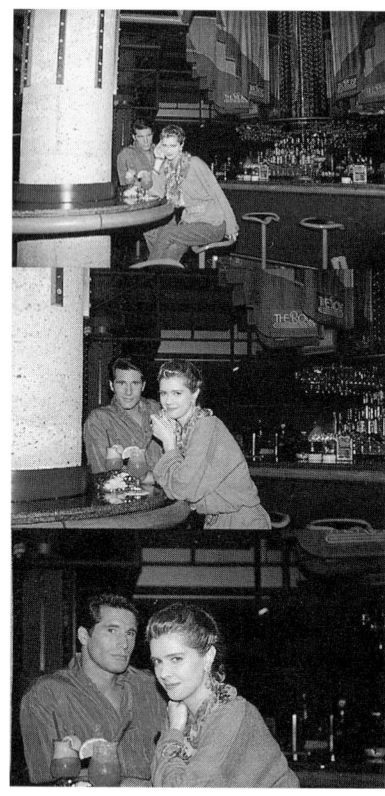

Power zoom reflector
The integral zoom reflector automatically adjusts the coverage angle over the full range of the camera's standard 28-80mm lens.

Automatic power zoom reflector

Like the Minolta 3200i and 5200i program flash units, the 3500xi and 5400xi also adjust their flash reflectors automatically to match the selected focal length of the lens. When the unit is mounted on the camera the reflector is set to the correct value as soon as the autozoom control system preselects a focal length. If this is adjusted within a range of between 28 (24 for the 5400xi) and 105mm the power zoom reflector automatically matches this setting, using data transmitted via the hotshoe contacts. Apart from more even illumination, this provides better guide numbers and greater coverage for telephoto subjects by concentrating the light. For special applications or in remote control mode the reflector can be adjusted manually to (24 on the 5400xi), 28mm, 50mm or 105mm focal length.

Bounce flash

The flash reflector of the Minolta 5200i and 5400xi program flash units can be tilted upwards from its standard position by up to 90°, or set at 45°, 60° and 75° in between. So you can point the flash at the ceiling of a room or a white wall to achieve soft, indirect lighting to tone down the harsh shadows often found with direct flash. Bounce flash is suitable for many subjects, especially portraits. Never aim the flash at coloured surfaces for indirect flashing as the colour will also be reflected. And this may leave you wondering where that seemingly inexplicable colour cast came from. Where the flash-head tilts to 90°, flash accessories such as 'Lumiquest' pocket bouncers are most useful

AF illuminator

With dark subjects or those lacking in contrast the integral flash unit automatically emits white metering flashes to support the autofocus system. A clip-on flash emits a red stripy pattern across a distance of about nine metres and so enables correct focusing even in complete darkness.

Guide number and output of the Minolta 3500xi program flash unit

Guide numbers (in metres and at ISO 100/21°)

Coverage	28mm	35mm	50mm	80mm	105mm
Output NORMAL	22	26	29	33	35
Output LOW	5.5	6.5	7.3	8.3	8.8

Range 0.7m to 21m (at ISO 100/21° and with 50mm,f/1.4 lens)

The Minolta 3500xi program flash unit can also be used with the 7000i and 8000i series Minolta cameras, although the remote control function is not available. Used in conjunction with the 9000, 7000 and 5000 models, the auto flash-activation function in program mode is not available either.

Guide number and output of the Minolta 5400xi program flash unit

Guide numbers (in metres and at ISO 100/21°)

Coverage	24mm	28mm	35mm	50mm	70mm	85mm	105mm
Output NORMAL	28	32	36	42	46	52	54
Output wireless	22	25	28	33	36	41	42
Output 1/2	20	23	25	30	33	37	38
Output 1/4	14	16	18	21	23	26	27
Output 1/8	10	11	13	15	16	18	19
Output 1/16	7	8	9	10.5	11.5	13	13.5
Output 1/32	4.9	5.7	6.4	7.4	8.1	9.2	9.5

Range up to 37m (at ISO 100/21° and with 85mm,f/1.4 lens at maximum aperture)

Capacity: 100 to 3500 flashes, recycling time between 0.2 of a second to 11 seconds with alkaline-manganese batteries; 4 to 1200 flashes and recycling times between 0.2 of a second and 6 seconds with Ni-Cad rechargeable batteries

Program flash unit 2000xi

The Minolta 2000xi program flash unit is only mentioned here for the sake of completeness; it has a capacity of only just twice that of the integral flash and so provides no real alternative. But the unit is equipped with an AF illuminator which allows focusing in

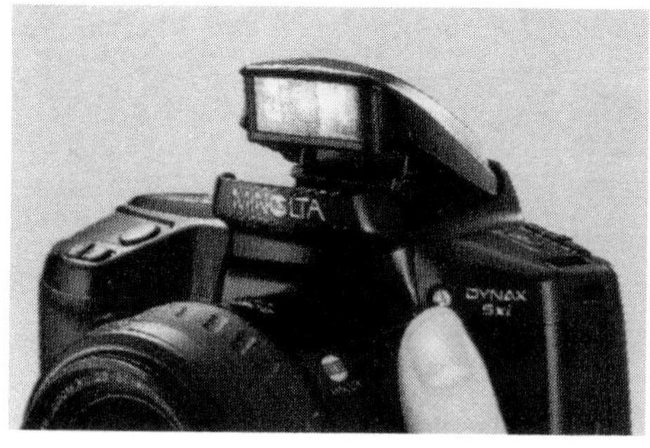

The integral flash unit can be activated manually with the flash pop-up button.

complete darkness, and so enabling you to save the battery of the camera itself. It is also activated automatically by the camera as soon as this is made necessary by light conditions or subject contrast. When the unit is switched on its functions correspond to those of the integral unit of the 5xi, although remote flash control is not possible. A set of four fresh 1.5-volt AA batteries lasts for between 300 and 5000 flashes, depending on the flash output used. Recycling times are between half a second and 4 seconds, depending on the charging state of the batteries and the ambient temperature, and the unit has a maximum range of 14m at ISO 100/21° and a 50mm,f/1.4 lens.

Working with the Minolta 5400xi, 5200i and 3200i program flash units

The 3200i and 5200i program flash units can be used with the 5xi with only a few functional restrictions. To be sure flash unit and camera are set to automatic program flash simply press the program-reset button when the flash unit is mounted. Normally you will not need to make any settings on the flash unit itself, except to use the **ON/OFF** button if you do not want flash. The 3200i also has the reduced output button.

The powerful Minolta 5400xi and 5200i program flash units, however, have quite a few additional functions. The 5400xi is the successor of the 5200i and, apart from several other improvements, the main difference is the fact that the 5400xi can be used for wireless remote TTL flash control and as a control unit for all other units which offer this remote control facility.

To look at, both units appear fairly similar, although several additional buttons promise further features. Four of these buttons have a dual purpose and their function is changed by pressing the MENU button, which is next to the main on/off switch.

When the units is first switched on the buttons are labelled LIGHT, TTL/M, ZOOM, and LEVEL on the 5200i, and TTL/M, ZOOM, LEVEL, and WIRELESS on the 5400xi. Because of the wireless function the 5400xi has an additional button to operate the LCD panel light.

The TTL/M button enables the flash to be switched from TTL automatic control to manual exposure control, provided your

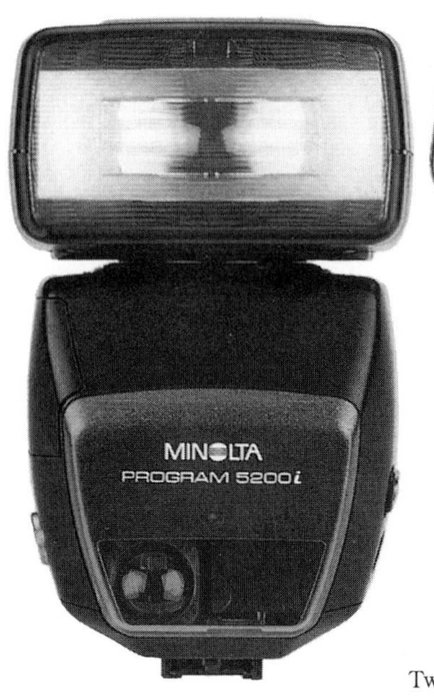

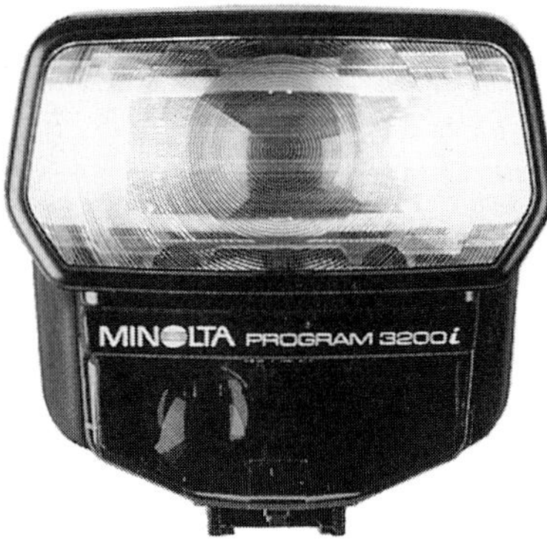

Two of the flash units available for the 5xi.

camera is set for manual exposure. ZOOM enables the angle of coverage of the flash head to be altered manually, if you want to use a different setting from the one the camera has chosen. Pressing the LEVEL button allows you to select lower power settings down to 1/32 of full power. The LIGHT button illuminates the LCD panel so that it can be seen in low light. These buttons appear on both models. The 5400xi has an additional button marked WIRELESS for selecting remote cordless TTL operation.

Pressing the MENU button provides a second set of functions, and these are the same on both models. MULTI sets the flash to fire a succession of low-power bursts during a single exposure. REPS determines the number of flashes which will be fired, and FREQ alters the rate at which they will be fired, between 1Hz (i.e. one flash per second), and 50 Hz (or 100 Hz on the 5400xi). The flash output is automatically set to 1/32 when this function is selected, and the flash is set for manual exposure. The LCD display will indicate the distance at which exposure will be correct, depending on which aperture is set. The camera must be set the manual exposure in order to use the MULTI function, and a relatively long exposure is needed. Your instruction manual will indicate what speed is required, depending on the number of bursts and the frequency you have selected. The last button is marked RATIO. If another flashgun is connected to the accessory socket on the side of the flashgun, or if you are using the 5400xi in wireless mode to control an off-camera flashgun, this button enables you to set a 2:1 or 1:2 lighting ratio between the two units, for a professional lighting effect.

All relevant data for the flash exposure is indicated on the LCD panel of the flash unit. You can even switch from metric to imperial measures by operating a switch in the battery chamber, if you prefer your distance data in feet.

Both the 5200i and 5400xi program flash units have a guide number of 42 at ISO 100/21° and with a 50mm lens. Used with a 50mm,f/1.4 lens their range is approximately 30m. Four AA alkaline-manganese, or four 1.2-volt Ni-Cad rechargeable batteries of the same size, produce between 100 and 3500 flashes at a rate of between 0.2 of a second and 11 seconds, depending on shooting distance and ambient light. The units also have a connection for an external battery pack which is available as an accessory.

The AF illuminator helps the AF system of the 5xi with low subject contrast or when in darkness.

The reflectors of the 5200i and 5400xi program flash units have internal power zooms which automatically adjust their angle of coverage to match the focal length of the lens between 24 and 85mm, and as much as 105mm on the 5400xi. Changing the coverage angle alters the guide number, and consequently the maximum range of the flash unit - the most important values are shown in the table. But more important than the guide numbers is the option of adjusting the angle of coverage manually, to 24, 28, 35, 50, 70, and 85/105mm. This is particularly useful for bounce flash where light is reflected off a ceiling or wall to achieve softer shadows. With this technique the best results are obtained if the reflector is set to cover a shorter focal length than is actually used on the lens. This ensures that the subject is covered completely by the bounce flash light and will create the softest possible shadows. Practical experience has shown that setting the reflector some two focal length values wider than the lens works well.

A further notable feature is the miniature stand MS-2 supplied with the 5400xi program flash unit. It is connected directly to the clip-on foot of the unit and used to position the 5400xi when it is not mounted on the camera. The MS-2 also has a tripod thread so the flash unit can easily be mounted on a tripod.

Macro Flash 1200 AF Set N

The Macro Flash 1200 AF Set N makes close-up flash photography with the 5xi easier. It is technically identical to the Macro Flash 1200 AF, which is available for the Minolta 7000, but includes Flash Shoe Adapter FS-1100 to enable it to be fitted to Maxxum/Dynax models. Its advantage, apart from fully-automatic TTL flash control, is its extremely compact construction. The four flash tubes, arranged in a square around the optical axis, can be switched on and off individually, enabling you to illuminate the subject in different ways. The unit itself consists of two main components, the flash head and the control unit, the latter is attached to the

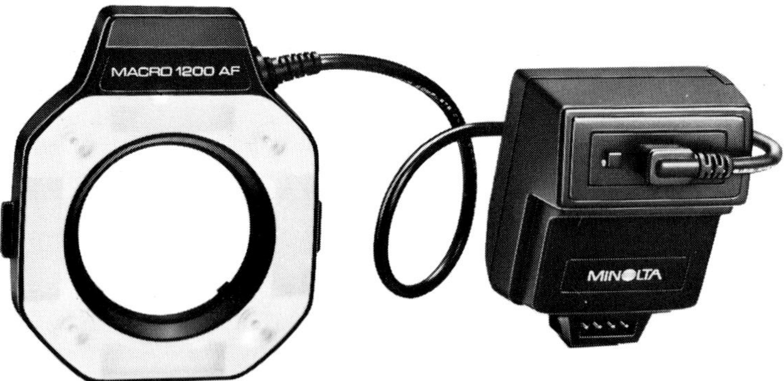

The Macro Flash 1200AF Set N has four flash tubes which can be switched on and off independently, and four modelling lamps. It allows a multitude of different lighting effects.

accessory shoe of the Dynax 5xi via the Flash Shoe Adapter FS-1100, just like any other flashgun. The flash head is attached by a special adapter ring to the filter thread of the 50mm,f/2.8 or the 100mm,f/2.8 macro lenses. The flash head can be moved around the lens for the best possible illumination.

To assist focusing there is a focusing lamp at each corner of the flash head. These also help to decide on the correct framing if the lighting conditions are poor. They are automatically extinguished when the shutter release is lightly pressed or has not been touched for 30 seconds. During the actual exposure they are switched off, but they can also be switched off manually by a button at the rear of the control unit.

Automatic flash metering is controlled by the TTL flash control of the camera. Indications of flash-ready and correct flash illumination are displayed in the viewfinder. In addition to these indications, flash-ready and confirmation that the flash illumination was sufficient are displayed on the back of the control unit. The correct aperture settings for various macro ratios may be read off the table at the back of the control unit.

The Macro Flash 1200 AF Set-N has a guide number of 12 at ISO 100/21° with all four flash tubes switched on. The power supply is by four 1.5-volt AA-size batteries or by equivalently sized rechargeable batteries. For continuous operation there is a power unit that can be plugged directly into the mains.

To save energy the flash will automatically switch itself off if the shutter release has not been activated for about one minute. Recharging begins as soon as the release is pressed. For macro flash work with regular flash units, 'Stroboframe' Lepp II brackets provide total control. Two flash units mounted as you require them each side of the camera.

Interchangeable autofocus lenses

You need the right lens on the right camera to make the most of your equipment. This applies more than ever to the 5xi because the ASZ - auto stand-by zoom - function from Minolta can only be fully utilized if camera and lens are perfectly tuned to work together.

The xi lenses are designed to work with the 5xi. Each of these small, compact zoom lenses turns camera and lens into a photographic system whose 'intelligently' controlled automation goes beyond focusing and exposure to include focal length control.

Why interchangeable lenses?

The creative possibilities of an SLR camera can only be fully utilised with interchangeable lenses. Using different focal lengths allows you to alter perspective without changing your position. By shifting the focal length the photographer can tighten or widen the field of view.

Lenses are grouped into roughly five categories according to their focal length and special characteristics: wide-angle, standard, telephoto, macro, and zoom lenses.

Wide-angle lenses are those whose focal length is 35mm or less. As you might expect, these lenses have a wide angle of view and allow photographs of large subjects at short distances. The shorter their focal length the wider their angle of view. The so-called fish-eye lenses are a special group within this category and have an angle of view of 180° or more. However, fish-eye lenses are characterized by pronounced barrel-shaped distortion which means that all lines not running through the centre of the image are curved.

Standard lenses have focal lengths of around 50mm and their angle of view of approximately 45° corresponds roughly to that of the human eye.

The telephoto category starts from around 80mm. Telephoto lenses allow frame-filling photographs of subjects from a greater distance.

Macro lenses, on the other hand, are available in all focal length ranges. Macro lenses with focal lengths of 50mm and 100mm are available for the 5xi. They are specialist lenses for use at close range and allow frame-filling reproduction of small subjects at a ratio of up to 1:1.

Zoom lenses have variable focal lengths. They can be continuously adjusted, within a certain range, to suit the photographic situation. In recent years enormous progress has been made in the design of zoom lenses. Not only have they become smaller and lighter but their optical qualities are now comparable to those of fixed focal lengths. They are therefore among the most popular interchangeable lenses. Minolta have developed the xi range of zoom lenses with motorized focal length adjustment specifically for the Maxxum/Dynax xi generation of cameras. The auto standby zoom function of the 5xi only works with these lenses.

Reproduction ratio and perspective

Shooting distance and focal length determine how large a subject will be captured on film. The relationship between subject size and reproduction size is called the reproduction ratio. It makes no difference to the reproduction ratio whether a subject is photographed with a long focal length at a great distance or with a short focal length at close range. By changing their position the photographer can use different focal lengths to capture a subject at exactly the same size. But photographs of a subject taken from different distances are still fundamentally different.

A change in the shooting position is automatically accompanied by a change in perspective. Perspective controls the relative size of objects, placed at different distances in a three-dimensional subject, when they are reproduced on a two-dimensional photograph. If the distance between subject and camera changes the relative sizes of objects at different distances from the camera will also change. Perspective therefore doesn't depend on the focal length, only on the subject distance.

If there were no limits to enlarging negatives telephoto pictures would not require long focal lengths, we would simply enlarge the subject in the wide-angle exposure to the desired reproduction ratio. It would have the same perspective as a telephoto picture taken from the same shooting position. The shorter the shooting distance the more obvious the change in relative sizes within the subject will be.

The xi autozoom lenses

Compared to other zooms, a lot has been changed on the Minolta autozoom lenses. There is, for example, the ergonomically designed non-slip zoom ring, which does away with the need for separate controls for focal length and focus setting.

But a lot has changed in electronic terms too. While earlier Minolta lenses were equipped with a ROM-IC, a fixed value memory, the new lenses have been upgraded with computer technology and have their own 8-bit microcomputer which constantly exchanges data with the camera's computer. Each of these new lenses also has its own zoom motor. In conjunction with the new xi-series cameras, including the 5xi, these new developments enable the lenses to offer the auto stand-by zoom function which is not available with the 12 earlier zoom lenses, which are still in the Minolta range and can be used on the 5xi without any loss of their functions.

But not all three of the new photographic techniques offered by the xi-series lenses can be accessed with the 5xi. If you want to make use of the third mode, the wide-view mode, you need to have the top model in the range, the 7xi, or the professional model, the 9xi (correct at time of publication).

Zoom lenses allow the continuous adjustment of the focal length within a certain range. They can be used to change the image size, and therefore the reproduction ratio, without any change in the photographers position. Previously, this adjustment was made manually by the photographer, and we were always advised, where possible, to start with the longest focal length for focusing. The experienced photographer only selected the optimum image size after focusing at the longest focal length. But fuzzy logic control brings innovation in this area too. The autofocus system feeds the subject distance to the auto stand-by zoom as soon as the sensor on the viewfinder eyepiece has activated the 5xi. On the basis of this the ASZ (Auto Stand-by Zoom) program selects a focal length to ensure a balance between main subject and surroundings. You can, of course, switch this function on and off whenever you like.

Image size lock is a special technique that involves the reproduction ratio of the main subject being stored in the camera's memory, and any changes in the subject distance are automatically compensated for by adjusting the focal length accordingly. This function means that the reproduction ratio of the main subject remains constant - and all you have to do is to hold the lens-function button. This facility is, of course, restricted by the focal length range of the lens you are using: if the end of the range is reached during an exposure sequence, whilst the lens-function button is pressed, the focal length adjustment stops and the characters **ISL** appear on the body data panel and in the viewfinder. If the subject comes back into range, and you are still holding the lens-function button, the image size lock function will resume its work and the letters **ISL**

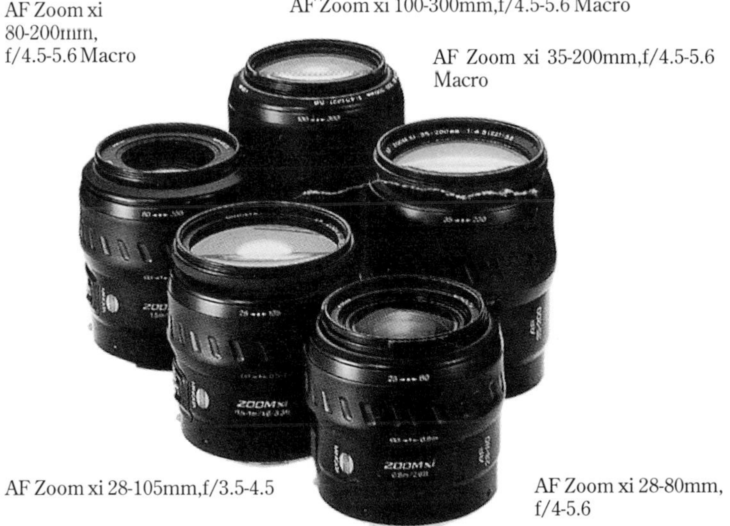

AF Zoom xi 80-200mm, f/4.5-5.6 Macro

AF Zoom xi 100-300mm,f/4.5-5.6 Macro

AF Zoom xi 35-200mm,f/4.5-5.6 Macro

AF Zoom xi 28-105mm,f/3.5-4.5

AF Zoom xi 28-80mm, f/4-5.6

On will reappear on the body data panel and in the viewfinder.

But as photography is also supposed to be a creative activity the xi lenses can be manually adjusted. This applies to manual motorized zooming as well as manual focusing, which is also done using the zoom ring.

For manual power zooming the zoom ring can be turned to the right and left by up to 5°, and the zoom speed changes in propor-

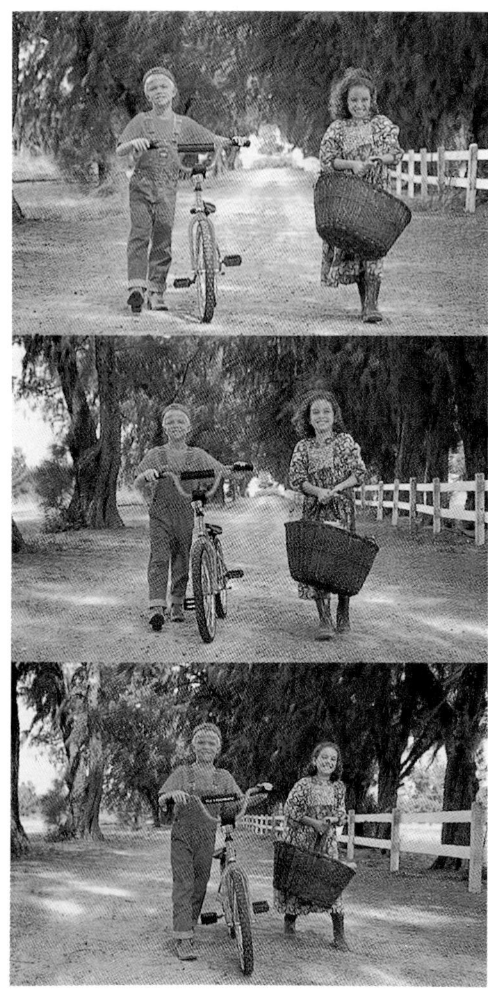

Even if your subject is moving towards or away from the camera you can maintain the desired framing, simply by pressing the lens function button located on the barrel of any Zoom xi lens.

tion to the degree of the turn. This means that large changes in focal length can be carried out with the same ease as precise fine-tuning. Whilst this takes some getting used to, it very quickly proves a lot more convenient than the turning and pushing we've been used to.

For manual power focusing, and non-slip focal length, the focus ring is simply pulled towards the camera and turned slightly in the desired direction. As with the motor zoom the setting speed of the power focus varies with the degree of the turn. So you can either focus very quickly or set the focus very slowly and precisely. This manual power focus facility allows for the confirmation of the final autofocus setting, as pulling the zoom ring towards the camera uncouples the autofocus system.

The new lenses combine surprisingly wide focal length ranges with compact design. Five xi zoom lenses were available in mid-1992.

AF Zoom xi 28-80mm,f/4-5.6
AF Zoom xi 28-105mm,f/3.5-4.5
AF Zoom xi 35-200mm,f/4.5-5.6
AF Zoom xi 80-200mm,f/4.5-5.6 Macro
AF Zoom xi 100-300mm,f/4.5-5.6 Macro

These light and easy to handle lenses fulfil the most varied requirements, and so every Maxxum/Dynax photographer will be able to find a favourite among them. All the xi lenses can also achieve surprisingly large reproduction ratios. This means that macro lenses are often superfluous for photographing small subjects.

AF Zoom xi 28-105mm,f/3.5-4.5 and AF Zoom xi 35-200mm,f/4.5-5.6

The two new lenses are varifocal designs with rear element focusing. Both lenses use a single compound aspherical element, and their compact construction owes much to the use of the unusual electronic focus compensation method. Unlike conventional zoom lenses, where the focus is kept constant during focal length adjustment by mechanical couplings, the focus is adjusted electronically. During focal length adjustment an autofocus motor simultaneously tracks the focus.

Thanks to their wide zoom range and large reproduction ratios these two lenses can be used for a multitude of applications, ranging from close-up photography to sports or landscape photography.

Whilst the 28-105mm xi lens offers a speed of f/3.5 at 28mm focal length and f/4.5 at 105mm, the wider focal length range of the 35-200mm xi lens costs you a whole stop in speed. You'll hardly miss this if you always take photographs in relatively good weather, but if you like moody light in your pictures you'd appreciate the extra stop. At 450g and 500g respectively, the difference in weight between the two lenses is substantially less than the different number of elements in their optical construction would suggest: 13 lenses in 10 groups, and 17 lenses in 15 groups respectively. The maximum reproduction ratio is also worth noting. It's 0.1 on the 28-105mm lens, and as much as 0.16 on the 35-200mm. The closest focusing distance of both lenses depends on the focal length set, and changes continuously from 50cm in the wide-angle setting to 100cm at the maximum telephoto focal length.

AF Zoom xi 100-300mm,f/4.5-5.6 Macro and AF Zoom xi 80-200mm,f/4.6-5.6 Macro

If you need medium to long focal lengths these light and compact lenses are the best choice. Both are extremely easy to handle and are ideal for 'snapshot', sports and travel photography. The AF 100-300mm xi not only has a 3x focal length range, it can also capture small subjects on film at almost one quarter of their original size.

Weighing 440g the 100-300mm lens is exactly 140g heavier than the 80-200mm. Despite the more complex construction of 11 lens elements in 9 groups used by the longer focal length lens, compared to the 9 elements in 9 groups of the 80-200, the design differences are surprisingly slight. This is also reflected by their identical close focusing distances of 1.5m. But the smaller focal length range allows the 80-200mm to be some 2cm shorter and measure in at exactly 8cm. So it is amazingly compact and is set to become one of the most popular lenses in the xi autozoom range.

AF Zoom xi 28-80mm,f/4.5-5.6

Minolta expect the compact (67.5mm long) and light (275g) AF Zoom xi 28-80mm,f/4.5-5.6, with its popular focal length range, to become **the** standard autozoom lens for many photographers. An aspherical composite lens contributes to a compact optical design of 7 elements in 7 groups. The lens allows close-up work with a reproduction ratio of up to 1:10 and a closest focusing distance of 0.8m. It offers a zoom range from wide-angle to medium telephoto and is therefore ideal for many types of subjects, from landscapes through group photography to portraits.

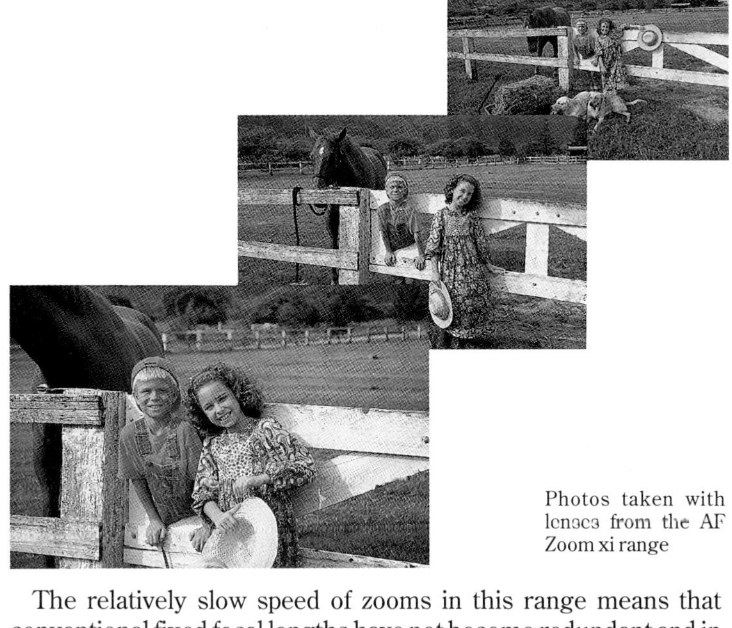

Photos taken with lenses from the AF Zoom xi range

The relatively slow speed of zooms in this range means that conventional fixed focal lengths have not become redundant and in fact the opposite is more likely. If you're a fan of extreme sharpness and therefore of slow films, you are bound to find the right fixed focal length in the Minolta AF lens range. The difference in speed at 80mm between f/5.6 on a zoom and f/1.4 on a fixed focal length is four full aperture stops. In order to achieve the same shutter speed in critical light conditions you have to use a film speed of ISO 50/18° with a lens aperture of f/1.4 compared to ISO 400/27° for the f/5.6 zoom.

Power Zoom lens

Like the new Minolta xi lenses, whose design it follows, the cheaper Minolta AF Power Zoom 35-80mm, f/4-5.6 Macro also offers motorized focal length adjustment. The focal length is also selected via the large ring on the lens barrel, and the focal length adjustment speed is variable. The further the non-slip ring is turned, the faster the motor works. The ring can be turned by approximately 5° for focusing and about 15° for focal length adjustment. If you let go of the ring, it automatically returns to its original position.

The focal length adjustment and manual focusing are not, however, carried out by a motor integrated into the lens. As soon as you turn the zoom ring, a coupling system diverts the power of the autofocus motor in the camera from the AF system to focal length adjustment or manual focusing. This approach allows the weight of the lens to be reduced, despite motorized power. A further reduction in weight was achieved by the special optical construction, which includes two aspherical elements. The zoom weighs just 175g. Eight individual elements were used in its optical construction, which includes two aspherical elements. The zoom weighs just 175g. Eight individual elements were used in its optical construction and its closest focusing distance is 0.5 metres. The auto stand-by zoom function is not available on this lens.

One feature that can often be quite useful is the ability to stop autofocusing, to lock it and correct it. It is possible to stop the AF setting without switching to manual focus mode, by simply pulling back the zoom ring and correct it, when necessary, by manually turning the focus ring. As soon as you let go, the camera will automatically switch back to automatic focusing. If you don't want it to do so, you need to push the AF/M switch - set at the bottom next to the camera bayonet - in order to switch to manual focusing.

AF zoom lenses

Apart from the five above-mentioned autozoom lenses, developed specifically for the xi generation of cameras, Minolta also offer a further 12 zoom lenses with different focal length ranges. A few of these lenses are bound to be replaced by new designs at some point in the future, in order to give the camera owner full access to the convenience and technical possibilities of the xi series in all focal length ranges.

AF 24-50mm,f/4 - The Minolta AF 24-50mm,f/4 wide-angle zoom is a real reporter's lens for capturing photographs in the centre of the action at fun fairs, festivals, in marquees or interiors. It is also ideal for landscape or architectural photography, and the relatively high speed of f/4 ensures a reasonable flash range in poor lighting conditions. Like many of the Minolta zoom designs

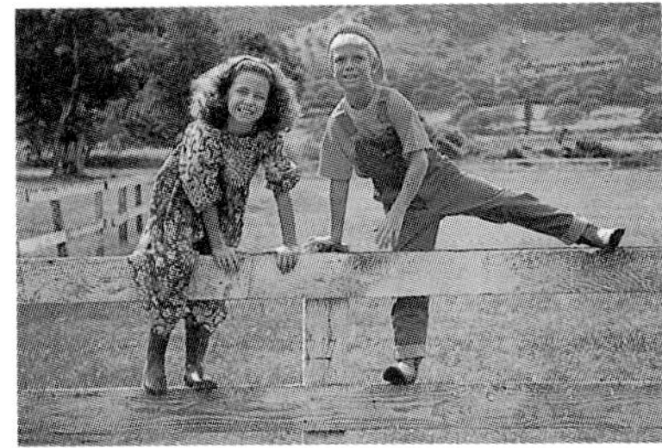

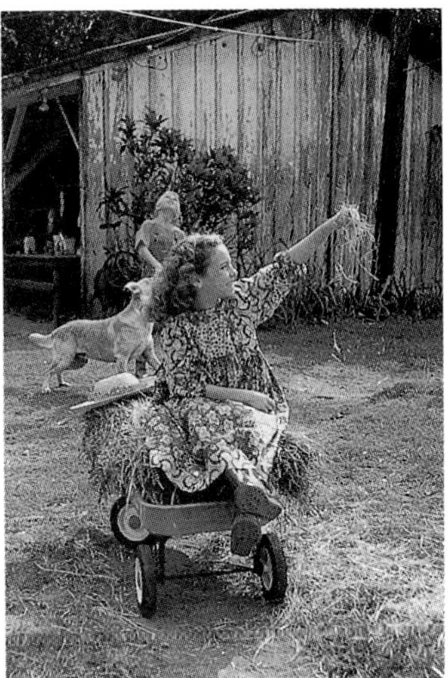

Auto stand-by zoom (ASZ) - the camera selects the optimum framing as soon as it is on the eye.

this particularly compact zoom contains an aspherical lens element which allows faster focusing as well as helping to deliver good optical performance. At a length of just 60mm and a weight of 285g you can take it anywhere, so it is ideal for the travel photographer. The filter size is 55mm.

AF 28-85mm,f/3.5-4.5 (new) - This Minolta lens covers a focal length range of more than 3x, from wide-angle to portrait telephoto. It is equipped with an improved focusing mechanism to give a higher focusing speed and is excellent in a variety of

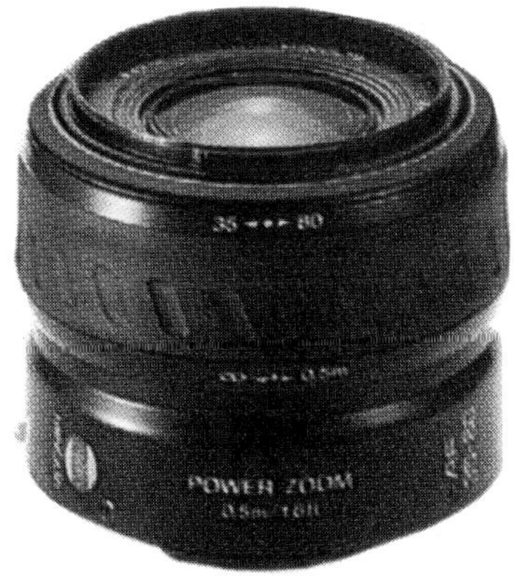

AF Power Zoom 35-80mm,f/4-5.6 Macro. The AF Power Zoom from Minolta is an extremely light and compact lens with easy manual-motorized focal length adjustment. The ASZ function is not available with this lens.

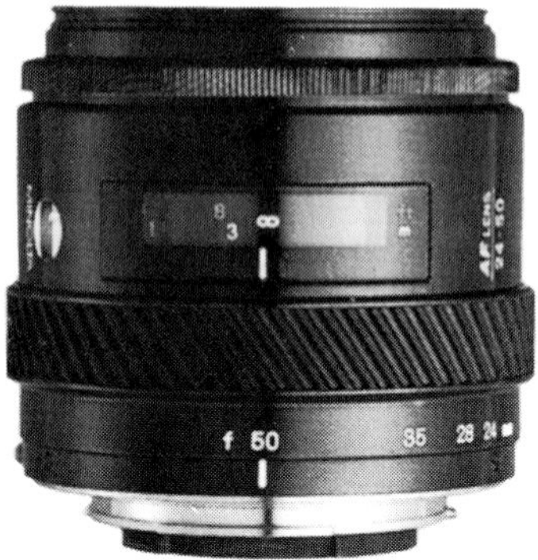

AF 25-50mm,f/4

situations for applications ranging from interior, to group photography and frame-filling portraits. Even close-up pictures are easily achieved with the macro setting, which goes down as far as 25cm at a reproduction ratio of 1:4. Its relatively high speed is useful for fast 'snapshots' and good flash coverage with medium- to high-speed films.

AF 35-80mm,f/4.5-5.6 - The smallest and lightest lens in the Minolta zoom range has an integral front element protector and a focal length range of 35-80mm, covering more than half of all average photographic situations. The range of this universal lens is sufficient for group photography and frame-filling portraits, as well as landscapes and 'snapshots' of children playing in the distance. In the close-up range the lens can achieve a maximum reproduction ratio of 1:6.

The integral sliding lens cap keeps the lens safe from dirt, dust, and scratches. It also speeds up lens changes and prevents accidental fingerprints, finally putting an end to the search for the lens cap. The slide switch on the side ensures fast opening and closing. The two slats of the protector simply move up or down in a similar fashion to a cigar-cutter. The cover behind which the two slats disappear double as an effective stray light hood. The filter size is extremely small and so allows the use of inexpensive 46mm attachments.

The focal length is changed with a wide ring with non-slip rubber coating. For manual focusing, however, the photographer has to make do with a fairly narrow focusing ring without the non-slip coating.

AF 35-105mm,f/3.5-4.5 - Despite its faster speed and wider focal length range, this lens is only 1.5mm longer and 4mm wider than the 35-80mm lens. The difference in weight is just 95g.

The construction involves an aspherical composite lens, which is the reason why it is so compact. Its 3x focal length range and relatively high speed make it a universal lens. And the close-up setting increases this versatility. Close-up setting distances also ensure rapid automatic focusing. The closest focusing distance is just 85cm, allowing close-up work with a reproduction ratio of 1:6.

AF 70-210mm,f/3.5-4.5 - Despite its 3x focal length range this telezoom is relatively fast, allowing fast shutter speeds for quick action pictures with medium speed films, even on overcast days. It weighs just 420g and is only 10cm long. It also has a special autofocus control button which causes Maxxum/Dynax series cameras to stop the focusing process to allow the shutter to be released straight away, suspending the camera's focus-priority function.

The filter size is 55mm and the focal length ring is fitted with a non-slip rubber coating. The closest focusing distance is 1.1m.

AF 80-200mm,f/4.5-5.6 - This zoom lens with the classical focal length range of 80-200mm already has a counterpart in the xi lens series. It is an ideal complement to the 35-80mm zoom and has a similar construction as well as the same integral front element protector. With a weight of just 290g and a length of 78mm it falls into the category of small, light lenses. It also has the small filter size of 46mm and works in the double telezoom system which allows particularly fast autofocusing. Its low weight and compact design make it an ideal lens for travel photography. And the closest focusing distance of 1.5m allows frame-filling pictures of relatively small subjects. The maximum reproduction ratio of this lens is 1:6.25.

AF 80-200mm,f/2.8 Apo - The lens is a heavyweight, but a real optical treat. Its extremely high speed and a special element made of AD glass to suppress chromatic aberration give this high performance lens a special place amongst zoom lenses. Its expensive construction consists of 16 elements in 13 groups, which accounts for its weight. If you want to enjoy the benefits of this high optical quality lens all you have to do is carry around 1350g and be

AF 28-85mm,f/3,5-4,5

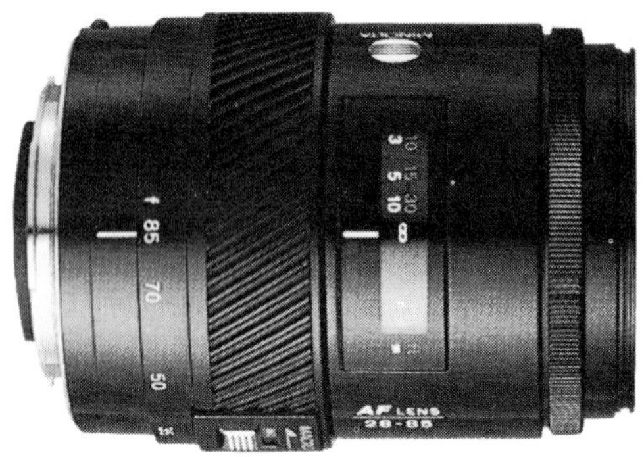

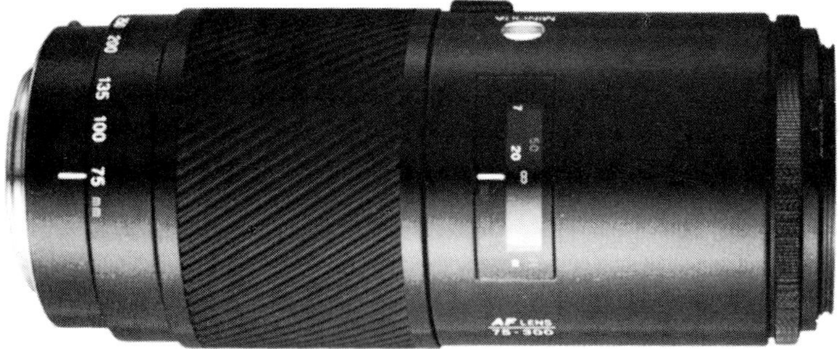

AF 75-300mm,f/4.5-5.6

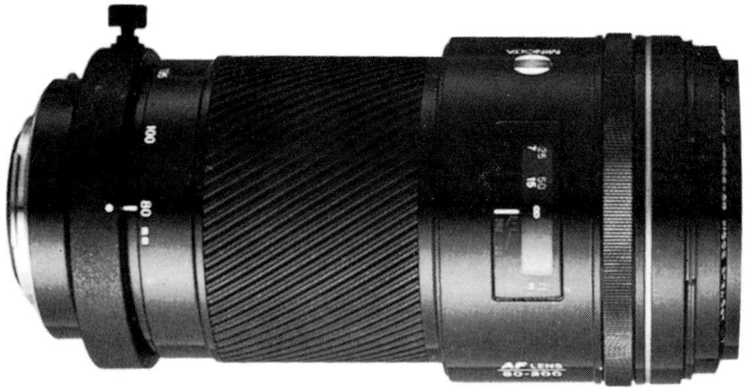

AF 80-200mm,f/2.8 Apo

able to aford the high financial outlay to acquire this exceptional optic in the first place.

AF 75-300mm,f/4.5-5.6 (now discontinued) - Minolta's well-proven 75-300mm telezoom has a focal length range that is 25mm longer than that of the more recent 100-300mm zooms. It is the ideal lens for sports or animal photography but its expensive construction of 13 elements in 11 groups means that it is more than twice as heavy, and more than 6cm longer, than the new 100-300mm zoom. A special feature of the lens is the switch on the lens tube which allows you to limit focusing range. It offers two positions, one for the close-up range from 1.5m to 3m, and one from 4m to infinity. This feature increases the autofocusing speed, useful for sports, wildlife, and action photography, because the lens never has to travel over the whole focusing distance.

AF 100-300mm,f/4.5-5.6 - Sports, animal, and landscape photography are the strengths of this telezoom with a 3x focal length range. Thanks to its sophisticated double telezoom construction it manages to be the same length as the 70-210mm zoom, as well as 10g lighter. Like the 70-210mm it has the new autofocus control button for suspending the focus priority of the camera. Its filter size is 55mm, and a closest focusing distance of 1.5m provides a maximum reproduction ratio of approximately 1:4.

Thanks to its extremely compact construction and low weight this lens is an ideal companion, especially when travelling. Used with the 35-105mm zoom it replaces a range of five fixed focal length lenses (100mm, 135mm, 180mm, 200mm and 300mm).

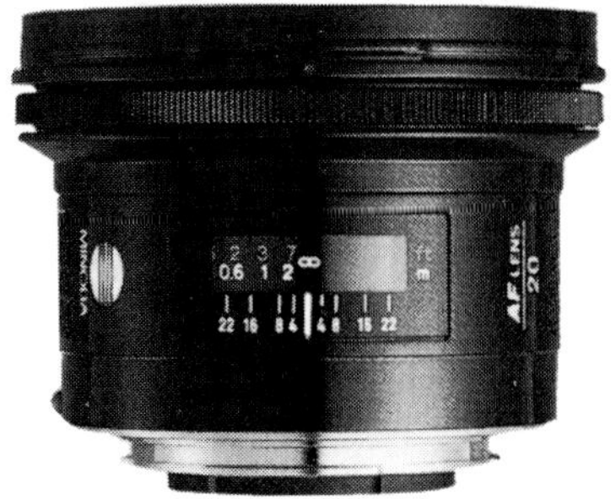

AF 20mm,f/2.8

Wide-angle lenses

AF 16mm,f/2.8 Fisheye - This lens has an extremely wide angle of view of 180° across the diagonal. Unlike many other fisheye lenses it fills the entire film format. The extreme angle of view and the altered perspective, which does not correspond to normal geometric perspective, do lead to strong barrel-shaped distortion. This means that all lines not running through the centre of the image are reproduced as curved to a greater or lesser extent. The closest focusing distance of this 400g lens is 20cm. The peculiar perspective allows the photographer to create surprising effects, but fisheyes should be used sparingly as these effect quickly become tiresome. They are best suited to landscape or interior photography.

This lens has an integral lens hood and an integral filter revolver with four filters, which are moved into position by turning a ring. The filters are integrated into the optical construction which means that a filter has to be used all the time, this explains why one of them is colourless. The other three are orange (for black-and-white and infrared use), pale pink (for colour photography in fluorescent light), and blue (for colour photography with tungsten light when using daylight film).

AF 20mm,f/2.8 - This extreme wide-angle lens has an angle of view of 94°, and its large depth of field makes it versatile for use in architectural and landscape photography, as well as photojournalism. It also comes into its own for tight interior work.

As focusing takes place using the rear element the close-up quality is excellent, and the speed of automatic focusing is in-

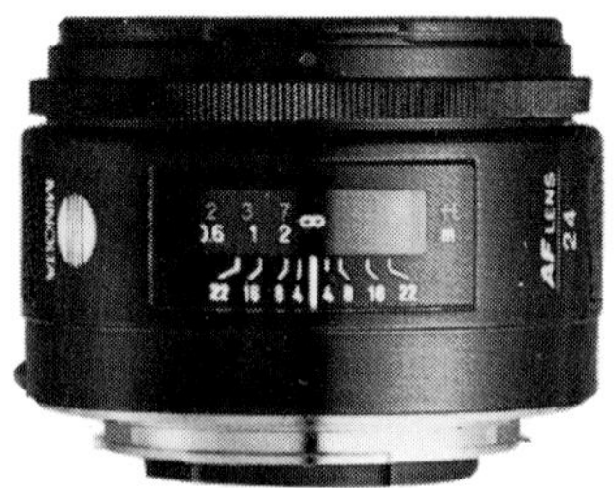

AF 24mm,f/2.8

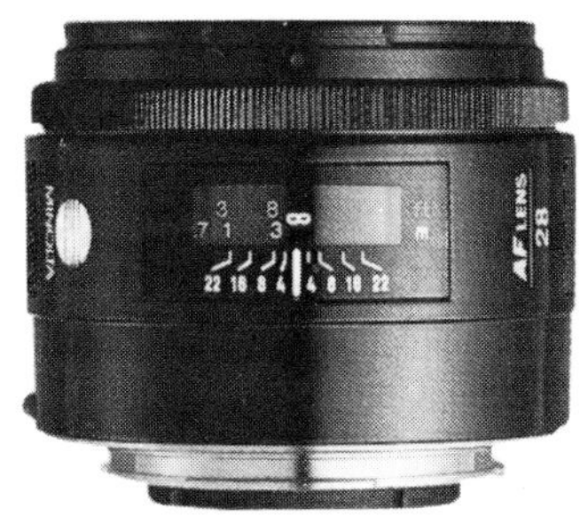

AF 28mm,f/2

creased. The essential lens hood supplied with the lens can be collapsed, for transport purposes, and the closest focusing distance is 25cm. The expensive optical construction of this fast 285g super wide-angle lens comprises 10 elements in 9 groups.

AF 24mm,f/2.8 - This compact and light 24mm lens has a slightly more moderate angle of view of 84°. It is ideal for photojournalism and 'snapshots', as well as for landscape and architectural photography and for tight interiors. When it comes to picture composition, particular care should be taken with the foreground in the lower third of the frame. The closest focusing distance is 25cm, and at just 215g this relatively fast lens is a real lightweight.

AF 28mm,f/2 - The Minolta AF 28mm,f/2 is suitable for wide-angle photographs in low light, like in twilight or poorly lit interiors. The angle of view of this particularly fast 285g lens is 75°, and its optical construction comprises 9 elements in 9 groups. Its closest focusing distance is 30cm.

AF 28mm,f/2.8 - This 28mm AF lens is a whole 100g lighter and 7mm shorter than the previous one, but is also one stop slower. It is useful for the same reasons as the more expensive option of the same focal length, but it falls behind for available light photography when you want to take atmospheric photographs without flash. Travel photographers, who appreciate every gram, will probably go for the AF 28mm,f/2.8 lens, which weighs just 185g. Landscapes, interiors, and 'snapshots' at close range are the strengths of this universal focal length.

AF 35mm,f/1.4 - This wide-angle offers extremely high speed, normally only available on lenses around 50mm focal length. It is an ideal replacement standard lens, particularly suited for atmospheric landscape photographs in twilight, or for use without flash in poorly lit interiors. Its expensive optical construction of 10 elements in 8 groups make this lens relatively heavy: at 470g it is the heaviest wide-angle in the Minolta AF range. Like the AF 28mm,f/2, the AF 35mm,f/1.4 also has floating elements in its construction to improve optical quality in the close-up range. The lens also has an aspherical element in its rear element focusing system which helps image quality and reduces focusing time.

AF 35mm,f/2 - This has a maximum aperture one stop smaller than the AF 35mm,f/1.4. And weighing less than half a pound makes it almost ideal if you don't work in extremely demanding conditions, like shooting in the poorest light conditions without flash. Like its faster 35mm counterpart this lens also offers excellent field flatness. For many photographers the weight of a lens is a decisive factor and the reduction in speed by one stop reduces the weight by almost half. Although at 55mm and 30cm respectively, filter thread and closest focusing distance are identical with the faster 35mm wide-angle.

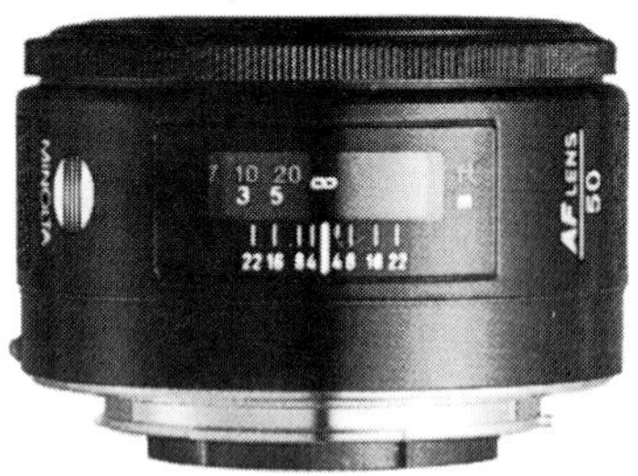

AF 50mm,f/1.4

Standard lenses

AF 50mm,f/1.4 - Standard lenses are wrongly becoming increasingly unfashionable. These versatile lenses are usually fast and have an angle of view that roughly matches the human eye. This means that many photographers find standard lenses with focal lengths around 50mm boring, but there are few lenses available which offer more possibilities than the much-maligned normal or standard. These usually very fast and compact lenses are especially useful for available light photography without flash. Conversely, their wide maximum apertures provide large flash ranges.

Fast standard lenses with a maximum aperture of f/1.4 even allow photography by candlelight.

AF 50mm,f/1.7 - This standard lens is still relatively fast - only three lenses in the whole Minolta range offer a wider maximum aperture. It has the same dimensions as the faster lens above and shares its close focusing distance of 45cm, but it is a full 65g lighter. One advantage of a half-stop less speed is, of course, price. High speed, low weight, and low price are the main arguments in favour of a standard lens. But remember, the 50mm focal length is covered by several zoom lenses in the Minolta lens range.

Medium telephoto focal lengths

AF 85mm,f/1.4 - The super fast 85mm telephoto lens in the Minolta lens range, weighing 550g, is particularly favoured by professionals. Its high speed is suitable both for atmospheric photographs in low light and for making use of differential focus. Here the advantages of a wide maximum aperture become very apparent in portrait photographs, where a cluttered background dissolves into unsharpness. Another advantage is the ability to work with fast shutter speeds, even in poor lighting conditions. A so-called floating effect, where elements move in different directions relative to each other during focusing, was used in the design of this lens to improve optical quality.

AF 100mm,f/2 - Although it has a focal length 15mm longer and a maximum aperture of f/2, the 100mm telephoto lens is 70g lighter

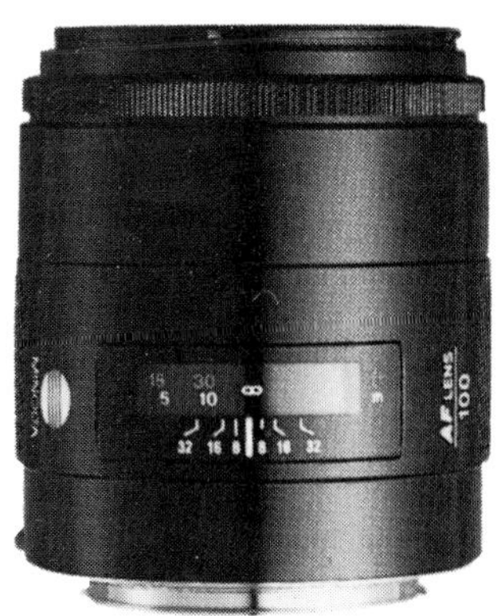

AF 100mm,f/2

than the super fast 85mm, and at 55mm its filter thread size is exactly 17mm smaller. Which one of these two very similar lenses you go for all boils down to photographic preference. Both lenses are excellent for portrait and landscape photography. Decide on whether you prefer the slightly longer focal length or the higher speed, or the lower weight. Price, too, will be an important factor for your decision, but both the 85mm and the 100mm are top class performers.

AF 135mm,f/2.8 - The slightly slower AF 135mm,f/2.8 is an inexpensive alternative to the shorter 85mm and 100mm lenses. It is just over one-third of their price, but weighs 365g (185g less than the 85mm lens) and is less than a centimetre longer. This lens, like the other two, is excellent for portrait photography, and can also be used for sports and action pictures over medium distances. As its closest focusing distance of 1m is the same as that of the 100mm lens, it even provides a greater magnification in the close-up range. This means that subjects smaller than an A5 sheet of paper can fill the frame.

Apochromatic lenses

Chromatic aberration is a reproduction fault that has caused optical designers many problems. Although spherical aberration has been largely eliminated in modern lens designs by special aspherical elements, chromatic aberration is corrected by using glass with special refractive characteristics.

Chromatic aberration is a colour fault which manifests itself in the following way. Different colours of the spectrum are refracted in different ways when passing through the lens. This has the effect of producing differently coloured images which are different in size and at different positions along the optical axis. These are called magnification and focus differences, and such faults are evident in colour fringes and unsharpness in the photograph. The effect becomes particularly noticeable on longer telephoto focal lengths.

Page 101
Because of their graphic shapes and different colours doors are an ever-popular subject for photographers. Telezooms facilitate spontaneous changing from overview to detail.

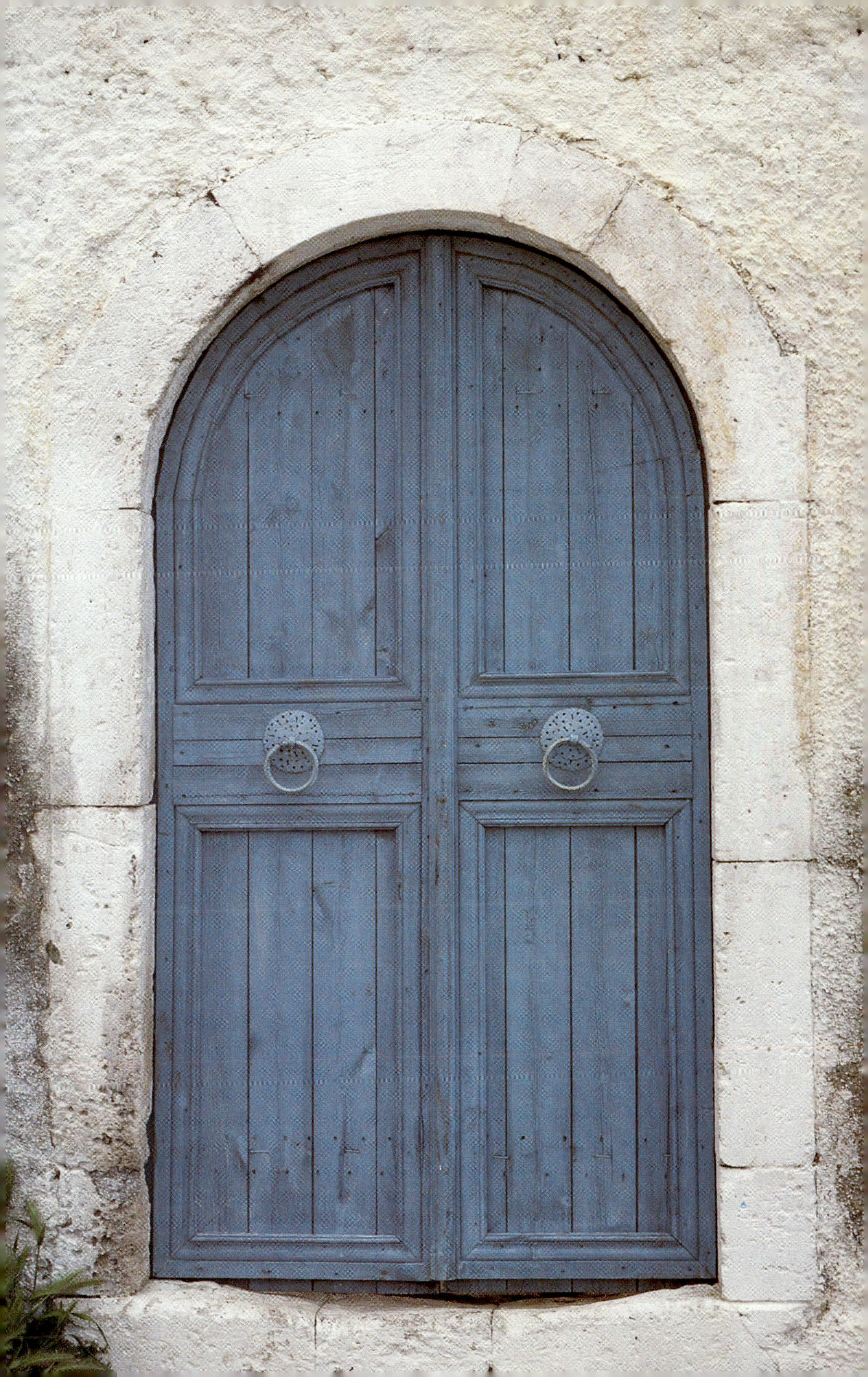

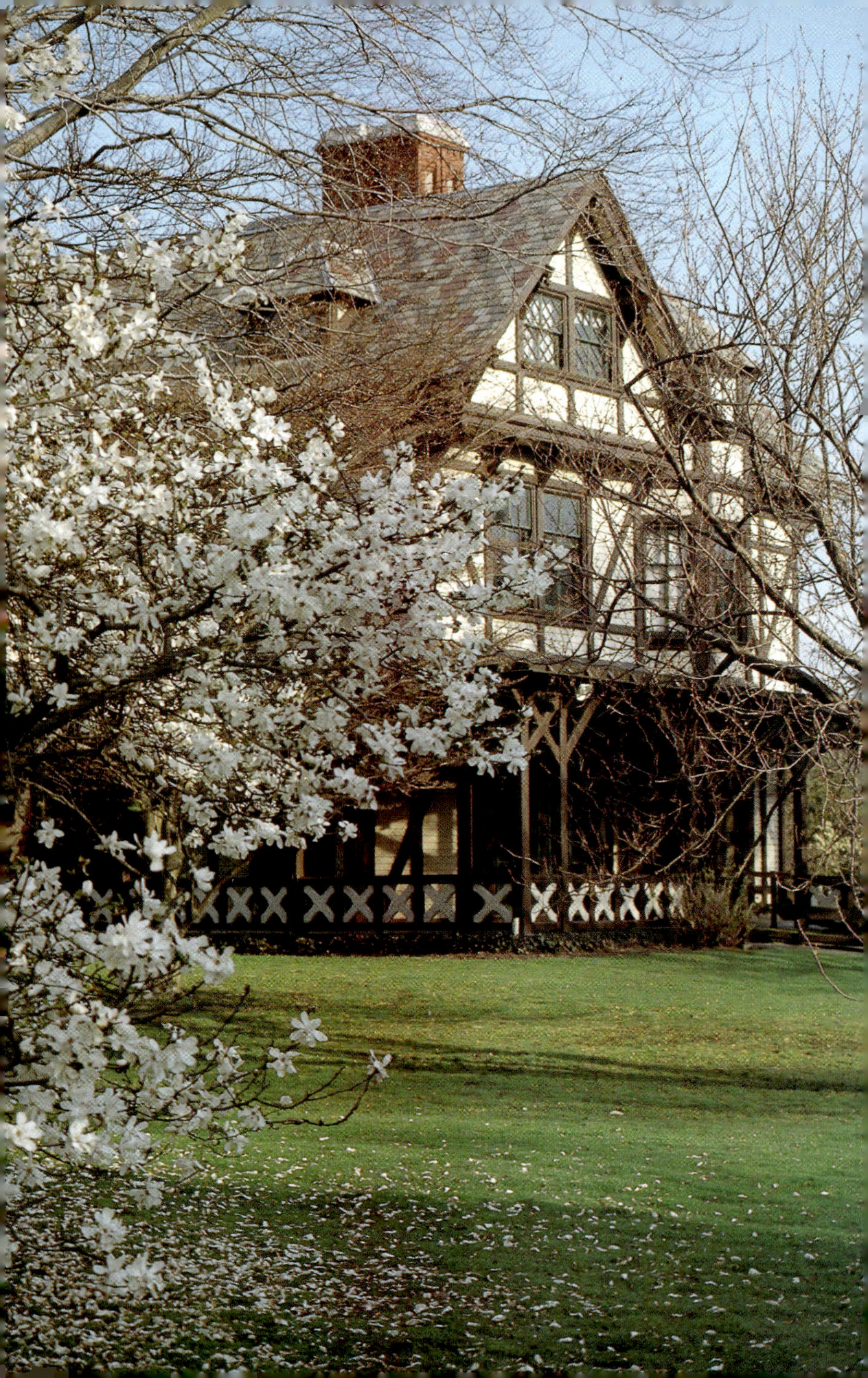

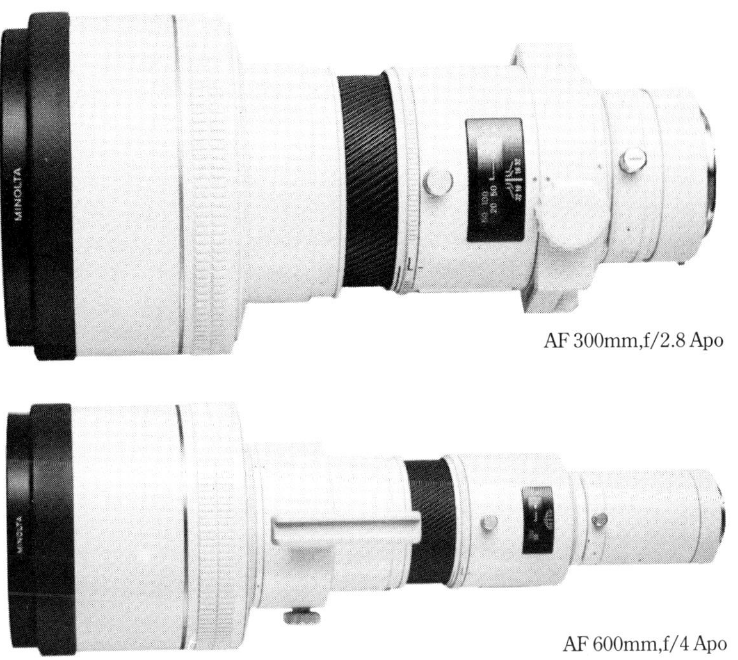

AF 300mm,f/2.8 Apo

AF 600mm,f/4 Apo

On most lenses this fault is only corrected for two colours, and this generally produces an acceptable impression of sharpness. The correction is achieved by combining several elements which cancel out each others faults. Lenses which are corrected for two colours - usually yellow and purple - are called achromatic lenses. The combination of positive convex and negative concave elements, made from different types of glass, is usually sufficient to achieve the correction. The correction of chromatic aberration for the whole spectrum of blue, green and red is far more difficult. Lenses corrected in this way are called apochromatic lenses. Minolta offers this type of correction in the AF 80-200mm,f/2.8 Apo and all fixed focal lengths above 200mm.

Page 102
With the Automatic Depth Control Card the Minolta 5xi automatically selects an aperture which reproduces foreground and background as sharply as possible. (This card has now been replaced by the Travel Card which effectively achieves the same result).

AF 200mm,f/2.8 Apo - The fast AF 200mm,f/2.8 Apo was designed for the special requirements of photojournalists and wildlife and sports photographers. Internal focusing is particularly fast and accurate and can be speeded up even more by preselecting the focusing range. This is done by selecting the largest or smallest focusing distance via a special ring so that focusing never travels across the entire focusing range. As you may know, the focusing movement is normally longer in the close-up range than in the far range. And so by limiting the close-up range to 5m for sports use, the focusing speed is at least doubled. Apochromatic correction is achieved by using two elements made of AD glasses (glass with 'anomalous dispersion'). These lenses are more heat-sensitive than others and for this reason the lens tube is beige to reflect heat rays more effectively than the usual black finish.

AF 300mm,f/2.8 Apo - The 300mm telephoto lens is the most commonly used focal length amongst sports photographers. A high speed, to allow fast shutter speeds, is a basic requirement as sporting events often take place in poorly lit halls and freezing fast movement is often a necessity. Like the 200mm lens, Minolta's AF 300mm,f/2.8 Apo includes two AD glass elements which give particularly good colour correction. The focusing range of this lens can also be limited. Thanks to internal focusing, where only one element group inside the lens is moved, the length of the 300mm remains constant. Its weight of almost three kilograms and the long focal length generally necessitate the use of a tripod. The lens has a special tripod ring of its own as it could damage the camera bayonet if it were supported by the camera alone. This ring is placed in such a way that the centre of gravity is positioned perfectly. The lens can be turned in the tripod ring for changing between landscape and portrait format.

Because of its size it is not advisable to use this lens with the integral flash unit of the 5xi, or other similar cameras, as the lens would cast a shadow on the lower part of the photograph. This will not happen with clip-on flash units, particularly if they are used for bounce flash.

AF 600mm,f/4 Apo - This super telephoto lens is twice as heavy as the 300mm. As the longest telephoto lens in the Minolta range, it is also one of the fastest of its kind. Its main uses will be in the fields of professional sports and animal photography, but because it is almost prohibitively expensive (in roughly the same price bracket as a small car) this optical delicacy will remain a rarity even among professionals. The lens is also constructed using AD elements. In addition, it has an achromatic coating which improves its colour reproduction and contrast. Like the other Apo telephoto lenses it has internal focusing, focusing range preselection, and a tripod ring.

But it's not only the photographer's wallet that is stretched to the limits by this lens as it weighs in at 5.5kg. As handheld shake free use of this lens is impossible, a particularly sturdy tripod needs to be added to the weight of the lens. The integral flash of the Minolta 5xi is no use with this lens either, as it cannot illuminate its entire image area. The large and expensive front element is protected by a colourless filter supplied with the lens. The lens also comes with six glass filters which slot into the lens tube. They are part of the optical construction of the lens which means that one always has to be in placed. The set includes one colourless filter (Normal), one yellow (Y-52), one orange (O-56), a red (R-60), a neutral density (ND-4X), and a skylight (1B) filter. The lens has a sturdy handgrip for easy transport and a storage case is also supplied.

AF Apo tele converters

Tele converters are a useful invention which allowing the focal length of a lens to be increased by a certain factor. Such converters, placed between camera and lens to increase the focal length, used to have the disadvantage of reducing the speed of the lens and its reproduction quality.

Although the loss of speed with an increase in focal length is an inescapable optical law, the AF Apo converters for Minolta Apo lenses are designed to be part of the lens construction. Like the

AF 2X Tele Converter II Apo
AF 1,4X Teleconverter II Apo

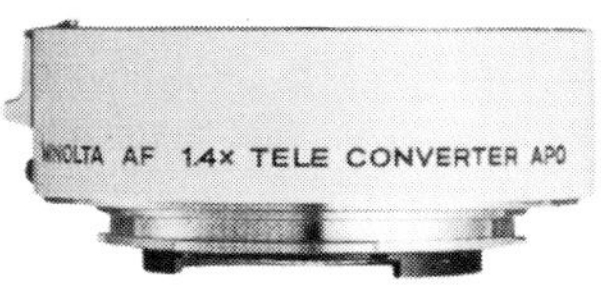

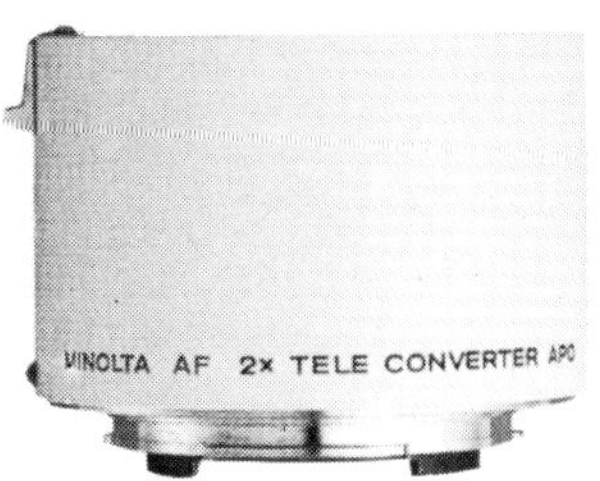

lenses themselves they have an integral ROM-IC which feeds into the camera all data necessary for focusing and exposure control, including the actual aperture and focal length value. This means that the actual aperture value is displayed on the data panels of the camera, making manual correction unnecessary. Their computer-designed optical construction from special glass with achromatic coating guarantees sharp reproduction with plenty of contrast and excellent colour reproduction, even at maximum aperture. The autofocus function is also hardly affected by the use of Apo tele converters. A transmission mechanism in the converter connects the AF coupling devices of camera and lens. Minolta's range includes two such converters, with factors of 1.4X and 2X.

AF 1.4X Tele Converter II Apo - This tele converter is specifically designed for Minolta AF Apo lenses with focal lengths above 200mm, and increases their focal length by a factor of 1.4. This means that the 200mm lens becomes a 280mm lens, the 300mm a 420mm, and the 600mm a 840mm, with the speed reduced by one stop in each case. But as all Apo lenses are very fast to start with, this does not make much difference. The converters have the same beige-coloured design as the Apo lenses, so they form a harmonious unit when used together.

AF 2X Tele Converter II Apo - The AF 2X Tele Converter Apo doubles the focal length, and is also designed specifically for Minolta's Apo telephoto lenses with focal length above 200mm. It turns the 200mm lens into a 400mm lens, the 300mm into a 600mm, and the 600mm into a super telephoto lens with 1200mm focal length. At two aperture stops the loss in speed becomes more noticeable, but thanks to the high speeds of Minolta's Apo telephoto lenses, the speeds are still quite acceptable. They compare favourably with those of the original focal lengths of other manufacturers. The 2X converter also has its own ROM-IC which transmits all data relating to the increase in focal length to the camera's computer so that the data panels of the Maxxum/Dynax show the actual values, and so again conversion is not necessary. It should be noted that the AF system does not function when the 2X converter is used with the 600mm,f/4 APO.

The high optical quality of the converter allows unrestricted use with full aperture, a fact which makes the loss in speed even more acceptable.

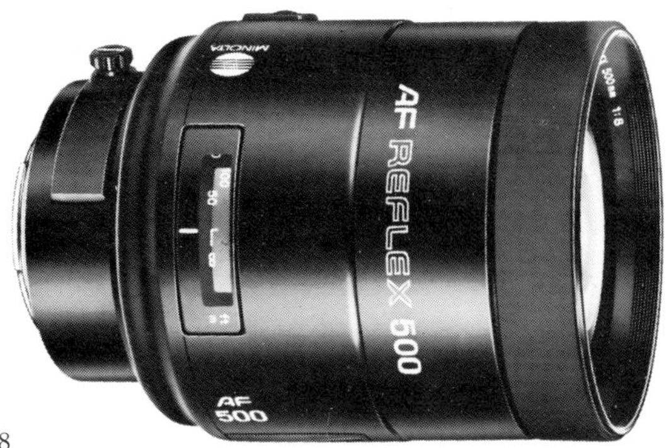

AF-Reflex 500mm,f/8

Reflex lens

AF Reflex 500mm,f/8 - The size and weight of very long telephoto focal lengths makes them more difficult to use, particularly for travel photography. This is why Minolta's lens range includes one real speciality, the Minolta AF Reflex 500mm,f/8, the first reflex lens for an AF camera. Reflex lenses are relatively small and light, and the Minolta AF Reflex 500mm weighs just 665g. Used on the i and xi series Maxxum/Dynax cameras (except the 3000i) it focuses automatically, but on older Minolta AF models it has to be focused manually. It consists of 7 elements in 5 groups, including two concave mirrors which divert the path of the light through the lens. The special construction of this lens means that it cannot have an iris diaphragm and so a filter is part of the optical construction. This also means that a filter needs to be in the compartment in front of the lens bayonet at all times. The closest focusing distance is about four metres.

As this lens does not have an iris diaphragm it is always used at full aperture. A consequence of this is that the depth of field is fixed and cannot be increased in any way. The neutral density filter ND4-X, supplied with the lens, reduces the speed to imitate a smaller aperture, but does not affect the depth of field. The exposure is always determined by the shutter speed - even if the camera is in P mode.

Photographs taken with reflex lenses are particularly easy to recognize if highlights or light reflections are included in unsharp areas of the picture. These highlights don't appear as bright spots, but as bright rings or 'doughnuts', an effect which can create interesting photographs. This lens does take some getting used to, but once you have discovered the appeal of reflex lenses you won't want to do without this Minolta speciality, particularly in the medium distance range.

AF macro lenses

Minolta offers two macro lenses of different focal length for its autofocus SLR cameras. The shorter 50mm model is suitable for copying applications where you are working with relatively short shooting distances from the repro stand. A longer focal length, such as the 100mm lens, is to be recommended for close-up nature photography where you have to keep your distance from the subject. Both lenses allow life size reproduction as their largest

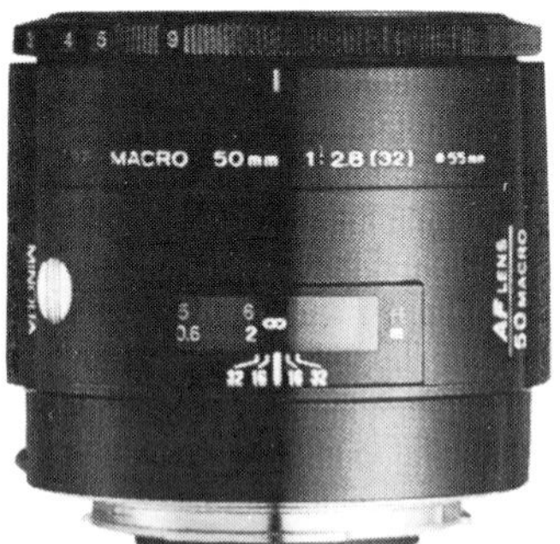

AF 50mm,f/2.8 Macro

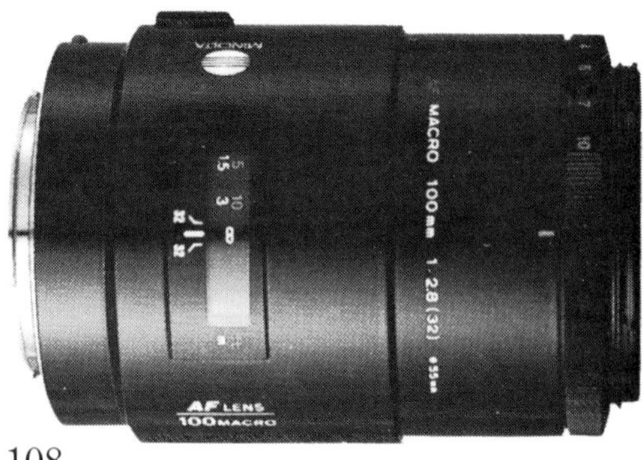

AF 100mm,f/2.8 Macro

reproduction ratio is 1:1. Which lens you go for depends on the potential application, as well as weight and price considerations. If you only take photographs of flowers - which don't run or fly away like beetles or other insects - you will be well served by the lower-priced 50mm. If you have to keep your distance you'll benefit from the telephoto macro, otherwise, both offer the same reproduction ratio and a speed of f/2.8.

AF 50mm,f/2.8 Macro - The AF 50mm,f/2.8 Macro can be focused continuously down to life-size at a distance of 20cm. Thanks to a special "double floating system" aberrations such as curvature of field and spherical aberration are largely eliminated. As three element groups move in relation to each other during focusing, the lens offers fast focusing as well as high speed. The closest focusing distance is defined as the distance between the subject and the film plane. As the lens tube is extended to its maximum length to achieve the largest reproduction scale, the distance between the front element and the subject is substantially reduced, which restricts the ways you can light the subject. As the reproduction ratio increases the depth of field becomes more and more shallow.

The exact reproduction ratio is shown in the position of the focus ring. The engraving 1:1 indicates actual size, 1.2 means five-sixths of actual size, and 1.5 two-thirds. It gets easier after the 2, which indicates a reproduction ratio of 1:2; three then stands for 1:3 and so on down to 1:9, where the subject is reproduced on the film at one-ninth of its actual size. For optimum flash lighting the Macro Flash 1200 AF can be attached to the 55mm filter thread.

AF 100mm,f/2.8 Macro - With the longer 100mm focal length and the 1:1 reproduction, the distance between film plane and subject is approximately 15cm larger. This has many advantages including, less problems with lighting, the smaller background area is easier to dissolve into unsharpness, and most importantly, the greater shooting distance is vital for close-up pictures of small animals. However, the longer focal length is also substantially more expensive and means that the lens is almost twice the price of the 50mm macro.

Like the 50mm macro the sophisticated optical construction of the 100mm includes a "double floating system", necessitating 8 freely moving elements. Three lens groups move simultaneously during focusing which allows the lens tube to be kept relatively short.

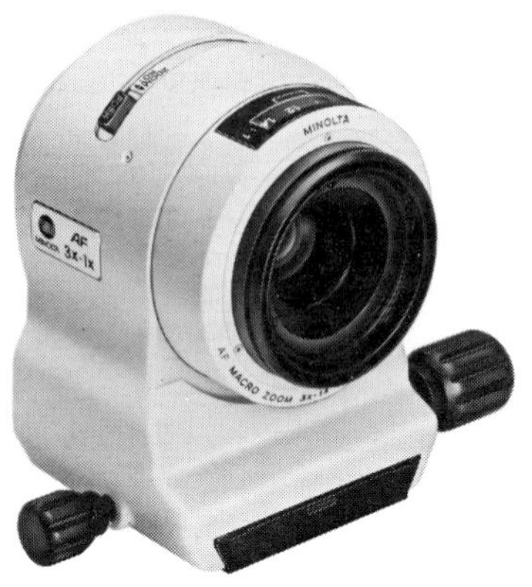

Minolta AF Macro Zoom 3X-1X,f/ 1.7-2.8

The first autofocus lens worldwide for reproduction ratios between 1:1 and 3:1 (actual size and 3x magnification).

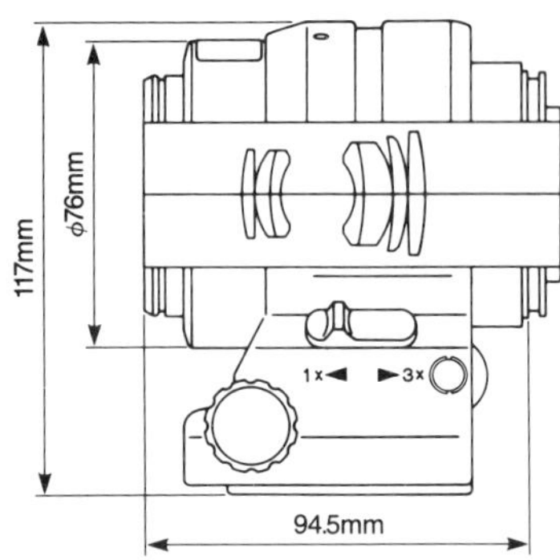

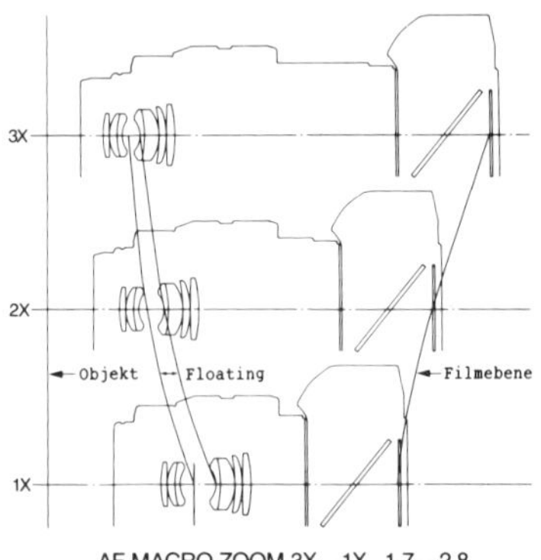

AF MACRO ZOOM 3X—1X 1,7—2,8

In the zoom setting the front and rear mounts carrying the camera body and optical system move in opposite directions along the axis. The central mount, which has a tripod connection, remains in a constant position in relation to the subject plane. A floating system is used to reduce spherical and chromatic aberration. In this system the distance between the two components changes in relation to the reproduction ratio.

The AF 100mm,f/2.8 Macro has the same focusing range limiter as the Apo telephoto lenses, substantially increasing the focusing speed and making for better handling. For short distances the focus range can be limited to 54cm, and for photographs across greater distances the range can be limited from 59cm to infinity. Macro lenses generally offer excellent optical quality at a distance, making the Minolta AF 100mm Macro an excellent portrait lens.

AF Macro Zoom 3X-1X,f/1.7-2.8

This particularly fast lens for special applications in the extreme close-up range works with limited reproduction ratios from 1:1 to 3:1. This means that it allows photographs from actual size up to three-times magnification. If you want to attach this lens to a Minolta 5xi - because of the slightly protruding integral flash - you need to select a reproduction ratio other than 1:1.

Photography with large reproduction ratios is normally very difficult and cumbersome but a number of the settings needed are handled automatically by this AF Macro Zoom. For example, the motor zoom carries out the axial movements of the front mounting, which carries the optical system, and the rear mounting, that carries the camera body. The middle mounting, which should normally be attached to a tripod, remains in a fixed position relative to the subject plane. The reproduction ratio can be selected continuously between 1:1 and 3:1, and is shown on the reproduction ratio scale of the lens.

Once the reproduction ratio has been selected, automatic focusing works as with other AF lenses. The autofocus has a type of internal focusing which keeps the relative positions of subject, lens, and camera body constant. If desired, the lens can also be focused manually with a knob which causes lens and camera to move together along a focusing track.

The optical construction includes floating elements to reduce spherical and chromatic aberration. The working distance of the lens is between 25.1mm (at 3:1) and 40.1mm (at 1:1).

The lens can be used in either autoexposure or manual mode. The camera automatically compensates for the loss of light which occurs at large reproduction ratios. This means that you do not have to calculate magnification factors. Another unique feature of this Minolta AF Macro Zoom is the motorized framing. As it is often quite difficult to precisely determine framing for magnification photographs, this lens can automatically adjust the camera position. By using a slide switch on the lens base (the same switch as is used for zooming) the camera body can easily be turned to the desired angle over a 135° range. The filter size is 46mm.

The power required for the zoom motor and for moving the camera is supplied by a 6-volt lithium battery which is inserted into a battery chamber on the lens mount facing the camera body.

But all these features, plus the extremely high speed (f/1.7 at a reproduction ratio of 3:1, f/2.8 at 1:1), have their price. The lens is really only used for specific professional applications and very rarely by amateur photographers. This 1100g lens is supplied with a dedicated macro tripod which allows the camera/lens unit to be positioned above the subject, in a similar fashion to a microscope.

The special Minolta Macro Flash 1200 AF can be attached to the front of the lens for macro flash photography. But you should remember that the autofocus will not work on predominantly red, yellow, or white subjects if it is used in conjunction with modelling lamps.

Although the speed of the lens changes with the reproduction ratio, it is not difficult to determine the exact exposure with a manual exposure meter. With this lens, unlike with conventional bellows, the aperture shown in the camera viewfinder or on the body data panel is always the actual aperture.

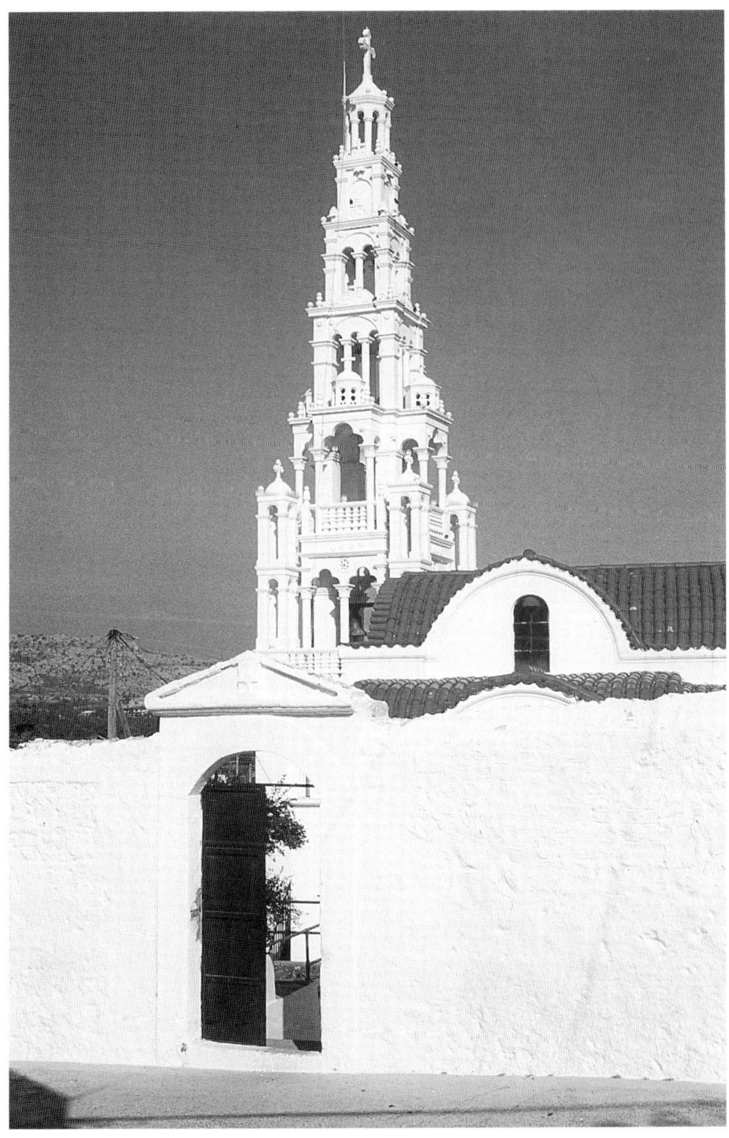

Strong contrasts, particularly white or black portions in the centre of the subject, cause most other exposure systems to fail. The Minolta 5xi easily masters situations such as this.

Expansion cards

Expansion cards are available only with Minolta Maxxum/Dynax cameras. They give you the opportunity to adapt your 5xi for special applications by programming the automatic functions of the camera. So far a total of 20 cards are available, of which more than half can be used with the 5xi. All Special Application Cards can be used with the 5xi, but so far only four of the Feature Cards expand the camera's functions, but the customized function cards cannot be used with this camera at all.

The microprocessor of each expansion card controls the circuits stored on them. When the expansion card is activated data is transmitted between the main computer of the camera and the microprocessor of the card. The cards may influences autofocusing, exposure control, or film transport, depending on how they are programmed. All cards with the xi suffix have autozoom functions included in their programing, which means that they can only be used fully with the Minolta xi camera series. Some of these cards (e.g. Travel Card) will function with earlier models but their autozoom functions will only work with xi camera's.

To activate an expansion card simply insert one into the small slot at the top of the card door. Once fitted its functions are automatically activated and the indication **CARD** is shown in the bottom left-hand corner of the camera's body data panel. The English abbreviation of the card name is shown on the body data panel for approximately five seconds. If a Feature Card is being used, adjustments to its program are made by pressing the card-adjust button inside the card door. No additional setting is necessary for the Special Application Cards.

A simple numerical menu system eases the programming of the desired function modifications, and the special functions can be cancelled at any time. In order to return to the standard setting temporarily, you simply press the **CARD** button next to the body data panel. This restores all the basic settings of the camera. All modifications of these special cards are also cancelled when the camera is switched off. But if you have modified the program of a Feature Card, the program remains altered (on the card, not on the camera) even when the card is turned off or removed.

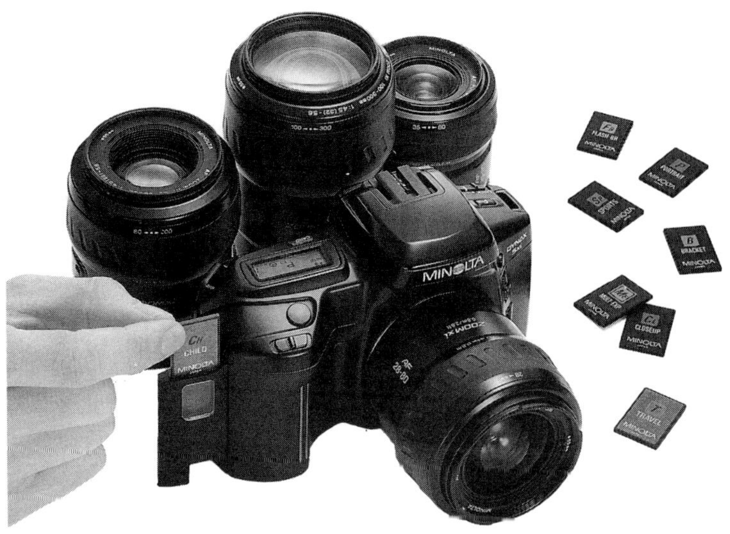

Thanks to the possibilities of the different creative expansion cards the 5xi can be fully adapted for special photographic applications.

A small window on the card door allows you too see which card has been inserted without having to open the card door. With all expansion cards on the 5xi, the functional modification is only maintained while the card is inserted

Feature cards

The largest group of expansion cards are the feature cards which expand the functions of the Minolta 5xi beyond its already substantial creative possibilities. These cards turn the camera into a specialist tool, without the need for the photographer himself to be a specialist.

For the 5xi there is a card for automatic exposure bracketing, one for automatic flash bracketing, a new card for exposure bracketing with or without flash, and another one for multiple exposures.

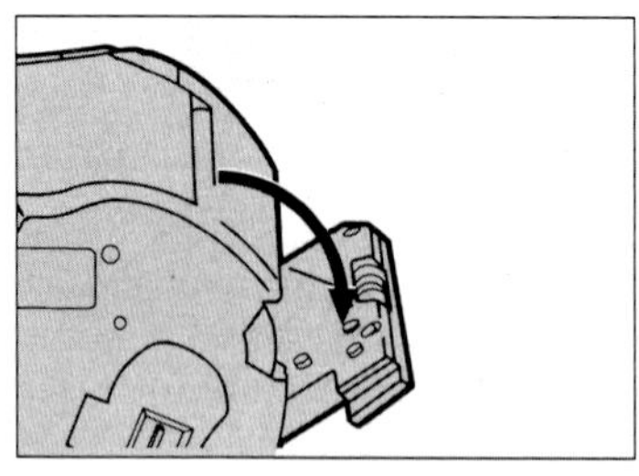

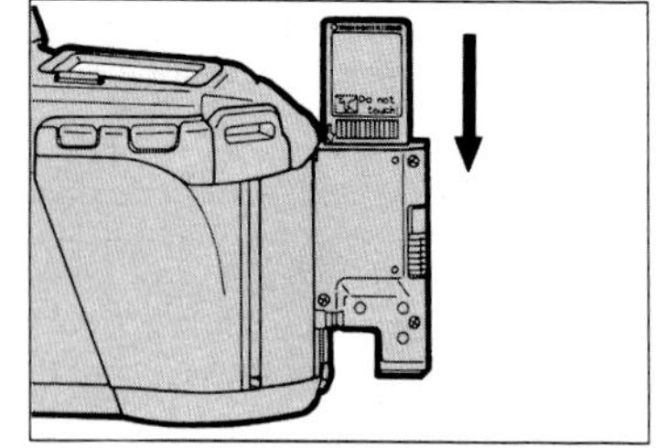

To activate an expansion card, insert it into the open card door from above. **CARD** will appear on the body data panel.

Exposure Bracketing Card

Correct exposure is often not a question of correct metering but a matter of taste, especially within the extended speed range of modern films. With slide films particularly, slight underexposure can produce punchier, richer colours, while minimal overexposure can lead to better results for examining photographs on the lightbox or for enlarging on reversal paper. Even professionals rarely rely on exposure measurements and experience alone, but take exposure sequences to be on the safe side. This means that they take a number of photographs of a subject, systematically varying the exposure from one frame to the next. In this way they can be sure to get an optimum result every time.

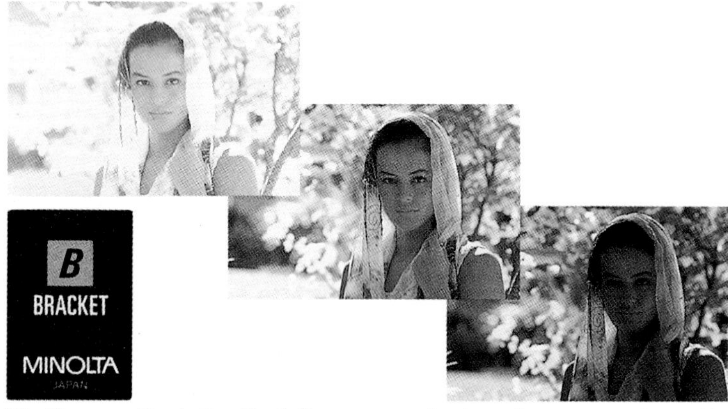

The Exposure Bracketing Card allows you to take three, five or seven shots with different exposures.

With the help of the Exposure Bracketing Card the Minolta 5xi can automatically produce such exposure sequences. This card allows the photographer to shoot automatic sequences of three, five, or seven frames whose exposures differ by either one-third of a stop, half a stop, or a full stop. The first frame is always exposed in the way the camera considers correct. Half the others are exposed more tightly while the rest are exposed more generously, each by the preselected step up or down.

When used in this way the camera automatically switches to continuous drive mode. If you let go of the shutter-release button before the bracket is completed the camera stops and interrupts the exposure sequence. The aborted sequence is not continued when the shutter-release button is pressed again, but instead, the camera starts a new sequence. Exposure bracketing sequences are not possible in single-frame mode and the focus of auto bracketing sequences is locked before the first frame.

Like all other expansion cards, the Exposure Bracketing Card is inserted into the card door with the camera switched on. The abbreviation **brAc** and the standard setting of the card then appear on the body data panel. If the standard setting is not changed the display disappears after approximately five seconds. In order to switch off the expansion card function simply press the card-on/off button, the **CARD** indicator on the body data panel will then disappear and the camera will once again be working 'normally'.

In its standard setting the Exposure Bracketing Card is programmed for automatic exposure sequences of three frames with an exposure variation of one light value each time. If you want to change this setting you have to open the card door and press the card-adjust button. The card and exposure-adjustment indicators will now flash to signal that the setting can be changed. At this point the shutter-release button and autofocus will remain locked.

On the 5xi the exposure is changed with the shutter-setting control, in increments of 0.3, 0.5 and 1EV. When the adjustment has been made, press the card on/off button. The card and card-setting indicators will then flash on the body data panel. You can now use the shutter-setting control to select the desired number of exposures - three, five or seven. To confirm your selection you need to press the card-adjust button once again and close the card door. The exposure variation and number of exposures will stay in the memory until it is changed again. If the programming process is interrupted for more than 20 seconds, the body data panel returns to the normal display and the card retains the last selected settings.

Automatic exposure bracketing is possible in all exposure modes, except TTL flash control, for which a separate card is now available. In programmed autoexposure mode aperture and shutter speed are controlled automatically. In aperture priority the camera varies only the shutter speed to achieve the different exposures, in shutter priority the aperture is changed. In manual mode the shutter speed is changed.

Flash Bracketing Card

The Flash Bracketing Card allows the camera to be programmed in such a way that it produces sequences of three, five or seven photographs whose exposures differ by a half or full stop. The first exposure is always the normal, while the second and third are lit so they are over and underexposed either side of the normal value. This means that the main subject is exposed by a half or full stop

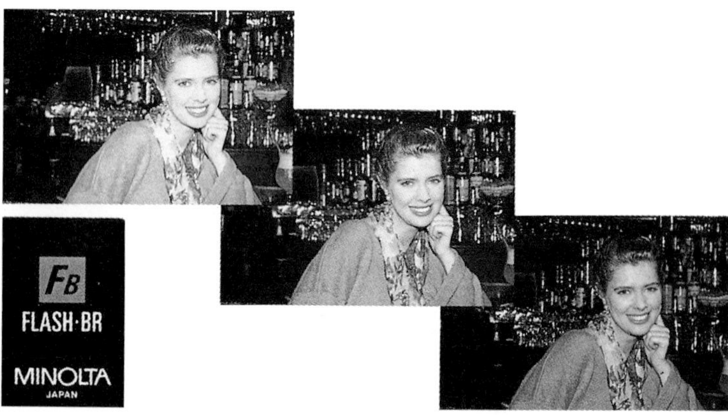

The Flash Bracketing Card facilitates shot sequences with different flash exposures.

Page 119
Zoom lenses do away with the need for a whole outfit of bulky fixed focal lengths and allow fast and flexible framing in travel photography. Photos: Ingrid Heinzelmann.

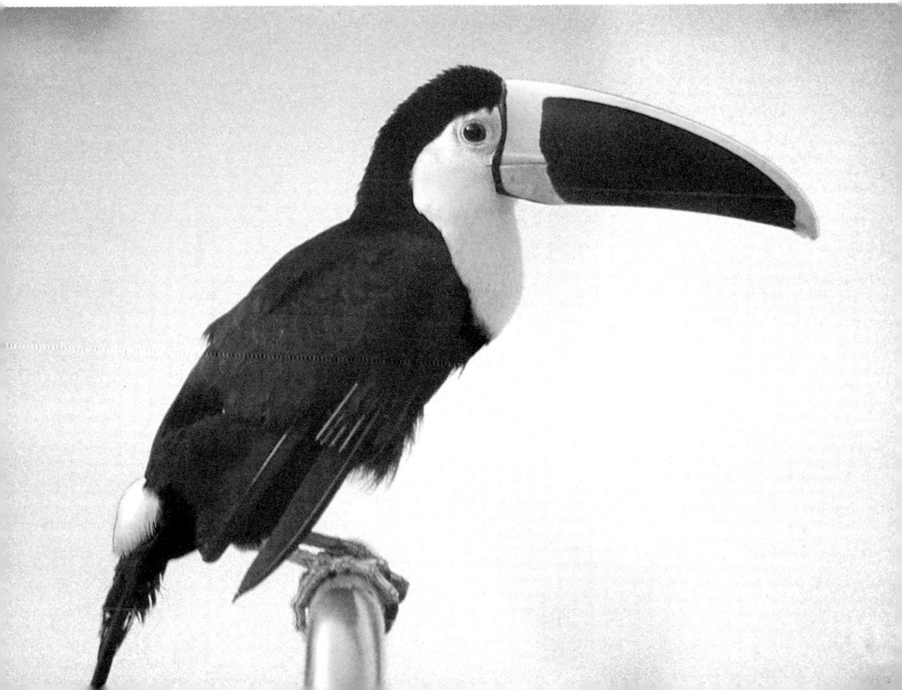

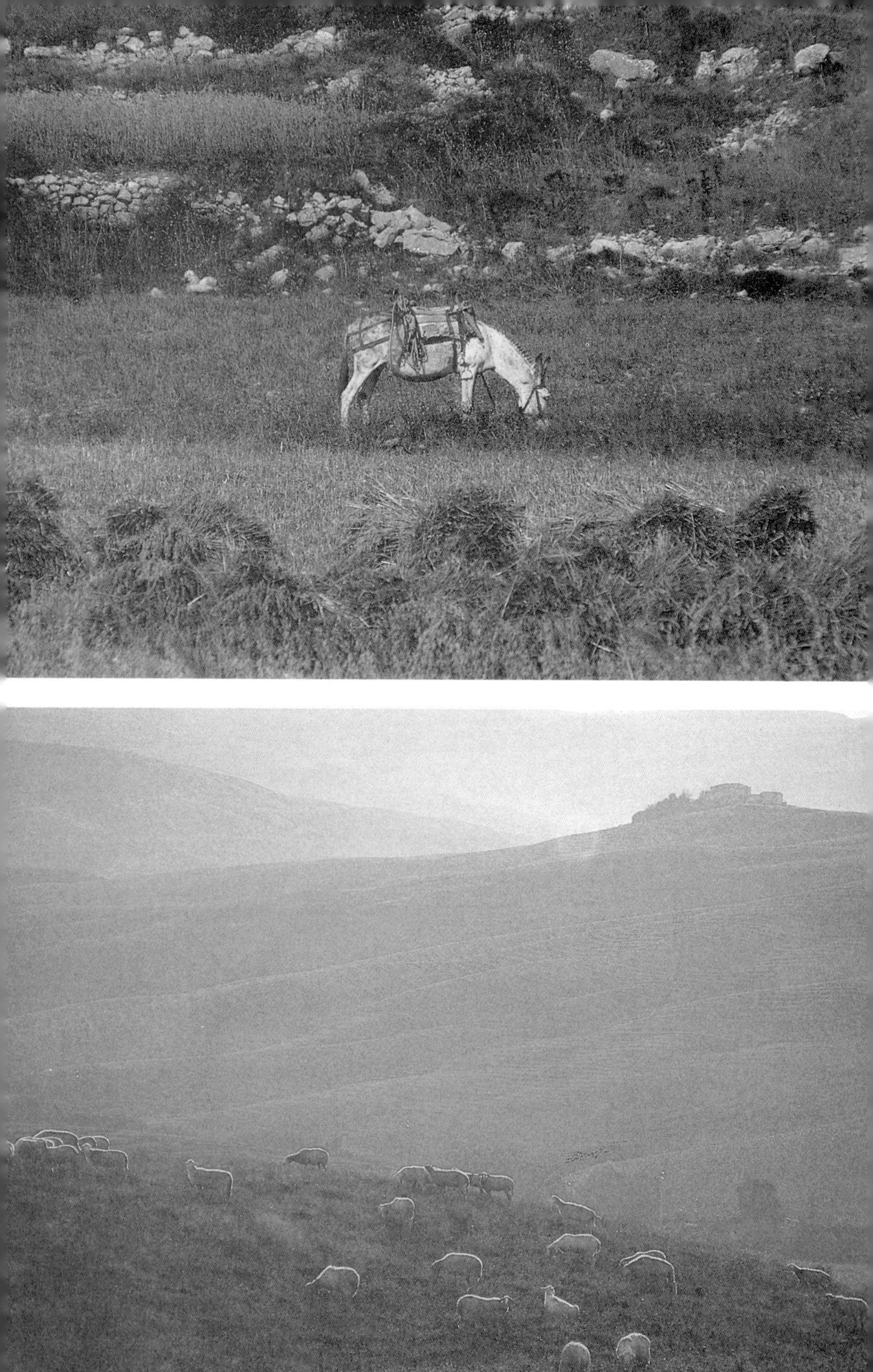

more generously in the second, fourth and sixth exposure, while it is exposed less in the third, fifth and seventh exposure. The tighter and more generous flash illumination only applies to the main subject. Here the camera makes an exposure measurement taking into account the subject background each time the shutter release button is pressed half-way. The change in exposure is controlled by the TTL flash metering system of the camera, and the aperture and sync speed selected remain constant. In P and A mode this also works with slow shutter sync, just as long as you use the SPOT button.

As the varied exposure effect is achieved by controlling the flash duration, the flash coverage range is also affected. A positive correction demanding more light and so reduces the flash coverage, whereas a negative correction increases the coverage. If the correction is +1/2EV the factor to calculate the new flash coverage is 0.7, if it is -1EV the factor is 1.4. None of these changes in the flash coverage affect the closest subject distance.

In this function the camera only makes one exposure, even if it is switched to continuous mode. When you let go of the shutter release button the new exposure and frame number are displayed for approximately five seconds. Short, fast flashing in the viewfinder between frames indicates that a correct exposure was made. But if you release the shutter before the flash unit is fully recharged

---

Page 120
Subjects like the one top left cause no problems for automatic exposure programs. The atmospheric light in the shot bottom left, however, requires deliberate adjustments in the light and shadow parts. The Minolta automatic exposure system masters even situations such as these surprisingly well.
Bottom shot: Detlev Motz.

- indicated by the flash symbol in the viewfinder - the flash is not fired and the card program automatically moves on to the next frame in the sequence.

System flash units cannot be set to reduced **LO** output. If the output of the flash unit is too high or too low - which is possible if the camera is programmed for seven exposures in 1EV increments - a complete exposure sequence may not be possible. This means that the 0.5EV increment is more sensible for long exposure sequences, both in terms of capacity and usually also in photographic terms. When an exposure sequence is completed the data panel indicates **End** for approximately five seconds. Any exposure sequence can be terminated by simply taking your eye from the viewfinder and letting go of the shutter-release button.

Bracket 2 Card

Apart from the two separate cards for exposure bracketing, with and without flash, there is now a single card for the Minolta 5xi which allows both options. The Bracket 2 Card allows sequences of three, five or seven photographs in maximum increments of 1EV. For flash bracketing sequences you can select increments of 0.5 or 1EV, whereas normal ambient light bracketing is possible in steps of 0.3, 0.5 and 1 EV. Ambient light bracketing sequences are taken automatically in fast continuous mode, whereas the card works in single-frame mode for flash bracketing to ensure full flash charge for each frame.

Multiple Exposure Card

The Multiple Exposure Card allows up to nine exposures to be made on the same frame. Although you have a choice of three exposure modes, you should spend a little time to consider multiple exposure technique.

The main problem is that the exposure setting you give each separate photograph is not necessarily determined by the number of images combined, but by the number of overlapping images. So if you want to photograph a person in front of a dark background eight times, so they appear to be standing in line, you will need

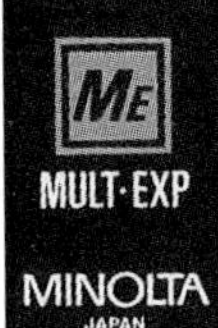

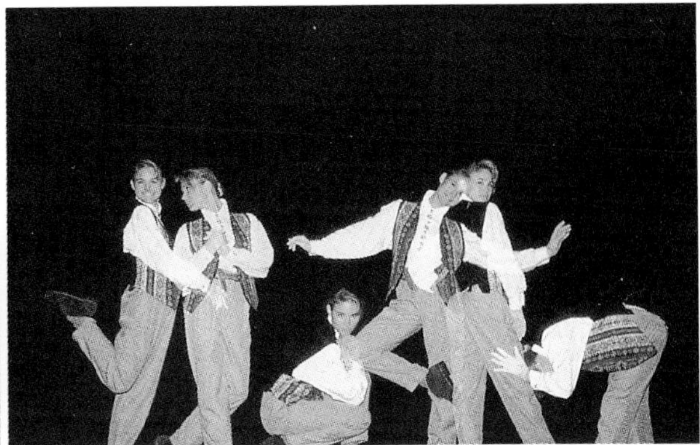

With the Multiple Exposure Card you can achieve interesting effects.

eight normal exposures. But if the separate exposures of this sequence overlap then you will need to use an exposure correction. This in turn depends on the number of subject overlaps. If, for example, the person overlaps four times, each time with their immediate neighbour, you only have to make a compensation for a double exposure. But if the eight people standing in a row turn into two overlapping groups of four, the exposure has to be adjusted as if it was a four-times multiple exposure. The amount of overlapping exposures is the factor by which the selected ISO value has to be multiplied to produce the new working speed to allow automatic exposure. Bright backgrounds should be treated as an additional multiple exposure. This is the easiest formula for multiple exposures, but in practice a negative exposure correction should be added to it. To achieve successful results the photographer needs to master technique by practice, but this is not easy. The Minolta expansion card offers two simplified options which produce a different effect, although both are multiple exposures.

To start with the card always anticipates a normal multiple exposure with non-overlapping subjects on a dark background. And all partial exposures of a sequence have the same intensity and are normally exposed as indicated on the body data panel.

In fade-in and fade-out mode, on the other hand, the partial exposures within a sequence are exposed more and more or less and less, depending on the selected mode. The first partial exposure in fade-out mode and the last in fade-in mode are once again exposed normally. With this technique you can slowly make a subject visible, fade in, or seemingly make it disappear into darkness, fade out.

Special Application Cards

Apart from the function cards described above, there are also a number of special application cards. Six of these cards can help you perfect your photographic technique with the 5xi for special tasks.

Travel Card

The Travel Card 'rationalizes' photography on holiday or when travelling. Many photographers like to have a family member or friend pose in the foreground of an interesting landscape. In such situations the manual settings necessary to ensure that the depth of field extends from the foreground to the distant landscape can often be rather time-consuming and nerve-racking. The Travel

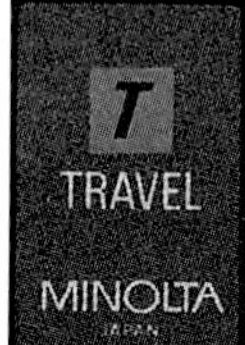

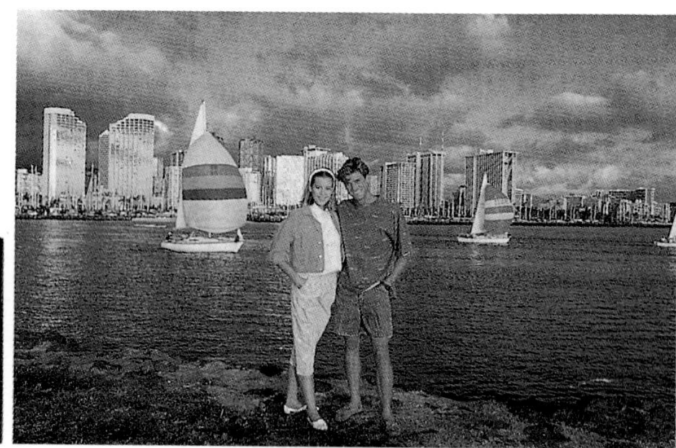

The Travel Card ensures maximum depth of field.

Card selects exposure combinations so that the depth of field extends as far as possible. But unlike on the top-of-the-range model 7xi or the professional 9xi, the Travel Card does not cause the 5xi to select a faster shutter speed when you are photographing from a moving vehicle, like a car or train. When using this card with xi-series lenses on the 5xi, as soon as you put your eye to the viewfinder the lens sets the programmed focal length adjustment.

To activate the expansion card you simply insert it into the card door with the camera switched on. The abbreviation **trvl** will then appear on the body data panel for approximately five seconds. And as with the other cards the **CARD** indicator appears in the bottom left-hand corner to remind you that the card has been activated. If you press the card-on/off button next to the panel the function is suspended and the card indicator disappears.

If the Travel Card is used with an 8000i, 7000i, or 5000i, the body data panel indicates **dPth** for maximizing the depth of field. The camera is always set to programmed autoexposure. Unlike the Depth Card the Travel Card does not work with infinity, but instead tries to maximize the depth of field behind the metered subject, and will also use flash if necessary. Focusing works with focus lock, via the shutter-release button, but manual focusing or the use of the focus control function is not possible.

Depth Card

(now discontinued and replaced by Travel Card)

Although the camera focuses precisely on a subject, a certain amount of space in front of and behind a subject will always appear in equal focus. This space is called the depth of field and is dependent on the shooting distance, the focal length of the lens, and the selected aperture. Long focal lengths, small shooting distances, and wide apertures reduce the depth of field, which you used to be able to check by operating the depth-of-field preview button. In the Maxxum/Dynax range only the professional 9xi features this button. But the Depth Card automatically controls the depth of field, setting focus and aperture to maximize the depth of field behind the main subject.

Like all the other expansion cards, the Depth Card needs to be inserted into the card door of the camera while the camera is switched on. The letters **dPth** will appear on the first line of the body data panel, as well as the **CARD** indicator in the bottom left. You can, of course, de-activate the card by pressing the card-on/off button, in which case the card indicator will disappear from the body data panel.

With the card activated the camera automatically switches to programmed autoexposure mode - you cannot then select any other exposure mode. The predictive autofocus system is also disabled; the camera will always focus to infinity initially and then move to the required focus setting from this position. The infinity focus setting was selected because at greater range, from about three metres onwards, the setting distances are substantially shorter than at close range. The functioning of the Depth Card is, of course, limited by the light conditions. In low light the depth of field is limited by optical laws, and the wide apertures required in these situations can cause the background to blur. So unlike other systems, the Depth Card can't be used to precisely determine the area that is to be in focus, but instead it optimizes the depth of field behind the focused subject. This card is particularly suitable for landscape and architectural photography, whilst a special Closeup Card is available for macro applications, where great depth of field is also an important concern.

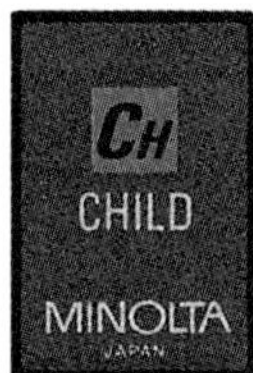

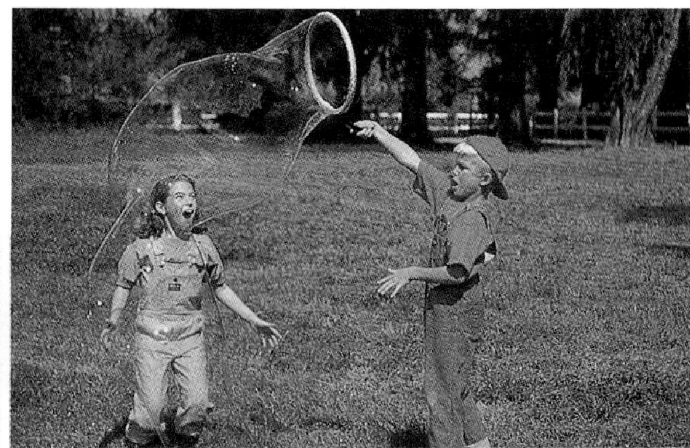

The Child Card automatically activates the image size lock function.

Child Card

This special application card makes spontaneous photographs of children at play easier and ensures action-packed photographs. It is often all too easy to miss the best moment because you're busy setting the focal length.

With the Child Card the advanced program zoom (APZ) automatically and continuously adjusts the focal length to the subject distance, even if the subject is moving. The image size is also controlled automatically to suit, enabling the photographer to concentrate fully on the subject and the right moment for releasing the shutter. This is why using this expansion card only makes sense in conjunction with one of the new xi zoom lenses. If the camera is set to continuous advance and you leave your finger on the shutter release button, three frames will be exposed one after the other.

Closeup Card

The depth of field is reduced as the macro ratio is increased, or the closer the reproduction size is to the actual size of the subject the

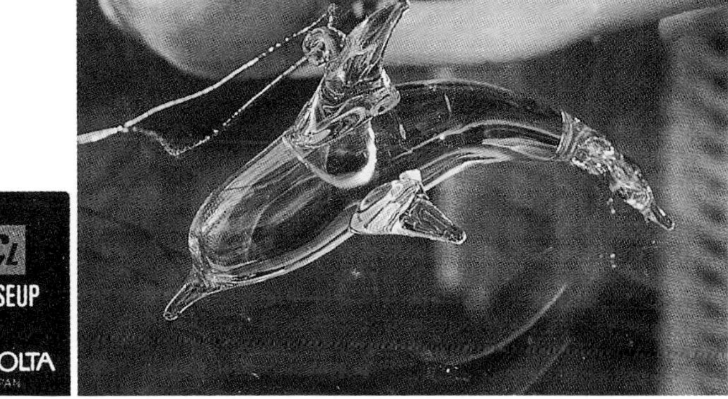

The Closeup Card optimizes the depth of field at large reproduction ratios.

more narrow the depth of field. The Closeup Card for the Minolta 5xi takes this fact into account and controls the aperture so that optimum depth of field is always guaranteed.

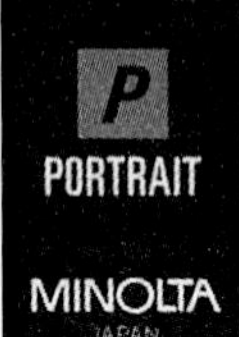

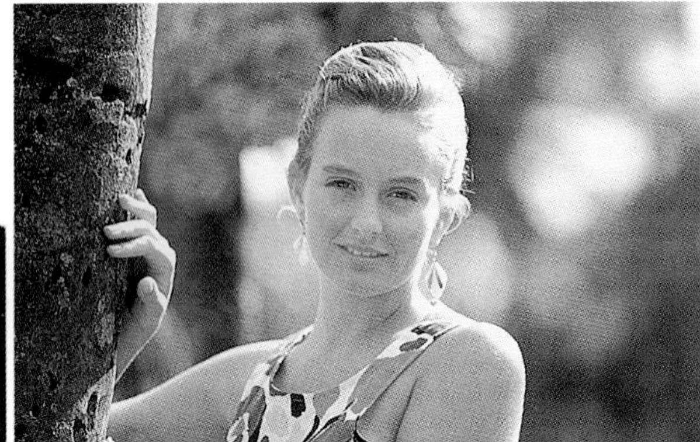

The Portrait Card reproduces the subject in the foreground in focus and dissolves the background into unsharpness.

When the card is activated the camera automatically switches to programmed autoexposure mode and the AF control system is set to standard mode, without predictive autofocus. The letters **CLOS UP** on the body data panel indicate that the card has been activated. Switching to a different exposure mode is not possible. This card does not shift the focus to achieve a greater depth of field in the background, but instead the depth of field is entirely extended by selecting a smaller aperture. The shutter speed is selected so that handheld exposures without camera shake are still possible, which seems sensible for autofocus close-up work.

Portrait Card

Like the Closeup Card, the Portrait Card is designed for optimum control of the aperture depending on the shooting distance. But unlike the other cards, the Portrait Card keeps the depth of field as shallow as possible so that a sharp subject is clearly separated from its out-of-focus background. But when working close to your subject the aperture has to be stopped down enough to maintain sufficient depth of field for eyes, nose, and mouth. This is why the apperture is always selected automatically, taking into account the magnification and the focal length of the lens used. The card also ensures that handheld pictures can be taken without any risk of camera shake.

If the Portrait Card is inserted the body data panel shows the abbreviation **Port** and the card indicator will appear. While the Portrait Card remains in the card door, its special functions can be switched off by pressing the card-on/off button.

Sports Action Card

If you want to avoid speed blur on sports and action pictures you will need fast shutter speeds as well as fast reactions. If you don't want to miss the decisive moment you will need to be ready to shoot at any time, which means there's usually no time for lengthy shutter speed and aperture setting. Whether you want to catch a high-jumper going over the bar, or a bird in flight, or a surfer on the crest of a wave, or a horse in mid-gallop, your concentration on the right moment to release the shutter should never be disturbed by thinking about exposure settings. In such cases the Sports Action Card is a useful tool.

This card switches the Minolta 5xi to programmed autoexposure mode with a preference for fast shutter speeds that takes into account subject distance and focal length. This means that the automatic system prefers an extremely fast shutter speed for large magnifications, but as this magnification decreases the shutter

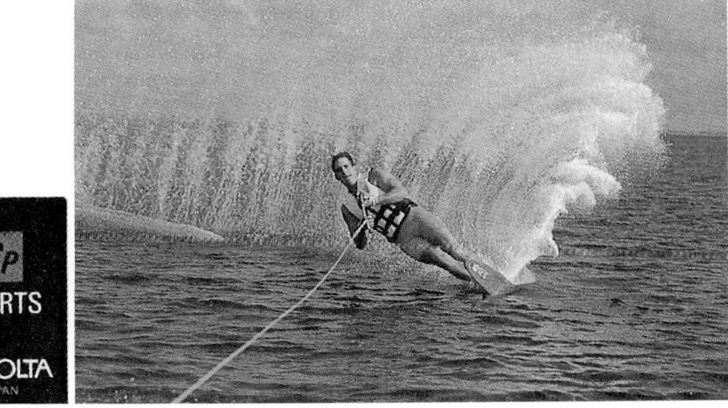

The Sports Action Card prefers fast shutter speeds.

speed will become noticeably slower. Once the card is inserted the card-on/off button can be used to switch to P mode with fast shutter speed preference. With the card active the program shift is switched off and the continuous autofocus is permanently activated so that it can follow the movement at any time. Manual focusing is possible with the card activated, but it is definitely not advisable.

Another feature of the Sports Action Card is that it automatically switches off the flash unit. If flash is to be used it has to be switched on manually, using the main switch of the flash unit. But even in

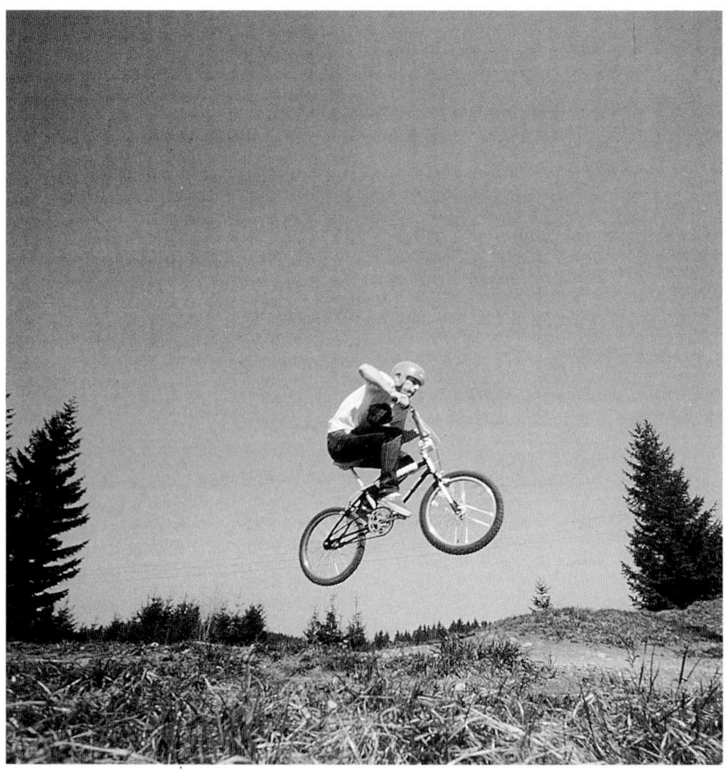

The SPORTS-2 Card can effectively freeze fast movements, working with an exposure program that utilizes fast shutter speeds.

this case the flash will only fire on poorly lit subjects. The suppression of the autoflash function seems very sensible because fill-in flash would automatically switch to the required sync speed of 1/90 sec which is too slow for sports and action photographs. Another factor is that most sports and action photographs are taken from distances far in excess of the flash coverage range. Other automatic exposure programs cannot be used with the Sports Action Card.

When working with the Sports Action Card it is advisable to use faster films to enable the automatic program to select the fast shutter speeds required for freezing movement.

When the Sports Action Card is inserted the body data panel will display the abbreviation **SPrt**, as well as the card indicator to show the card is activated. No further settings are necessary. You can return to the standard setting of the camera at any time by pressing the card-on/off button, and the special functions of the card are also cancelled when it is removed.

Sports 2 Card

With the Sports 2 Card capturing sporting events on film is even easier, thanks to the advanced program zoom function (APZ). When shooting sports and 'snapshots' it is all too easy to miss the best moment because of the difficulty in changing the focal length fast enough to follow the movement of the subject and adjusting to changes in subject size. The advanced program zoom function automatically ensures suitable framing by continually matching the focal length to the subject movement. But as APZ won't always produce ideal framing, you can also switch over and adjust the focal length manually. The Sports 2 Card prefers fast shutter speeds to render the subject in optimum focus.

Tips for better pictures

Whilst the first part of this book is largely devoted to the technology of the 5xi, the following pages are given over to photographic practice. Even if the majority of settings on the 5xi could be largely automated, the final results would be strongly dependent on whether photographers use the many automatic functions sensibly and for the right subject.

As not every photographer has the same interest in all subject areas, the preferences of each person will determine how their photographic equipment is put together and used. The animal photographer, for example, will need different lenses and accessories than someone who is more interested in landscape photography. Travel photographers will appreciate lightweight equipment that can be used in many varied situations, and if you want to take frame-filling photographs of small subjects you will choose altogether different products. The technology of the 5xi is designed for general 'snapshot' and action photography. Its great strengths become apparent in conjunction with the new power zoom and xi lenses and the auto stand-by zoom function.

But the optimum selection of photographic hardware is not the only factor that determines the end result; it is also important to select the right exposure program and adapt it to the given situation. The question of whether you should use flash or make use of the ambient light to create an atmospheric photograph is just as important as your choice of film.

The tips given below on putting together the right equipment for certain photographic situations are only intended as a guide. Many areas overlap and many photographers are interested in more than one subject area. This is why the suggestions are put together so that they're as universally applicable as possible, while still relevant to the specialist applications.

Tips for better 'snapshots'

Fast 'snapshots' in programmed autoexposure mode are the real strength of the 5xi. Because of the auto stand-by zoom function and the automatic activation of autofocus and exposure metering system as soon as the camera is put to the eye, you can frame your subject and fire with almost no preperation. The integral flash unit ensures sufficient light and provides AF illumination even in darkness. You won't miss any subject simply because the camera wasn't ready to shoot at the decisive moment. Thanks to this technology 'snapshot' photography has come even closer to its age-old attraction: the documentation of the small things in life that would pass us by unnoticed were it not for photography and the attentive eye of the photographer. The meaning of such fleeting moments only becomes clear when they are captured forever in a photograph. 'snapshots' can be lovingly observant, ruthlessly revealing, or just humorous caricatures. A good photographer can tell a whole story with a single 'snapshot'.

The essential thing is to catch the moment that will document an event in such a way that a single picture is enough to present the entire gist of a situation.

Good 'snapshots' are therefore rarely achieved accidentally. An experienced 'snapshot' photographer anticipates how a situation will develop and is ready to press the shutter-release button at the right moment. The camera is always ready to shoot and so nothing will get in the way of taking the picture at the decisive moment. The fast autofocus of the 5xi is a welcome help on such occasions, but it is really the auto stand-by zoom function that turns it into a real 'snapshot' camera.

Even the integral flash, or a unit mounted on the 5xi, is activated and fired automatically. 'Snapshot' opportunities don't leave much time for fiddling with the camera. We have to be able to respond spontaneously and quickly and be able to anticipate how a situation will develop and when events will reach their climax. Good 'snapshot' photographers are experienced observers and excellent judges of character, they know the best vantage points and where the most interesting things will happen. They never go where everybody else is going.

Apart from an instinctive feel for a photographically promising situation and fast reactions, 'snapshot' photographers also need patience. Like a hunter they must be able to wait until the time is right to take a 'shot'; and that 'shot' has to be on target. You don't often get a second chance. 'Snapshot' photographers must have the gift of seeing what is special in everyday situations and not be content with voyeuristic observing. They look behind the surface of things by capturing on film the decisive moment that most people may not even have noticed.

The scope for 'snapshots' is huge. They can be affectionate or revealing portraits. They can show the behaviour of individuals or of groups of people, and can be found in sport as well as animal photography. And they are not called the high art of photography for nothing. The 'snapshot' is the one picture of an event that reveals its whole story.

How to take original 'Snapshots'

* Set the main switch of the 5xi to **ON**
* Select P mode

Equipment

Lenses

Minolta AF Zoom xi 28-80mm,f/4.5-5.6 and
Minolta AF Zoom xi 80-200mm,f/4.5-5.6 or
Minolta AF Zoom xi 35-200mm,f/4.5-5.6

Accessories

Minolta 3500xi program flash unit
Sports 2 Card

The tips on 'snapshot' photography also apply to the following areas:
* Action * Pets * Children * Markets * Travel * Party * Portrait * Sport * Wildlife * Fun fairs * Zoo *

Tips for better photographs of children

For a variety of reasons children are one of the most popular photographic subjects. It may well be that one of the reasons is because photography is an excellent medium for documenting how children change as they grow up. As these changes happen quickly, particularly when the children are small, you should grasp every opportunity to take a photograph, their value is only realized many years later. However, children can quickly get tired of being pursued by parents, relatives, friends, and acquaintances brandishing cameras. It's better in the long run to go without the odd picture rather than provoke a dislike of photography by being too

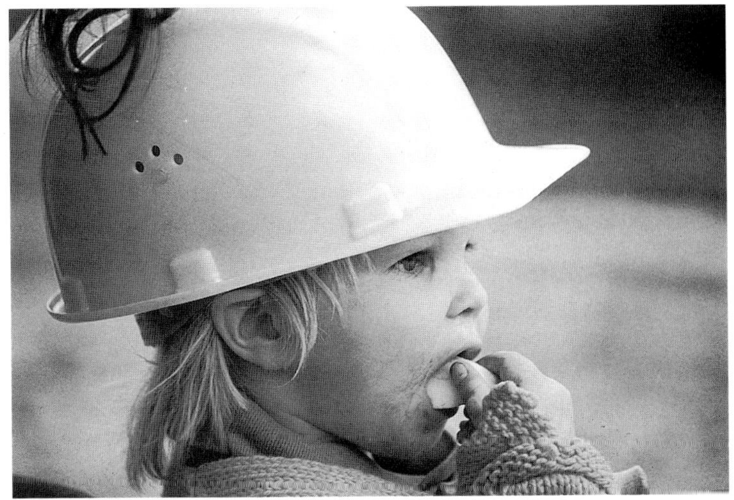

Snapshots are one of the strengths of the 5xi - in programmed autoexposure (P) pictures such as this can be achieved quickly and easily.

obtrusive. In general children like being photographed and taking photographs themselves. Their joy in posing and their natural behaviour in front of the camera are reasons why children like being photographed and, in turn, why there are so many successful photographs of children. Children don't tend to clam up in front of the camera because they're worried about looking silly. They become inhibited for completely different reasons, i.e. if the photographer asks them to do something that either doesn't seem natural to them or is just something that they don't feel like doing. But it can also happen when they're deliberately trying to pose and then become shy.

This is why being photographed should be something natural for children. It shouldn't prevent them from doing other things that might appear more important to them at the time. They should feel neither disturbed nor annoyed by the photographer. Even the dreaded sentence 'Give us a smile' can nip every smile in the bud. The more natural it is for the camera to be around, the more it is part of everyday life, the easier it will be to take a 'natural' photograph. Try and spend a little time with the children so that they get to know you.

However tempting it may be to take a surprise 'snapshot' of a child it's sometimes better to give it a miss. For children, like adults, should know they're being photographed, and that way you more often get a better reaction.

If you want to take good photographs of children you don't know well, you have to be prepared to sacrifice a great deal of time. You have to win their trust, and this can only be done if you do come down to their level. And this is one of the most common mistakes of child photography. Adults usually photograph children from above. Except in some instances this produces an ugly perspective with large heads and short legs, particularly with short focal lengths. If you come down to the child's own level by squating down a little, you'll notice that your photographs get better. There are two reasons for this: first, the perspective is more favourable, and second, the communication and 'contact' with the child is better.

Some of the points made on 'snapshot' photography equally apply to photographing children. You need a lot of patience for the right moment to happen; be it the desired facial expression or the expected gesture.

The most important thing is for the children not to lose their enjoyment of photography, and that the camera does not disturb them. Children should only be 'directed' with the utmost caution. After all, they don't understand why they're supposed to repeat what they just managed to do so brilliantly. The request 'Do that again, please' may be successful when the whole thing is fun, but it can just as easily provoke irritation.

At home, where you're photographing your own children, the camera should be ready to grab wherever the family spends most time. It's unlikely that you'll be able take a tidily stored camera out of the cupboard or photo bag for a spontaneous 'snapshot'. Keep a spare film and a fresh battery handy, and if you've only got two or three frames left at the end of the day, it's advisable to use them up. Just shoot what you've always wanted to photograph but which was never important enough to make you load a fresh film: the chaos left behind by your children, or the things your child is particularly fond of, such as a favourite doll or teddy bear. The most interesting subjects usually crop up when the film is full or the camera empty.

Child photographers must be able to respond quickly to spontaneous or sudden events. Extensive preparations with the camera are rarely possible, but are not necessary with the 5xi. The auto

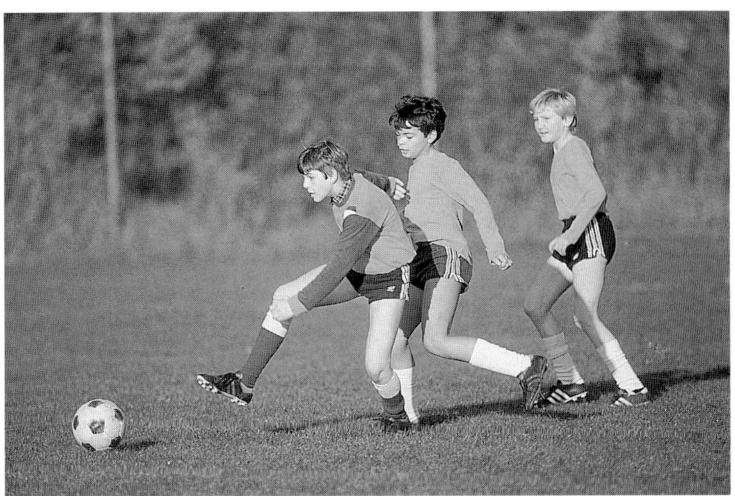

The Child Card and image size lock function together ensure constant reproduction ratios.

stand-by zoom function in particular can be a great help in child photography. It's always quicker to adjust the suggested focal length to the one you want than to adjust from an arbitrary focal length, but usually the camera's suggestion can be accepted without adjustment.

How to take impressive photographs of children

* Set the main switch of the camera to **ON**
* Auto stand-by zoom is activated

Equipment

Lenses

Minolta AF Zoom xi 28-80mm,f/4.5-5.6 and
Minolta AF Zoom xi 80-200mm,f/4.5-5.6 or
Minolta AF Zoom xi 35-200mm,f/4.5-5.6

Accessories

Minolta 3500xi or 5400xi program flash unit
Child Card

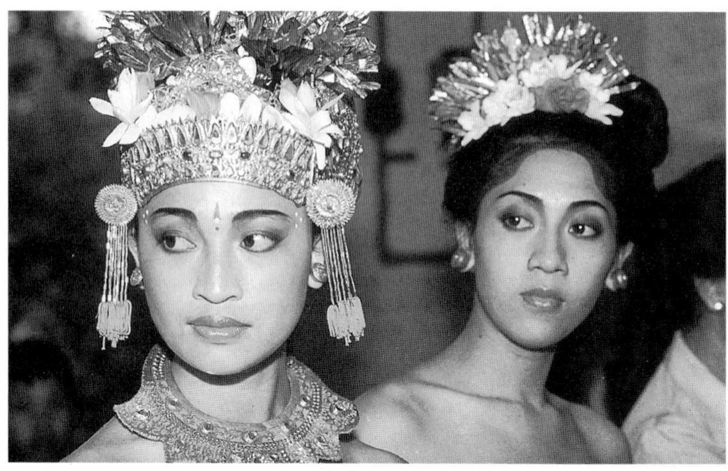

On holiday, too, portraits are ever-popular subjects, just as interesting as photographs of famous landmarks.

Tips for better portraits

Portraits are one of the classical photographic subjects. But really successful portrait photographs are far more than just natural pictures of faces. Ideally, portraits reveal the character and the typical behaviour of a person. A really good portrait presupposes that the photographer knows the subject, or at least has spent some time with them.

Portraits don't just give clues about the subject, they also contain information on their relationship with the photographer. Portraits can romanticize, flatter, and beautify. But they can also expose, reveal, caricature, or distort. Portraits that aren't just flattering, but allow a glimpse beyond the surface, are particularly in demand in photojournalism and news reporting. Conversely, you will usually try to show friends from their best side. And to do this there are a few simple tricks.

All too often photographers concentrate so hard on their subject that they forget to give any thought to creating a backdrop. Backgrounds for portrait photographs should be as unfussy as possible, and their colours should be balanced to the subject's hair and clothing. A dark background is usually a more favourable contrast to someone with blond hair, and conversely a light background suits someone with dark hair. But here, too, the exception proves the rule.

Short telephoto lenses are considered ideal focal lengths for successful portrait photographs. Focal lengths between 80mm and 200mm produce a natural-looking perspective and allow the photographer to keep a certain distance from the subject, so that they don't feel too threatened by the camera. But at the same time the distance isn't great enough to make communication between the subject and the photographer difficult.

Another argument in favour of telephoto lenses for portrait use is their shallow depth of field. If the iris diaphragm is opened fully the depth of field shrinks to a minimum, allowing the subject to be rendered sharp while the unsharp background appears as if it were translucent. To dissolve the background completely the subject should be sufficiently far from it, and even with flash a certain distance from the background is advisable to prevent ugly harsh shadows, or use diffused flash to soften shadows.

Unfortunately most portraits are more or less successful souvenir pictures. They are only of interest to people who know the subject and were present when the photograph was taken. It is often very disappointing when a third party is left unmoved by a photograph that shows the person the photographer loves most. If portraits are to be more than private souvenirs the photographer has to try a little harder.

The first rule is: limit yourself to what is essential. The tighter the framing, and the fewer details that say nothing about the subject, the more expressive the portrait will be. So if you want to show a face, it should fill the frame as much as possible. Subject with long hair can benefit from particularly tight framing such that the hair almost frames the face. If hard shadows are required then harsh direct lighting can be used, whereas if a soft effect is desired then indirect light is required. In the latter case it is advisable to use the remote control function for the Minolta 3500xi program flash unit and fill in with the integral flash unit. The integral flash can then prevent unflattering shadows under the eyes, whilst the main flash is 'bounced'. But the remotely controlled flash can also produce backlight effects at a ratio of 1:2, or be used to set highlights on the hair.

The character of the lighting is very important for portraits. Side or backlight is prefered by many portrait photographers as it makes the face look more three-dimensional, although directional light does tend to creates harsh shadows. But it would be a shame to remove these shadows completely with the integral flash unit. Instead, many photographers place cardboard or styrofoam boards, or white cloth near the sitter to help soften shadows. A 'Lumiquest' flash bounce also softens shadows.

Portrayer attachments in different strengths are available from Minolta to create particularly soft portraits. These lens attachments produce a gentle soft-focus effect, and can be used effectively not only in portrait photography but also in landscape and still life work.

Whilst you can influence the external conditions when taking portraits of friends, children, or acquaintances, the documentary portrait demands flexibility, spontaneity, and precision. We have all seen impressive photographs by travel photographers - the Moroccan water carrier, the Greek fisherman, or the Tibetan monk. But the vegetable seller in a local market, the coach-driver at the Munich beer festival, or the waitress at the restaurant can also be included in this subject area. These portraits demand a completely different technique from the photographer. Photo opportunities arise from every situation, but however tempting it may be to take a picture of somebody with a long focal length from a great distance, it is also impolite. There are good reasons why we have legal rights over photographs of ourselves.

But even basic politeness should prevent every photographer from simply photographing anybody. Even when abroad, where your linguistic abilities may be insufficient to ask permission, eye contact and pointing at the camera, together with a nod and a smile, are often enough to secure you subject's agreement.

But then, you need to be quick - few people spend time posing for a stranger. You'll have no choice but to improvise, making the most of the current light conditions and surroundings. In most cases you won't have enough time to look for a suitable shooting position either. A zoom lens, such as the Minolta AF Zoom xi 28-80mm,f/4.5-5.6, is ideal for such opportunities, allowing you to compose the framing at lightning speed. The Minolta AF Zoom xi 35-200mm,f/4.5-5.6 is also very suitable for such situations. The integral flash unit of the 5xi can be used to fill in, in order to prevent ugly shadows or excessive contrast.

The camera's automatic continuous focus function is a useful feature for photographs of subjects moving towards the photographer, and the subject will always stay sharp. The photographer can then concentrate fully on the facial expressions and the right moment to release the shutter. It is a good idea to set the camera to aperture priority mode and open the lens aperture fully to make intrusive details dissolve into unsharpness. The Minolta AF 85mm,f/1.4, the Minolta AF 100mm,f/2, and the Minolta AF 135mm,f/2.8 are also ideal lenses for portrait work.

How to take attractive portrait photographs

* Set the camera to aperture priority mode
* Preselect a wide aperture for shallow depth of field
* Use a medium to long focal length
* Fill in with integral flash unit in backlight and with excessive contrast

Equipment

Lenses

Minolta AF Zoom xi 28-80mm,f/3.5-4.5 or
Minolta AF Zoom xi 35-200mm,f/4.5-5.6 or
Minolta AF 85mm,f/1.4
Minolta AF 100mm,f/2
Minolta AF 135mm,f/2.8

Accessories

Minolta 3500xi or 5400xi program flash unit
Portrait Card

Tips for better sport and action photographs

Sport, along with travel and photography, is one of the most popular hobbies. So what could be more obvious than to keep alive your memories of sport in photographs. I'm not going to talk about professional sports photography, but about the souvenir photographs we, as active amateur sportsmen, like to take of our teammates and partners.

Sport means movement, and movement in turn creates unsharpness in photographs if we are unable to freeze it with particularly fast shutter speeds. The 5xi offers the photographer a top shutter speed of 1/2000 sec. Around 1/500 sec to 1/1000 sec will usually be sufficient for most types of sport such as surfing, skiing and all ball games. As long as the light conditions allow it the camera will always suggest a shutter speed that is fast enough to avoid camera shake, but this doesn't necessarily mean it will freeze all movement. It is therefore a good idea to set the aperture to the smallest f/number - that is, the maximum aperture - and to work in aperture priority mode when taking sports and action photographs. Alternatively, if there is enough light, a sufficiently fast shutter speed can be preselected in shutter priority mode while the camera automatically takes care of the aperture. But you should in any case occasionally check the shutter speed on the body data panel.

As for most subjects the rule in sports photography is: the less distraction from the main subject the better. This means taking frame-filling photographs wherever possible. This causes the sports photographer a dual difficulty. First, you need to keep a certain distance from events in order not to disturb or even impede the competitors, and second, the subject constantly changes its distance from the photographer. So telezoom lenses with a wide focal length range would be the ideal equipment for sports photography, only there is yet another compound problem - the fight with light and the fast shutter speeds required at the same time. If you're shooting outside in sunlight there's rarely any problems. Even with long focal lengths, fast films around ISO 400/27° can produce shutter speeds that prevent camera shake and speed blur. But things are different with sports events inside as only fast lenses used with fast films will produce the higher shutter speeds necessary to freeze the movement. The Minolta AF 200mm,f/2.8 Apo and the 300mm,f/2.8 Apo are the ideal equipment for such occasions, but unfortunately these top class lenses are also particularly expensive.

Photographs of sporting events take a fraction of a second out of a whole movement or sequence. So the phase of movement captured on film must represent what is typical, be it the climax of movement or the key fascination of the particular sporting discipline. So a good sports photographer needs to be familiar with the

In good sports shots detractions from the main subject are kept to a minimum.

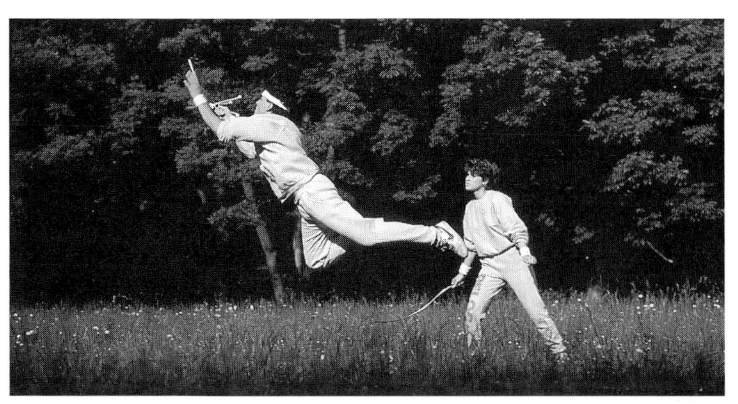

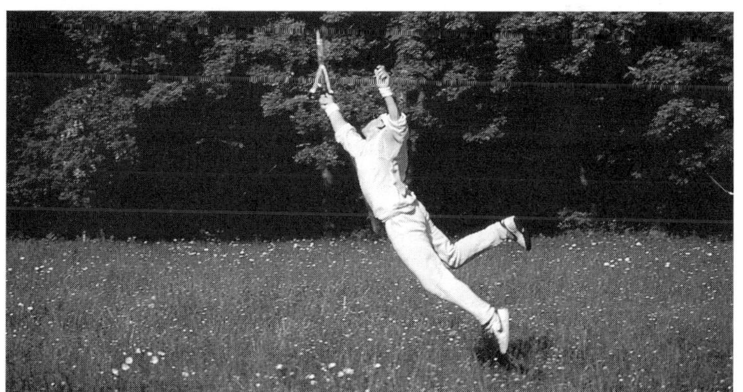

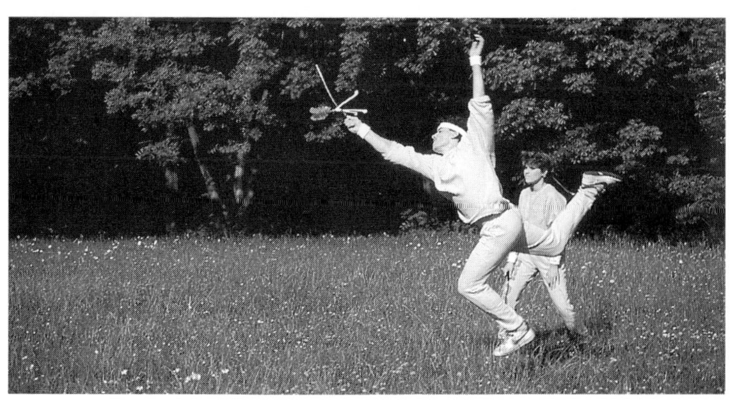

sport and be aware of what is important. So the pole-vaulter is less often photographed when the pole is put down, than at the point when it is let go and the vaulter is seemingly floating on air. And you wouldn't photograph the skier on a flat section of the piste, but when jumping over the edge. Equally, you'll try to catch the goalkeeper, not during a goal kick, but making a brilliant save. Good sports photographers need to know the sequence of events to be able to anticipate them and know which situations can produce spectacular photographs.

Movement sequences have a certain rhythm. They have a beginning, a climax, and an end. Usually these are also the three phases worth photographing. But the most impressive photographs will always be those that show the moment which decides on success or failure. So the moment when a movement reaches its climax (for example, when the pole-vaulter seems to be floating above the pole) is the one when you need to press the shutter release button. The moment for a successful picture isn't when the gymnast prepares for the piece de resistance on the horizontal bar, but when they posed above the bar doing a handstand.

Even the fastest autofocus may be too slow for fast sporting disciplines such as ice hockey or motor racing. An old professional trick of preselecting the focus will help here. Select a point, perhaps a bend on the race track, focus, and then wait until the subject reaches the area of sharpness. With the 5xi you can use the focus lock function, or push the AF switch downwards to manual focus after you have made the preselection. Alternatively, simply pull the zoom ring of a power zoom or xi lens towards the camera. If you don't use the AF switch the camera returns to AF mode as soon as you let go of the zoom ring. Having switched to manual focus you can release the shutter at any time. In this mode also the green LED in the viewfinder will confirm that the focus has been found.

Of course, it isn't just the highlights of a sporting event that will yield impressive photographs. Observations at the fringe of events can also produce good photographs: the competitors joy at their success, triumphantly throwing their arms into the air after victory, or the moments of disappointment, defeat, or exhaustion.

A series of photographs that show the entire development or the complete process of an event represent a challenge for every sports photographer. To document the training, the preparations, and everything that goes on at the fringes of an event can often express the mood and atmosphere better than the event itself. Photographs of the presentation ceremony and the subsequent celebration in the club house could well complete your documentary.

It doesn't always have to be the big events where good sports photographs are created. Sports day at school, the local club competition, the riding contest in your village, all these are opportunities that can fill whole albums. Don't be mean with your materials, but don't get sidetracked either. Have a feel for the essential, despite all the attention to detail.

Many sporting disciplines take place in badly lit halls so remember that the integral flash unit only has a limited range. More powerful flash units will only be sufficient when used with extremely fast film and in exceptional cases. Hall or stadium lighting often has the characteristics of artificial light which doesn't matter much with negative film. But when using daylight-balanced slide film the colour temperature can produce an unwelcome green or reddish-brown cast.

Filtering with so-called conversion filters is usually out of the question as these filters swallow so much light that they can lead to sluggish shutter speeds. Using artificial light slide film, on the other hand, isn't the ideal solution either as it is usually only available at slow speeds. One exception is the Scotch 640 T at ISO 640/29°.

How to take exciting sports and action photographs

* Select shutter priority mode and a fast shutter speed, or select a wide aperture for fast shutter speeds in aperture priority mode
* Use long focal lengths

Equipment

Lenses

Minolta AF Zoom xi 28-80mm,f/3.5-4.5 and
Minolta AF Zoom xi 100-300mm,f/4.5-5.6
possibly Minolta 300mm,f/2.8 Apo

Accessories

Minolta 3500xi or 5400xi program flash unit
Sports 2 Card

Tips for better animal photographs

Hunting with the camera is an experience of a special kind. It includes all the essential elements of a real hunt, but its outcome is a lot more positive. The hunter with the camera doesn't kill the prey, it is only the photograph that is taken home as the trophy. Photo tourism, still increasing in popularity, has contributed towards saving many species of animals from extinction. The photographs of the American scientist Dian Fossey, who lived with the mountain gorillas of Ruanda for many years, have touched millions of people worldwide. They have attracted visitors from all over the world and have drawn the public's attention to the plight of these threatened animals. Dian Fossey paid with her life for her love of the gorillas. But she awakened in many tourists the desire to observe these lovable apes in their natural habitat; and this finally made the governments of Ruanda, Uganda, and Zaire devote more effort to protecting these animals, and in the last few years the population of mountain gorillas has started to increase again for the first time. Without photo tourism in Africa the population of most game reserves would have decreased a long time ago. They would have been plundered by unscrupulous poachers, and bled to death by well-heeled hunters.

A photographic hunt for animals in the wild doesn't just require photographic know-how, but also a knowledge of the behaviour and habits of these animals. Not everyone who likes to watch animals with the camera has this knowledge, and it isn't always absolutely necessary either. In most game reserves the tourist isn't allowed to roam without a guide who knows the area and is familiar with the dangers of the wild and the animals living in it. And you don't have to be an enthusiastic animal photographer to cherish the desire to capture on film your safari experiences in Africa, or even the local wild park. Gamekeepers are familiar with the peculiarities of each animal and bring the visitor close enough to the subject so a super telephoto lens isn't really necessary.

In animal photography patience and fast reactions are important prerequisites for success. Animals don't understand the needs of photographers and so much patience and persistence is needed until you really get their best side facing the camera. And if they do show themselves the way you'd like to photograph them, it's usually only for a fleeting moment before they run of into thick shrubbery.

In the game reserves of Africa the photo hunt will usually take place from the safety of a car. In many places the animals are used to vehicles so remain undisturbed. In fact if you're in a car the chances are that lions won't give you a second glance, and elephants will rumble on undisturbed, as long as you respectfully keep the necessary distance.

To get good photographs in situations like this you don't need any wildly specialized equipment. The 5xi with the Minolta AF Zoom xi 100-300mm,f/4.5-5.6 is quite sufficient. Even the Minolta AF Zoom xi 35-200mm,f/4.5-5.6 will still produce presentable results. As for the technique, the same tips apply as for sports and action photography. The automatic exposure system of the 5xi will always suggest suitable shake-free shutter speeds with the telephoto lens in use. But as animals are most active in the morning or at dusk, using fast films is a prerequisite. Moreover, animals don't keep still and 'snapshots' of movement - a gazelle in mid-jump, a cheetah on the hunt, or an eagle in flight - are the most fascinating animal photographs of all.

To be sure of getting the fastest possible shutter speed it's advisable to shoot in aperture priority mode at maximum aperture.

But you don't have to go all the way to Africa to get good animal photographs. At home also a photographic hunt can be a magnificent experience. But you should remember that here, too, many species of animals are threatened with extinction. This is in no small part thanks to the ruthless methods of some photographers who don't think about the damage they cause by photographing young birds at the nests and breaking off twigs to get a better view. Others track down young deer in their hiding places, even chasing them into more photogenic positions. Today you won't get any recognition or admiration from animal lovers for photographs created in this way. In animal photography great emphasis is now placed on the 'species-friendly' photographs.

So enthusiastic wildlife photographers should also be enthusiastic conservationists, and manage without taking a picture if necessary. The good animal photographer selects their shooting position so that they don't disturb the animal's habitat. But this presupposes that they know the habits of the animal they are observing, that they have found out a great deal of information and consulted experts. If you can manage to go out on a trip with an

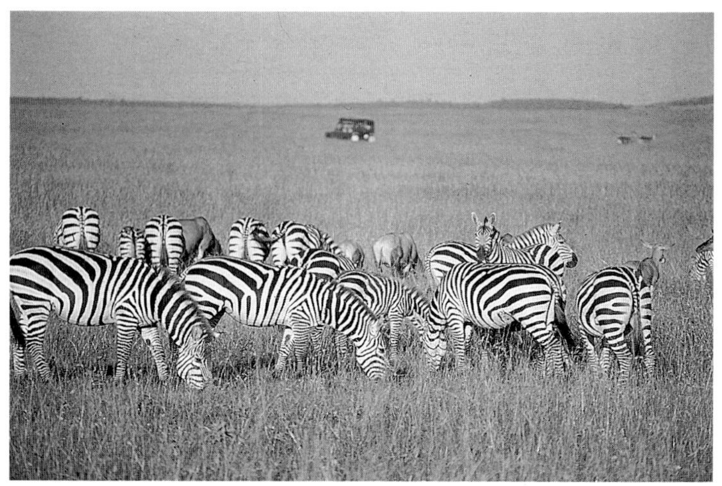

Shots of animals in the wild are only possible with long focal lengths, but on safari in game reserves focal lengths in the range between 200mm and 300mm are often sufficient.

experienced wildlife photographer you may gradually become a successful animal photographer yourself.

Before a photographic expedition you should also find out about all the legal aspects. In many countries it is now a punishable offence to disturb wild animals, particularly species threatened by extinction, in their hiding, nesting, breeding, or living places by tracking them down and photographing or filming them, or by similar actions.

It can be far less problematic, and certainly just as interesting, to photograph pets or animals in the zoo. The decree of all animal photographers also applies here: the more I know about the animal the more likely it is that I will get a good photograph. If you study the habits of your pets carefully and know precisely how they react, it's more likely that you'll be able to bag better pictures than someone who has not done this. One thing pets have in common with wild animals is that it never occurs to them to pose for a photographer, but it is easier to anticipate their reactions. So if you want to get a good picture you need to know what they do on which occasions. In this area of animal photography many 'snapshot' photography techniques apply. The photographer has to wait patiently for this opportunity and must make use of it very quickly when it arises.

Using aperture priority with the lens set to its maximum aperture is the most suitable exposure mode for photographing animals in movement, like a dog catching a ball, or a cat jumping from a window sill. This is most likely to secure a sufficiently fast shutter speed, but flash is also excellent for freezing fast movements in low ambient light.

One very interesting variant of animal photography is capturing small animals or insects on film. You don't have to travel too far for this as even your own garden can provide plenty of subjects. Beetles, bees, dragonflies, butterflies, and everything else that crawls or flies. However, a macro lens is important for frame-filling photographs of small animals. The Minolta AF 100mm,f/2.8 Macro, designed to give a maximum reproduction ratio of 1:1, is ideal for this. The shorter Minolta AF Macro with 50mm focal length is less suitable as shooting distances are too short. With normal flash, the 'Stroboframe' Lep II bracket is an ideal accessory.

The Minolta Macro Flash 1200AF Set N is a convenient ring flash unit which mounts on the front element of the macro lens. The unit has four separate flash tubes that fire simultaneously to give even lighting without shadows. The lamps can also be switched on separately for a more three-dimensional lighting effect, and a focusing lamp allows easy monitoring of the viewfinder image and helps the AF system.

Using flash for shooting small animals has several advantages. First, you can use narrow apertures in order to increase the shallow depth of field at high reproduction ratios. And second, flash light allows the use of slower films that offer greater sharpness and finer detail. This is essential for recording delicately-limbed insects, or the dainty structures of a dragonflies' wings, or that picture of a finely-spun spider's web.

Long focal lengths and high reproduction ratios are the reason for the shallow depth of field. This is why it is advisable to shoot the subject so that it doesn't extend too much into the depth of the frame. With a 600mm telephoto lens the stag shouldn't be photographed head-on but from the side, and the dragonfly from above, not from the front. This prevents the head from being in focus and the body disappearing into unsharpness.

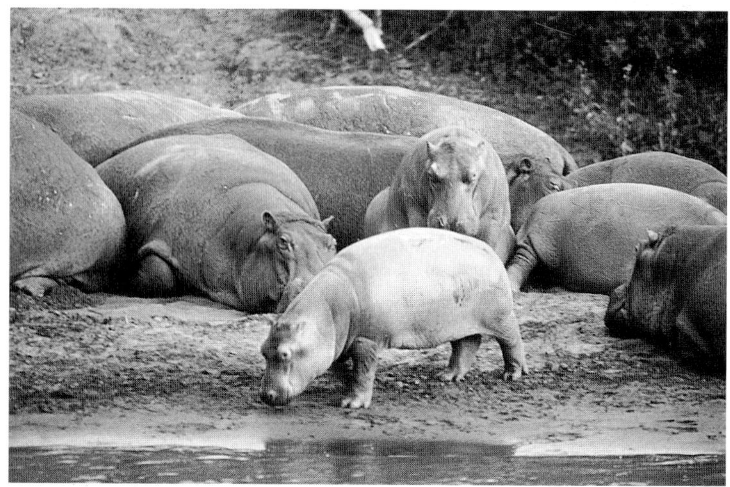

One problem in animal photography is the shallow depth of field at large reproduction ratios, another the danger of camera shake with long focal lengths. Tripods or monopods can help with both these difficulties.

How to take fascinating animal photographs

* Select aperture priority mode (A)
* Preselect wide apertures for fast shutter speeds
* Use long focal lengths
* Fast films from ISO 400/27° up
* Use a tripod or monopod with long focal lengths

Equipment

Lenses

Minolta AF Zoom xi 100-300mm, f/4.5-5.6 or
Minolta AF Zoom xi 35-200mm,f/4.5-5.6
Minolta AF 200mm,f/2.8 Apo or
Minolta AF 300mm,f/2.8 Apo or
Minolta AF 600mm,f/4 Apo and
Minolta AF 100mm,f/2.8 Macro

Accessories

Minolta Macro Flash 1200AF Set N
Minolta 3500xi or 5400xi program flash unit
Tripod or monopod
Sports 2 Card

Tips for better travel photos

Nowhere do we take more photographs than when travelling. This is understandable because who doesn't want to capture the most vivid memories from foreign countries, to keep them alive for as long as possible and let friends, acquaintances, and relatives share the experience.

Nothing is better than photographs for bringing to life memories of events in the distant past. The photographs you bring back from holiday are the most convincing way of sharing your experiences with someone else, and of showing them where you have been and what interested you there.

But travel photography demands a great deal of discipline from the photographer. If you simply start snapping away when you're on holiday, full of enthusiasm for the strangeness of the country you're visiting, your friends and acquaintances will greet the dreaded slide show with nothing but yawns. Piles of photo albums with pictures from the most exotic countries won't necessarily enthuse your friends. Unless photographers are able to create images that convey to the viewer what got them so excited in the first place, they will be nothing other than personal souvenirs. The viewer, who wasn't there when the picture was taken, won't feel the roar of the sea nor hear the chirping of the birds unless there is something in the photograph that conveys those feelings.

All of this atmosphere has to be achieved by the composition, by leaving out or adding certain creative elements. The tree in the foreground, bent by the wind, has to make you feel the storm; the flowers their fragrance, and the dusk the mild air of the summer evening. Of course, if you take photographs simply to aid your own memory you don't need to worry about such considerations. But if you want to share your experiences with friends and acquaintances, without running the risk of boring them with meaningless little pictures, then you do have to give some thought to the photographic interpretation of what you are seeing.

Travel photography goes back a long way. It is said that William Fox Talbot, the inventor of the photographic negative, only concerned himself with the development of the medium because he found his drawings of the banks of Lake Como too amateurish. With the help of photography we are able to record the world around us at the touch of a button, with unparalleled realism. Early travel photography acquainted people with countries, and the inhabitants of countries, that they never visited themselves. Today it seems as if every corner of the world has been photographed from every conceivable perspective. Travel photography snowballed along with the explosive development of tourism and now there are hardly any holiday-makers who go away without taking along a camera.

Holiday photographs capture your own experiences and in doing so encourage people to travel more. The many colourful books of the natural beauties of this world - the fascinating buildings of strange cultures and the people from exotic countries - have turned the desire to travel into an important economic factor. Holiday-makers are tempted with many colourful brochures. Magazines stimulate our wanderlust with images of our world in the most beautiful colours. It all seems as if there is nothing on this earth that hasn't fallen victim to photographers' enthusiasm a hundred times over. Yet despite the many brilliant photographs, some by excellent photographers, travellers continue to reach for their own cameras in order to capture the moments of their very own personal experiences. Translating personal experiences into pictures is the secret which dictates whether a photograph fascinates or bores its viewers. If you don't manage to capture what is special about your personal experiences you won't take good photographs home with you, only colourful pictures to help your own memories. The Leaning Tower of Pisa, the Grand Canyon, Niagara Falls, and the Pyramids have all been photographed countless times, and in a better way than you may ever manage yourself. But a good private travel photograph can still convey a fascinating message, both in artistic terms and in terms of content. Individual experiences turn personal holiday photographs into valuable documentation for the traveller themselves, as well as for the onlooker.

As long as you're reproducing landscapes and buildings you won't meet any particular problems. The things to watch out for are described in the sections on architectural and landscape photography. What causes problems when photographing abroad is the different culture of the country being visited, the customs and habits of the people, all of which the photographer will want to document in pictures.

Every travel photographer should realize that the search for unusual subjects should have its limits, dictated by respect for the

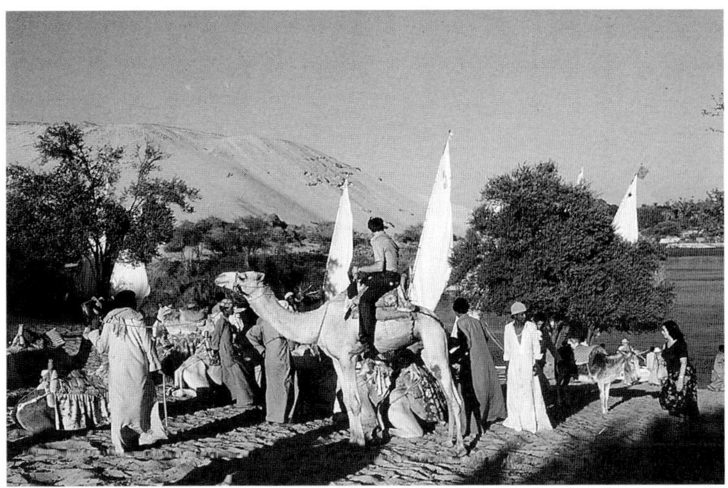

The best holiday memories are captured in successful shots to keep your unforgettable experiences alive for years to come.

feelings of the people. Quickly snapping photogenic people without their permission is a bad habit that is becoming increasingly widespread amongst tourists; it's no wonder if such angry 'photo victims' suddenly start throwing stones. It should be a matter of course for every photographer to ask permission if they want to take someone's picture, whether abroad or not. And this communication can also serve to put them more at ease with the camera. If you run around armed with a camera to collect photographs of places that have already been photographed countless times, you'll only end up with a good picture by accident. If you want to dig more deeply, spend time first finding out about the country you're visiting and its people. When you finally get there take the time to talk to the people. Most people like being photographed if you ask them nicely.

One reason why many photographers still continue to use telephoto lenses to take sneaky photographs of strange people is a fear that their subjects might lose their natural attitude and start posing as soon as the camera is noticed. But if you do spend some time with people their inhibitions will usually soon disappear and that natural smile will return. So if you want to get good portraits it pays to have a lot of time, patience, and above all, tact and sensitivity. Such pictures will show whether somebody is really interested in a country and its people or whether they are simply a photographic souvenir hunter.

The attraction of travel photography is the mixture of every conceivable subject area, from landscapes, buildings, people, and festivals, to the detailed pictures at very close range. So the travel photographer needs to be prepared for every eventuality. They needs to anticipate what sort of subjects they will come across, but must still be prepared for the unexpected and be able to respond spontaneously. Equipment, therefore, must be as versatile as possible yet still be easy to carry. With the compact Minolta 5xi and a zoom lens, or other similarly modern equipment, it is no longer necessary to carry a large amount of equipment. With the photographic equipment of today it is possible to master most photographic tasks with ease. The integral flash unit of the 5xi in particular makes hot-shoe mounted flashguns mostly superfluous. It is not only useful for 'on the move' photographs in badly lit rooms but can also provide effective foreground lighting at twilight.

One useful accessory no travel photographer should be without is a polarizing filter to eliminate reflections on non-metallic surfaces. Substantially richer colours result from eliminating reflections, the sky looks a deeper blue and the clouds become whiter, and green fields and trees will look more intense.

Experience proves that it is advisable to buy your film at home before you leave. When you're on the move it's often impossible to find the film type you're used to, while at home you know the dealer and know how the material is stored. In hot countries films that have been stored for too long are likely to have colour casts.

A spare battery is just as important as sufficient film because once the lithium battery is used up your 5xi will just stop. Not only are lithium batteries still extremely expensive in some countries but they may also be very difficult to get hold of.

Different countries have different customs, and something that's permitted at home may not be allowed somewhere else. You should remember this before you take a nude photograph of a partner on the beach, for example. Find out before you leave home what's permitted and what isn't. In some countries even photographing a train platform without permission can be enough to get you in trouble with the authorities. In other countries it's prohibited to photograph airports, harbours, or bridges, and many people refuse to be photographed for religious reasons.

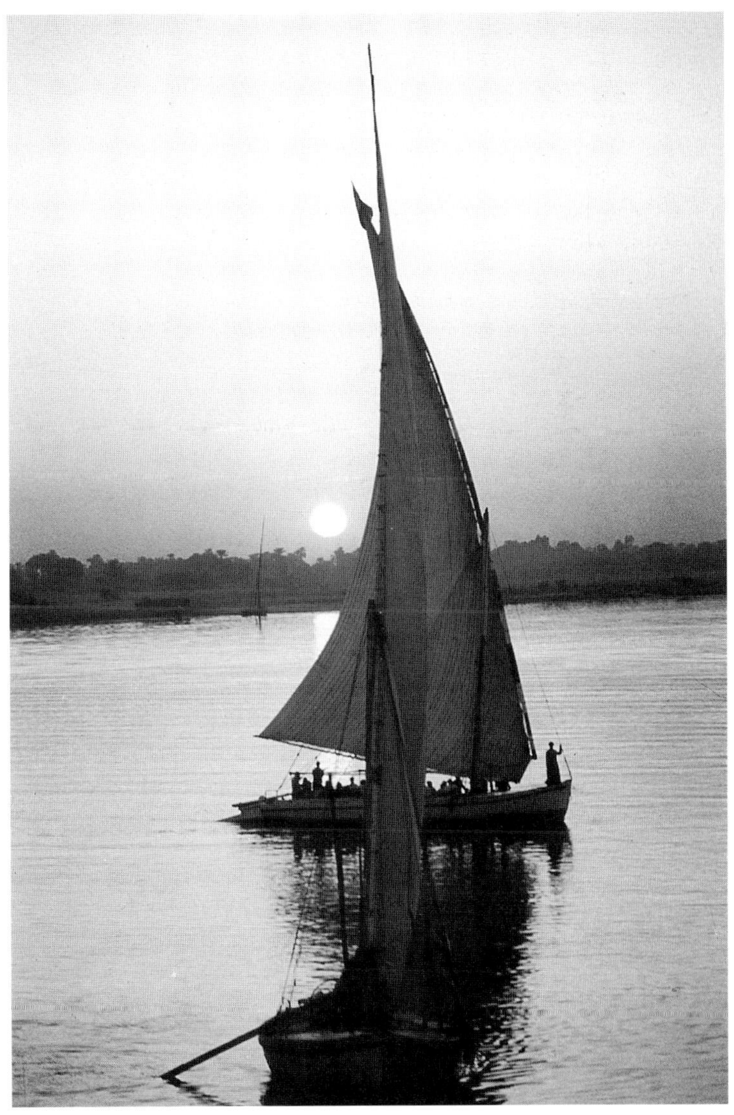

Romantic sunsets at a lake, a river or the sea are irresistible subjects.

How to take impressive holiday photographs

* Keep your equipment to a minimum so that you'll take it with you rather than leave it in the hotel out of sheer laziness
* Photograph your own personal experiences, don't try to imitate postcards
* Discover your subject with the camera, photograph it from different angles and positions
* Get close to your subject and show details
* Ask the permission of the person you want to photograph first and then take your time
* Use early morning and evening light
* Find out about any restrictions on photography before you leave

Equipment

Lenses

Minolta AF Zoom xi 28-80mm,f/3.5-4.5 or
Minolta AF Power Zoom 35-80,f/4-5.6 and/or
Minolta AF Zoom xi 35-200mm,f/4.5-5.6

Accessories

Minolta 3500xi or 5400xi program flash unit
Minolta mini tripod
Polarizing filter
Travel Card

Tips for better landscape pictures

Landscape photography has a long tradition and is still one of the most popular areas of amateur and professional photography. The constantly changing image of our earth has been captured in millions of photographs. We can see the changes in our environment in old and new pictures, welcoming or regretting this change. Although many famous landscapes have already been photographed thousands of times, no two pictures are the same. Landscape photographs can only be repeated to a certain extent because the landscape itself is constantly changing. This change is not only evident with the change of the season but also from one hour to the next. Landscape photography, as someone once said, is changes in weather on film.

The worst time for landscape photography is around midday on a sunny day. This is because at this time in the day the sun is very

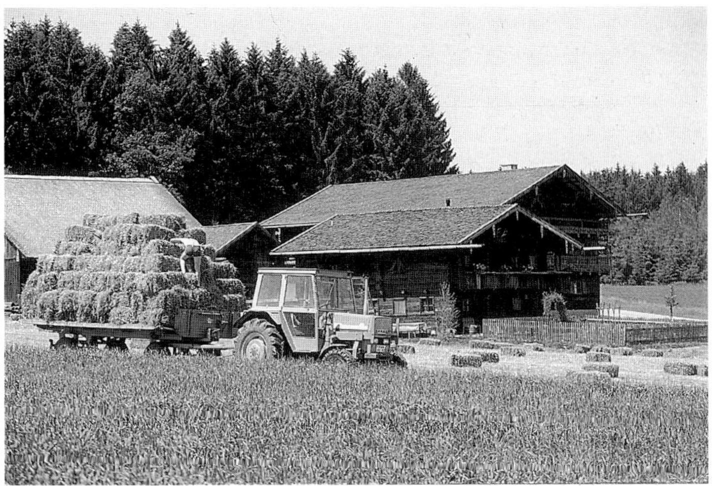

Early morning or late afternoon light is best for landscape shots.

high in the sky and so the shadows are short and almost imperceptible. And since the shadows normally help to give the landscape a feeling of depth, a photograph taken at this time will tend to appear two dimensional. Mountains, trees, and buildings appear flat and boring and a slight haze usually masks the view into the distance.

When the sun is lower down in the sky, on the other hand, the shadows become longer and objects in the landscape suddenly appear much more three-dimensional. The play of light and shade adds drama and tension to the photograph. Sunshine immediately following rain is also excellent for landscape photographs as the air is then clear and the wetness adds a fresh shine to everything, making the colours glowing.

The photographer needs to study the change in a landscape at different times of the day in order that they might know which cloud and weather pattern is most suitable for the effect they are after. They have to take their time, occasionally even risking a fruitless trip when the light wasn't quite right. But as landscape photography isn't necessarily quick and hectic the photographer can mount the camera on a tripod and take time to compose the framing.

One common mistake with landscape work is a grey-blue sky taking up the majority of the picture, causing nothing but yawns all round. Small white fleecy clouds can be a lot more interesting than monochrome blue, and dramatic cloud patterns add extra impact to your landscape. Whilst sunshine is usually good for landscape photographs, work in hazy conditions like fog, snow, or rain can also achieve fascinating results.

On the other hand, snowy landscapes without sunshine and under an overcast sky mostly look grey and lifeless because the diffused light removes all the contours. But for photographs at twilight an overcast sky can provide a light that causes the snow to look cold and blue, an effect that may contrast well with the warm yellow light diffusing from the windows of houses.

The horizon plays a very important role in landscape photography, but all too often photographers neglect to run it through the frame horizontally. Many beginners automatically place it in the centre of the frame but this mostly leads to dull photographs, except in certain circumstances. Blue sky taking up half of a picture also looks boring, although a seagull, or a flock of birds can help make such a 'sky-heavy' scene more interesting. In most cases dividing the frame into one-third sky and two-thirds landscape adds more interest to the photograph than a simple symmetrical division.

With landscape photographs the framing is particularly important because, after all, such pictures are supposed to convey an overview. Although many photographers tend to reach for wide-angle lenses for landscape work, short telephoto focal lengths can also be used effectively and have several advantages. First, tighter framing allows you to leave out unwanted areas of the subject and second, a telephoto lens concentrates perspective. This means that it compresses details placed at different positions in the depth of the view.

But the impression of depth is emphasized with a wide-angle lenses. The foreground takes up a relatively large proportion of the scene and distant objects appear small. The variety of detail in landscapes and their great spatial extension demand films that render details as brilliantly as possible and large depths of field. Photographers for magazines like *Geo* and *National Geographic* consider Kodachrome 25 as the ultimate film. But because of the long processing turnaround time many photographers have switched to Ektachrome material which can be developed within 90 minutes by a specialist lab. The Ektachrome HC 50 or the warmer Ektachrome 64X are favourites in professional circles. Another reason for this is the fact that these films are excellent for reproduction in print.

How to take magnificent landscape photographs

* Use the early morning and evening light
* Use a tripod
* Watch out for the horizon
* Use aperture priority mode with narrow aperture for great depth of field
* Use a polarizing filter
* Use films of the slowest possible speed

Equipment

Lenses

Minolta AF Zoom xi 28-105mm,f/3.5-4.5 and
Minolta AF Zoom xi 100-300mm,f/4.5-5.6 or
Minolta AF Zoom xi 35-200mm,f/4.5-5.6

Accessories

Minolta 3500xi or 5400xi program flash unit
Tripod
Circular polarizing filter
Travel Card

Tips for better close-ups

Small things greatly enlarged often make particularly attractive subjects. Things that escape a fleeting glance are only made truly visible by the camera, so an excursion into the world of macro photography can turn into something of an adventure. Close-up photographs are worthwhile in almost all subject areas. In travel photography pictures of architectural details or of traditional embroidery or of the exotic flora of a country can make fascinating as well as informative viewing. In close-up animal photography, the hunt for small animals, beetles and insects is highly rewarding. In documentary or sports photography also, close-up photographs can guide the eye to the many details that dramatize an event. A close-up picture of the chalk-whitened hands of a gymnast, or the

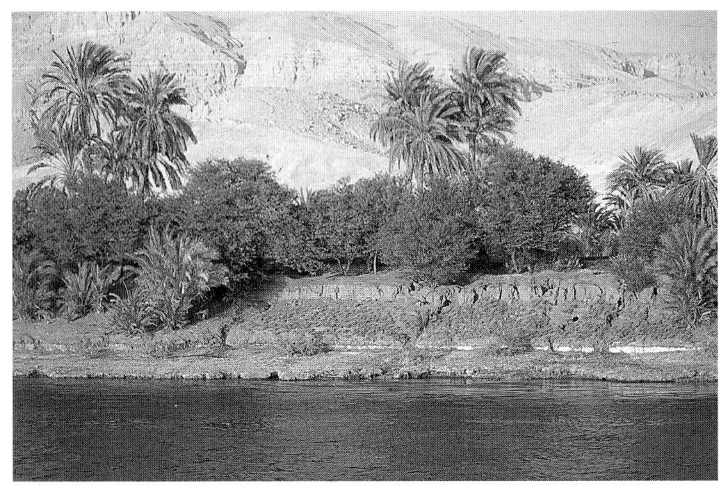

Landscape shots require great depth of field, which can be achieved with the Automatic Depth Control Card.

spikes on a sprinter's shoe, or a rifleman's finger on the trigger can all say more about an event than a normal picture.

The new Minolta zoom lenses allow very short shooting distances, and hence large reproduction ratios. With the Minolta AF Zoom xi 80-200mm,f/4.5-5.6 Macro the photographer can get as close as 1.5 metres to his subject, achieving a maximum reproduction ratio of almost 1:6.25.

The reproduction ratio of a lens indicates the ratio between the actual subject's size and its image size on film. So at a reproduction ratio of 1:4 the subject is reproduced on film at one-quarter of its actual size. At a reproduction ratio of 1:2 an object appears on film at half life size, and at a ratio of 1:1 the photograph is life size.

Normal lenses are not suitable for the extreme close-up range, reproduction ratios greater than 1:4, but there are a number of accessories which can extend the maximum reproduction ratio possible with a lens.

The easiest method is to use lens attachments, available from many manufacturers, which are simply screwed into the filter setting of the lens. This type of attachment reduces the minimum shooting distance and so increases the maximum reproduction ratio. They are available in different strengths, measured in dioptres, and several can be used together. Using lens attachments is unproblematic as they don't affect the autofocus or the exposure metering system, but their scope is limited.

The most effective and versatile way to achieve close-up photographs is by using a macro lens designed to work over short shooting distances. Two macro lenses are available for the Maxxum/Dynax models, including the 5xi, namely the Minolta AF 50mm,f/2.8 Macro and the 100mm,f/2.8. Both lenses allow you to shoot at life size, up to a reproduction ratio of 1:1, without the need for close-up accessories. These lenses don't only deliver excellent performance at close range but are also good for longer distance work.

Whilst the longer focal length is more suitable for photographing small animals, where you have to keep at a certain distance so they don't run away, the 50mm standard focal length lens is better suited for copying. Here short distances between subject and front element are necessary to avoid over-large copying stands. The 50mm macro lens is also well suited for close-up photographs of flowers and plants, as well as small objects, provided you don't need much space between the front element and the subject to squeeze in lighting equipment.

One ever-present problem with close-up photography is the depth of field which decreases rapidly as the reproduction ratio increases. Another factor is the aperture, and the wider this is the narrower the sharp zone either side of the point of focus becomes. This is why the camera should be set to aperture priority mode with as narrow an aperture as possible.

Large reproduction ratios also increase the danger of camera shake so it is advisable in close-up work to use a tripod or a very fast shutter speed whenever possible. But narrow apertures to give a large depth of field, combined with fast shutter speeds to reduce the danger of camera shake, means that plenty of light is required. As the graininess of high-speed film means that they are not an acceptable option for close-up work, where detail is important, you will need to use flash light in most cases.

The Minolta Macro Flash 1200AF Set N can help in these situations. The Macro Flash has four flash tubes which can either be fired together for shadow-free illumination or separately to provide a more three-dimensional effect. The flash head of the ring flash unit is screwed onto the lens like a filter and the power unit is mounted on the hotshoe of the 5xi with the Flash Shoe Adapter FS-1100.

How to take impressive close-up photographs

* Because of the shallow depth of field always shoot small subjects from the angle where they have the least depth
* Use flash light and preselect a narrow aperture in aperture priority mode
* Mount the camera on a tripod if possible and release the shutter with the self-timer

Equipment

Lenses

Minolta AF 50mm,f/2.8 Macro or
Minolta AF 100mm,f/2.8 Macro

Accessories

Minolta Macro Flash 1200AF Set N
Flash Shoe Adapter FS-1100
Tripod
Copy Stand II
Closeup Card

Tips for better architectural photographs

Nowhere is human creativity more convincingly and solidly represented than in fascinating buildings and monuments from different epochs. These impressive witnesses to human creativity are amongst the most popular subjects of amateur photographers. But it is often difficult to capture buildings in pictures because their surroundings prevent the photographer from shooting from the required distance. Wide-angle lenses are needed in order to be able to photograph large buildings at close range, and the shorter the focal length of a lens the shorter the possible shooting distance.

But apart from the distance needed, the height of a building can also be problematic. The optimum shooting position, in terms of the height, for photographs of buildings is roughly half their height. But usually the photographer will have both feet on the ground, with the building towering above them. To squeeze it all on film you need to tilt the camera upwards, but the more the camera is tilted the more unnatural the result usually looks. On the photograph the building will look as if it were falling over backwards. This effect, called converging verticals in photographic jargon, occurs whenever the back cover of the camera and the vertical lines of the subject are not parallel with each other. In other words whenever the camera is tilted (given vertical subjects).

This tilting of the camera can be avoided by selecting a raised shooting position. This is possible, for example, when you are able to take your photographs from the upper windows of the building opposite.

But even if the wide-angle lens is sufficient to capture all of the building with the camera held straight, low shooting positions hold a further disadvantage. As the optical axis is only parallel with the ground at eye-level, the ground will take up almost as much space in the frame as the building itself. Unless you're dealing with a particularly interesting forecourt with attractive paving, this unbalanced relationship between main subject and foreground is most likely to be unattractive. If you're shooting with negative film you can salvage such photographs in the darkroom by printing sectional enlargements to compensate for the perspective. But with slide film sectional duplicates are not only expensive but usually involve a substantial loss in quality.

Careful picture composition - the division of vertical and horizontal lines, and of shapes and structures - adds the special touch to a successful architectural photograph. Many architectural photographers use a tripod to avoid the effects of camera shake with long shutter speeds and to allow them to check their framing precisely and without hurrying.

With most buildings the beauty of their architecture is only fully revealed in the play of light and shadow, which maybe when the sun is low in the early morning or evening. The shadowless light of the midday sun directly overhead, on the other hand, will probably only produce interesting photographs of buildings with a lot of cornicing and distinctive ledges or bays.

As the reduced light of the morning and evening require slower shutter speeds, a tripod is a useful help to prevent camera shake at small apertures. Moreover, recording the structures and lines that lend special character to a building can only be achieved successfully with a fine grain, low speed film. Overcast grey skys and diffuse soft lighting are also generaly considered not very suitable for architectural photographs.

A whole series of photographs of a building taken at different times of day, or even different times of year, can show interesting changes. Photographs taken at intervals over several years can produce documentaries of great value, but the longer the intervals between each picture, the more important it is that the photographer makes accurate notes of the shooting position and focal length. The aperture can also play an important role in affecting the depth of field of such photographs. You should therefore always shoot from a tripod in the same position, and in aperture priority mode with the same aperture set, if you want to get identical framing with a constant spatial effect.

Buildings lit up at night can be fascinating, but can be given extra zest by changing the focal length during the exposure. In this case you have to work in manual mode to be able to set a sufficiently narrow aperture for the long exposure.

Remember that the wide spectrum of architectural photography doesn't just include overviews. Often it's the small details of a building that reveal the great skill of the architect and master builder.

Souvenir pictures of people in front of famous buildings are almost a must for every traveller. But many photographers make the mistake of placing their subject directly in front of the building where they'll be dwarfed by the huge structure. Here the photographer should use the laws of perspective to their advantage. As objects at different distances from the camera appear at different sizes on the film, you should compose the photograph so that the monument fills the frame in the background while the person is positioned close in the foreground. But make sure that the person doesn't cover up important parts of the building and that the preselect aperture guarantees a sufficient depth of field, such that both person and building are in focus. It can often be helpful to set the focus plane manually to slightly behind the person. This is because about one-third of the depth of field in the photograph will extend forward (towards the camera) from the focus plane and two-thirds behind it.

Interior photographs are also part of architectural photography. In large rooms - the nave of a church for example, or a theatre, or the great hall of a castle - you often have to do without flash, partly because of its limited range and partly because its use is not permitted. In this case you need to use fast films, such as the Kodak Ektar 1000, which delivers remarkable sharpness and good reproduction of detail, despite its high speed. Otherwise you must use a tripod.

If you need to use flash why not get yourself a slave? Such auxiliary flash units, fired by remote control from the camera's flash unit via a photo diode, are available from manufacturers such as Cullmann and are relatively inexpensive. The flash can simply be set up in a room so that it illuminates areas of the subject that the integral flash unit won't reach. Using the integral flash unit in conjunction with the remotely controlled 3500xi or 5400xi program flash unit is also a good way of lighting large rooms.

How to take impressive architectural phototgraphs

* Don't tilt the camera
* With tall buildings select a raised shooting position to avoid intrusive foregrounds
* Use morning and evening light
* Use a tripod
* Don't position people directly in front of a building but closer to the camera
* Use 'slave flash units' to light larger rooms

Equipment

Lenses

- Minolta AF Zoom 24-50mm,f/4
- Minolta AF Zoom xi 28-80mm,f/4.5-5.6
- Minolta AF Zoom xi 28-105mm,f/3.5-4.5

Accessories

- Tripod
- Polarizing filter
- Slave flash unit
- Minolta 3500xi or 5400xi program flash unit
- Depth Card

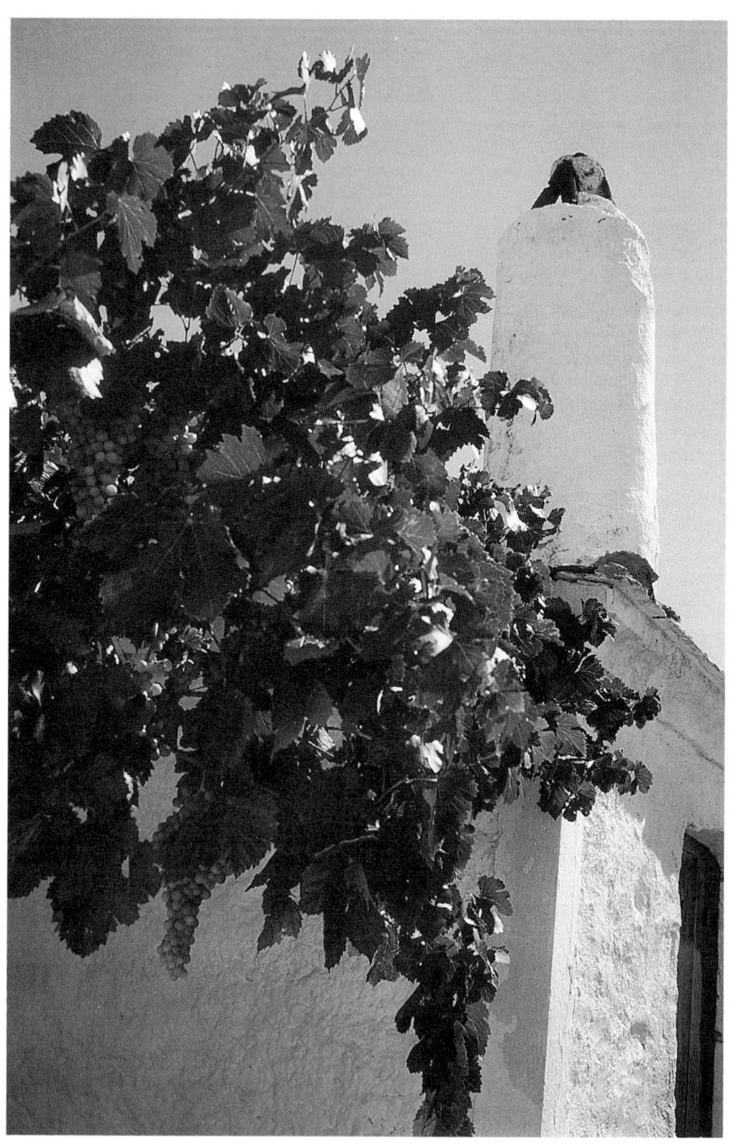

To improve sharpness the use of a tripod is advisable for landscape or achitectural photography.
Photo: Ingrid Heinzelmann

System accessories

Filters and other Lens Attachments

Minolta offer ten different types of filters for black-and-white and colour photography for the Maxxum/Dynax system. There are filters for colour that suppress colour casts and improve colour saturation. And there are also neutral filters to absorb UV radiation as well as special filters for black-and-white photography. Working with filters requires the photographer to know certain basic rules about their handling and their effect, and this knowledge is best acquired by carrying out your own tests and experiments. Further attachments for Minolta AF and xi lenses are achromatic close-up lenses, which decrease the close-up distance, and the underestimated lens hood.

UV Filter - Film emulsions used to react strongly to UV radiation giving heavy blue casts and a loss in sharpness. Strong UV radiation is often found in mountains and by the sea but nowadays modern films often include a layer that blocks UV radiation, making such filters superfluous. However, UV-absorbing filters are completely colourless and absorb no light, so they do not influence the exposure in any way, and so can just be kept on the lens to protect the front element.

Skylight Filter 1B/1A - These filters produce a slightly warmer colour rendering. They suppress blue with subjects photographed in so-called open shade, i.e. without direct sunlight, where the blue of the sky is reflected, and give warmer colours in dull and hazy conditions. The 1B filter has a slightly stronger effect than the 1A.

Conversion filters - These filters let you match the colour sensitivity of colour film to the colour temperature of the illumination. Filter type 80B (blue) is used to suppress the red bias you get when using daylight film in tungsten light. While Filter 85 (red) is for tungsten film in daylight use as it suppresses the heavy blue that would otherwise result.

Polarizing filters - These help to remove unwanted reflections from non-metallic surfaces. A picture taken with a polarizing filter usually has stronger colours and the sky will be a deeper blue. The effect of the filter can be varied by turning it but the strongest effect on a blue sky occurs when the shooting direction is 90° to the direction of the sun's rays.

There is one problem when using polarizing filters on an AF lens. The front barrel of some lenses rotates during focusing which means that the polarizing filter is turned as well. Consequently the filter has to be adjusted after correct focus has been set and so it may be more simple to change to manual focusing when using a polarizing filter. Alternatively, filter holders (available as accessories) enable the front element to move freely without affecting the filter.

The autofocus system and the exposure metering of the Minolta Maxxum/Dynax cameras will only allow circular polarizing filters to be used. Linear polarizing filters affect the AF and exposure metering of the camera and so are not recommended.

Neutral density filter ND-4X - These special filters are neutral grey and do not affect colour rendering. They are used in colour and black-and-white photography if the light is too bright, or to let you use large apertures or slower shutter speeds in bright conditions.

Filters for black-and-white photography - Minolta offer four filters of this type - yellow, green, orange, and red. Yellow improves the reproduction of blue sky and clouds. Green also darkens blue sky and lightens the greens of grass and foliage. Orange is often used for landscapes, producing dark dramatic skies.

Red filters have a similar but even more intense effect and blue sky appears very dark. Red filters are also used for infrared photography. Since all colour filters absorb light to varying degrees the exposure must be increased to compensate but this is automatically taken into account by TTL exposure control. The high density of some red filters can also affect the AF system of the camera.

Gelatin filter holders - Kodak offer 7.5x7.5cm light-balancing filters which can be clamped in special Minolta filter holders, and these holders in turn screw into the filter thread of the lens. These filters adjust the colour temperature of the illumination to match the colour sensitivity of the film emulsion.

Minolta Portrayer filters - As the word 'Portrayer' may already suggest, these are soft-focus effect filters used for portrait photography. Minolta offer two types giving different effects.

S1 and S2, supplied as a set, are intended for general soft-focus photography with lenses of focal lengths between 50mm and 210mm.

P1, P2, and P3, also available as a set, are for particularly flattering portraits where a special softening effect on skin tones is wanted. They are distinct from other filters of this type because the aperture does not influence the softening effect, although the focal length of the lens plays an important role. The soft-focus effect increases with increasing focal length. If a strong soft-focus effect is desired, more than one filter can be used. All Portrayer filters keep the centre in sharp focus, with the soft-focus effect increasing towards the edge of the frame.

Achromatic close-up lenses - These are used to decrease the closest focusing distance and thereby increase the reproduction ratio. The Minolta type consist of two cemented elements which are screwed into the filter thread of the lens. Compared with simple close-up lenses, achromatic lenses give a much better quality of reproduction. At f/8 and smaller apertures (larger aperture numbers) reproduction quality is very acceptable - larger apertures are not recommended.

Minolta offer three different lenses, each with a different magnification factor, which can be combined to obtain still more reproduction ratios. But if you do combine these lenses always attach the one with the smaller number first. Although the autofocus system is not adversely affected by using these attachments, it is important to stay within the restricted distance range where focusing is still possible.

They are available in 49mm and 55mm filter thread sizes and identified as 0 for +0.94 dioptres, 1 for +2.0 dioptres, and 2 for +3.8 dioptres.

Lens hood - This is a very useful and almost indispensable accessory. With some Minolta lenses the hood is already built-in, but others come supplied with a separate clip-on or bayonet-fitting hood. They prevent light entering the lens at an oblique angle which can refract and scatter inside the lens giving poor contrast and an impression of unsharpness. Lens hoods are another way of ensuring good quality pictures and are a simple, relatively cheap, and often underestimated accessory.

Eyepiece Corrector 1000 - Although the 5xi sets the focus automatically, photographers who wear spectacles often have problems assessing the picture through the viewfinder. For this reason Minolta offer nine eyepiece correction lenses with values between -4 and +3 dioptres for the Maxxum/Dynax cameras. These lenses simply snap onto the camera's eyepiece.

Flash accessories

Cable CD - This cable connects to the accessory socket of a 5200i or 5400xi flash unit. The four-pole sockets at either end of this cable allow the connection of a second 5200i or 5400xi flash unit, or the Off Camera Shoe OS-1100, so that two flash units can be used for studio-quality flash illumination. The 5200i program flash unit does not need to be mounted on the camera but can be controlled via the Off Camera cable OC-1100 and the Off Camera Shoe OS-1100. The EX extension cable is also available for off-camera flash work. A maximum of five EX cables can be connected together to extend the Off Camera Cable OC-1100 or the Cable CD.

In conjunction with the Off Camera Cable OC-1100 and the Triple Connector TC-1000, TTL control of up to three flash units (2000i, 2000xi, 3200i, 3500xi, 5200i or 5400xi) is possible. If a 5200i or 5400xi is mounted on the camera, Cable CD is sufficient to control the three flash units via the automatic flash control system.

Off Camera Cable OC-1100 - This spiral cable can be pulled to a length of about one metre and can, if necessary, be extended with five EX cables.

It allows more flexible lighting with the Minolta program flash units. The OC-1100 can be connected directly to the accessory shoe on the side of the 5200i program flash unit. For other Minolta program flash units the Off Camera Shoe OS-1100 is required.

Off Camera Shoe OS-1100 - This attaches to the end of Cable OC-1100 and allows an i or xi series flash unit to be fitted. It has a standard shoe base and a tripod socket.

Triple Connector TC-1000 - This distributor with a four-pole plug for OC-1100 or CD cables and three four-pole couplings for Cable EX is used to connect up to three flash units to Maxxum/ Dynax cameras simultaneously.

Flash Shoe Adapter FS-1100 - This allows the use of 1000 series flash units, such as the 1800AF, 2800AF, and 4000AF, with i and xi series cameras.

Bounce Reflector III and IV Set - These light, collapsible reflectors provide soft and indirect flash lighting everywhere, even outside. The Bounce Reflector III can be attached to the 5200i program flash unit while the Bounce Reflector IV fits the 3500xi program flash unit.

Ni-Cad Charger NC-2 and External Battery Pack EP-1 Set - If flash is used a lot, and if special functions like strobe flash are used frequently, it is advisable to use rechargeable Ni-Cad batteries instead of expensive standard batteries. Additionally, the external battery pack reduces the recycling times for the Minolta 5200i and 5400xi program flash units and increases the number of flashes possible between battery changes.

Slide Copy Unit 1000 and Macro Stand 1000

Minolta offer two accessories specially designed for the production of high-quality duplicates or copies. The Slide Copier 1000 and the Macro Stand 1000 can be used on all Maxxum/Dynax AF SLR cameras in conjunction with the AF 50mm,f/2.8 Macro, the AF 100mm,f/2.8 Macro, and the AF Macro Zoom 3X-1X.

Slide Copy Unit 1000 - This useful and practical device has a 35mm slide holder set above an opaque perspex screen which

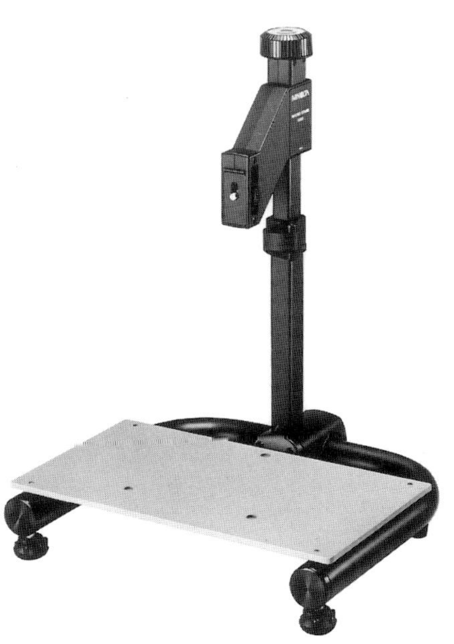

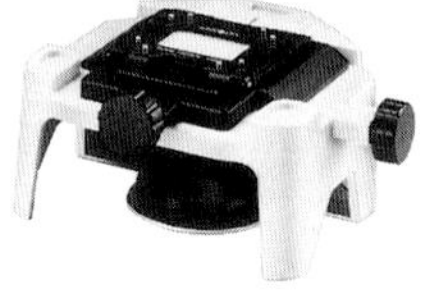

The Macro Stand and Slide Copier, used with the 5xi and a suitable macro lens, allows the simple reproduction of slides.

ensures that the slides are evenly lit. The original slide can be moved inside this holder easily and very precisely by turning setting knobs to adjust its vertical and horizontal position, this then allows you to achieve the optimum framing. The slide copier is mounted on a special stand designed so that the flash reflector of the Macro Flash 1200AF can be attached quickly and easily. This special macro flash unit is an excellent light source for evenly lighting original slides. The Slide Copy Unit 1000 can be used in conjunction with the tripod of the AF Macro Zoom 3X-1X,f/1.7-2.8 when this lens is used.

Macro Stand 1000 - The Macro Stand 1000 is a practical and easily operated accessory for macro photographs with the Minolta AF 50mm,f/2.8 Macro and the AF 100mm,f/2.8 Macro. The tripod socket of the camera body is connected to the adjustable arm of the rigid tube. The baseboard, with its integral 18% grey subject table, allows the subject to be carefully positioned before being photographed. Used in conjunction with the Slide Copy Unit 1000, this device allows fast and easy photographing at a reproduction ratio of up to 1:1.

Storing and caring for your camera

Minolta cameras are valuable precision tools, crammed full of the most modern electronics and precision engineering. You should always handle them with care. Shocks, high humidity, and dirt can affect the functioning of the camera, although the high-quality plastic body can cope with the odd rough blow. So you should always protect your camera against such factors. A lens hood is a good protection for the front element of the lens since it makes fingerprints and scratches less likely. The lens cap should always be in place when the camera is not being used.

Strong heat and high humidity are the enemies of every electronic system, so your camera should be stored in a dry place and at normal temperatures. The glove compartment or boot of a car parked in glaring sunshine are about the most unsuitable places.

Certain fumes and chemicals can also damage the camera body and its electronic system, and you must never oil or grease any camera component. The same also applies to lenses. The shutter curtains of the camera are particularly sensitive and you should always be careful not to touch them when loading a film.

Compressed air is unsuitable for cleaning precision instruments such as modern cameras. The air tends to swirl the dust around rather than blowing it away, and the concentrated stream directed into the interior of the camera could change some of the internal settings. A fine dust brush is still the best, and a dry, soft cotton cloth, possibly impregnated with silicon, is best for cleaning the exterior of the camera and lens.

But never use a silicon cloth for cleaning the glass surfaces, which are best treated with special lens cleaning tissues or cloths from photographic equipment dealers. If the glass surfaces of the lens or viewfinder eyepiece are heavily soiled, 'Prophot' is best, or use a liquid lens cleaner. Such cleaners must be applied to the cleaning cloth sparingly, they must never be applied directly to the glass surface. If soiling is very heavy, it is advisable to have the camera cleaned by an authorized Minolta service agent.

If you want to store the camera for a long period of time you should rewind and remove any film still in the camera and then take out the battery. The camera is best stored (in most climates) in an airtight container, together with some silica gel to absorb any humidity. Silica gel is available from pharmacies, and damp silica gel can be dried in the oven and re-used. This absorbent material is particularly indispensable for longer periods in humid climatic zones, like the tropics.

However, an airtight camera case can prove problematic in such situations. If its interior cannot be kept completely dry it will develop a climatic zone of its own, encouraging the formation of fungus on glass surfaces. Experience has shown that a cotton bag, which 'breathes', is a better way of storing the camera as it absorbs as well as gives off humidity. Domke bags are cotton canvas.

When the camera is to be used after a long period of time, check all camera and lens functions before taking any important photographs. This will help you become familiar with the camera again and will prevent any disappointment over spoilt pictures.

The liquid crystal display of the body data panel will normally function at temperatures between -20° and +50° Celsius. Below this minimum the contrast and speed of the displays will change, and the data may become difficult to read. At particularly high temperatures the data panel may temporarily go black so that the displays are invisible. But the displays will reappear once in normal temperatures and will again function perfectly.

If the camera malfunctions you must never attempt to repair it yourself. Instead, you should either send it to the nearest Minolta service agent or take it to a Minolta dealer. It is a good idea to keep the original packaging of the camera so that it can be packed securely for dispatch. To save unnecessary expense you should telephone the nearest Minolta service agent before posting the camera. This is because the camera may just have locked because of an operating error, and often you can get it going again by simply removing and re-inserting the battery, but in any case the agent may well be able to assist. For example, electronic circuits can switch themselves off, even though a battery with sufficient capacity is in the camera. In such cases you may only need to take out the battery and put it back again for the camera to resume normal operation. Minolta recommend that the camera should be cleaned and checked annually by an authorized Minolta service agent, especially if it is used a lot.

ACCESSORIES WELL WORTH LOOKING AT!

OP/TECH

The world's most comfortable cameras, bag and tripod straps (binoculars too). Op/tech has a built-in weight reduction system that makes equipment feel 50% lighter and 100% more comfortable. From the famous 'Pro-Camera Strap' to the 'Bag Strap' and the 'Tripod Strap', the style, colours and comfort which along with the non-slip grip, ensure that you have a wonderful combination of comfort and safety.

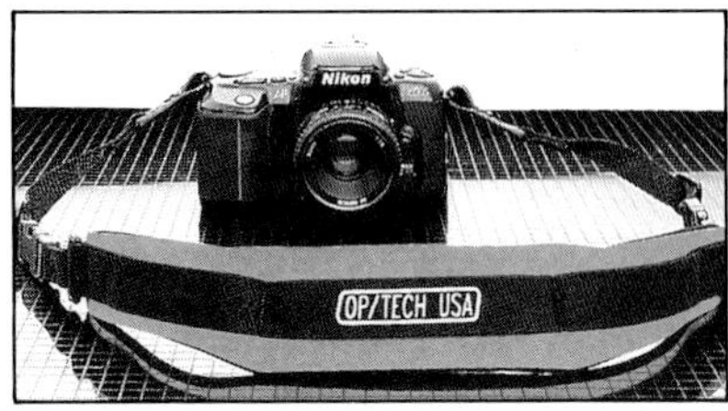

DOMKE

The favoured bag of the world's photo press. Designed to be used and made from all-natural materials, Domke has grown to become known as the 'workhorse' of all camera bags for it's toughness and durability. Made from 100% soft, supple cotton canvas which molds around its contents and hugs your body. Nature's perfect material is naturally water-resistant and will not harm either equipment or clothing. A non-slip shoulder strap is an added feature of all Domke bags.

LUMIQUEST

For any portable flashgun that has a bounce head, Lumiquest is an accessory system that has a place in everybody's camera bag. Not just to reduce 'red-eye', but from the simple 'Pocket Bounce' through to the 'Softbox', added diffusion for flash portrait or close-up's of still life can be achieved while at the same time Metallic Inserts in silver will give spectacular highlights and in gold, a warm sunset tone. Snoots and Barndoors are part of the system for the creative flash photographer.

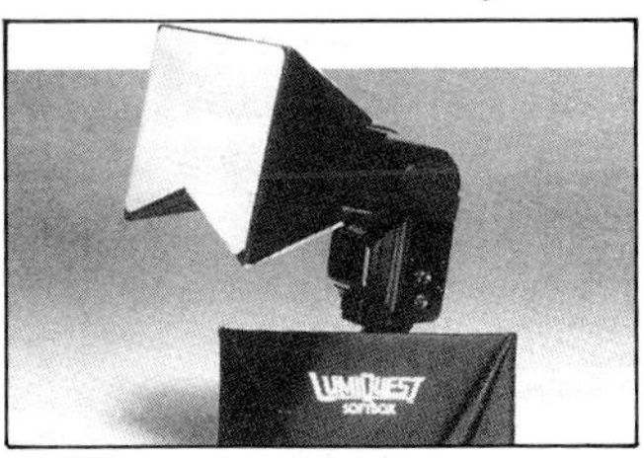

STROBOFRAME

The perfect partner for all 'off-camera' flash users. 35mm or Medium Format there is a Stroboframe bracket suitable for you. Getting a flashgun off a camera is vital for creative and studio-like effects. Camera mounted or side mounted flash will simply not give you the effects you are looking for. Stroboframe will. Also in the range is the famous 'LEPP 11' macro flash bracket that provides full creative lighting control when you need to get close. To make it easy to get the camera on and off a bracket, the 'QRC' Camera Auto Quick Release is a welcome accessory.

KINETICS

The tough hard-shell case (known as Tundra Sea King in the USA) that is favoured by all those who travel and have a need to fully protect valuable camera or electronic equipment. Made of hard industrial plastic that will withstand the rigours of travel, with the added advantage of being airtight, dustight and watertight when locked down. With a Kinetics case you can now enjoy taking your valuable equipment wherever you want in the knowledge that it will be safe from impact, dust and moisture.

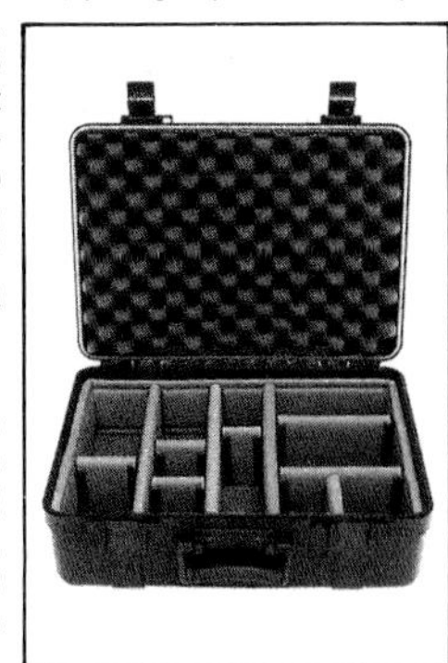